Microsoft Exam MD-100 Windows 10 Certification Guide

Learn the skills required to become a Microsoft Certified Modern Desktop Administrator Associate

Jeroen Burgerhout

BIRMINGHAM—MUMBAI

Microsoft Exam MD-100 Windows 10 Certification Guide

Commissioning Editor: Richa Tripathi
Acquisition Editor: Karan Gupta
Senior Editor: Storm Mann
Content Development Editor: Rosal Colaco
Technical Editor: Gaurav Gala
Copy Editor: Safis Editing
Project Coordinator: Deeksha Thakkar
Proofreader: Safis Editing
Indexer: Priyanka Dhadke
Production Designer: Shankar Kalbhor

First published: May 2020

Production reference: 1220520

Published by Packt Publishing Ltd.
Livery Place
35 Livery Street
Birmingham
B3 2PB, UK.

ISBN 978-1-83882-218-7

www.packt.com

Why subscribe?

Contributors

About the author

Jeroen Burgerhout is a Microsoft Cloud Consultant at SKS Professionals with great technical experience in Microsoft products. He is specialized in Azure, Hyper-V, Intune, Office 365, EMS, Windows 10, and Windows Server. He is currently working for the government in the Netherlands, working on the migration to Microsoft 365 with Microsoft Endpoint Manager, Azure Active Directory, and security features such as Azure AD PIM, Azure AD MFA, and Azure AD Conditional Access. Later this year, he will start with the new Modern Workplace concept, which is entitled to Windows 10, Windows Autopilot, Microsoft Endpoint Management, Office 365, and Azure AD. His Twitter account is @BurgerhoutJ.

I want to thank the people who have been close to me and supported me, especially my wife, Simone, and my daughter, Femke. I also want to thank my employer, SKS Professionals, for their confidence and the space that they gave me to write this book. I would like to thank Rosal Colaco and Storm Mann, for their dedicated work to improve the book's quality, as well as Shriram Shekhar, who convinced me to write this book.

About the reviewer

Chandra Mohan has over 12 years' experience in IT, including more than 11 workplace technologies. He has worked on SCCM/Microsoft Endpoint Configuration Manager Cloud Integration, Windows 10, O365, Azure, AWS, GCP, Microsoft 365, Modern Workplace, Windows 10 Migration, Windows as a Service, Office as a Service, Microsoft Intune, and BitLocker.

He also holds many certifications: Microsoft Certified: Exam 703: Administering System Center Configuration Manager and Cloud Services Integration, MD-100 Windows 10, MD-101 Managing Modern Desktops, Microsoft 365 Certified: Modern Desktop Administrator Associate, Azure Fundamentals, Azure Administrator Associate, Google Associate Cloud Engineer, and Amazon Web Services Cloud Practitioner.

Packt is searching for authors like you

If you're interested in becoming an author for Packt, please visit authors. packtpub.com and apply today. We have worked with thousands of developers and tech professionals, just like you, to help them share their insight with the global tech community. You can make a general application, apply for a specific hot topic that we are recruiting an author for, or submit your own idea.

Table of Contents

3
Customizing and Configuring Windows 10

Section 2 : Managing Devices and Data

4
Managing Local Users, Groups, and Devices

5

Configuring Permissions and File Access

6

Configuring and Implementing Local Policies

7
Securing Data and Applications

Section 3: Configuring Connectivity

8
Configuring Various Networks

9

Configuring Remote Connectivity

Section 4: Maintaining Windows

10

Understanding Troubleshooting and Recovery

11
Managing Updates

12
Managing Log Files

13
Mock Exam (A and B)

Assessments

Other Books You May Enjoy

Index

Preface

Complete with a clear, succinct explanation of key concepts, self-assessment questions, tips, and mock exams with detailed answers, this MD-100 study guide covers different facets of upgrading and deploying Windows 10. You'll learn how to manage devices and data, configure connectivity, troubleshoot the operating system and apps, and secure and maintain Windows 10 with updates and recovery.

You'll explore different Windows 10 editions and learn how to choose the best fit for your organization. This book will guide you through installing and configuring Windows 10 using different approaches. Toward the end of the book, you'll get to grips with managing local users and groups in Windows 10 and learn how to establish connections via different networks, such as a LAN or WLAN/Wi-Fi.

You'll learn how to deploy Windows 10 in a variety of ways, and to manage local users, groups, and devices. You'll also learn how to configure networking and remote connectivity, and gain insights into Windows 10 maintenance. You will also learn how to customize different Windows 10 features and become an expert at troubleshooting and recovery. Also, you'll get to grips with managing log files, and monitoring and managing Windows security.

You will learn about managing devices and data, configuring connectivity and security, and maintaining Windows 10 with updates and recovery.

By the end of this book, you'll have covered everything you need to pass the MD-100 certification exam and become a Microsoft 365 Certified: Modern Desktop Administrator Associate.

Who this book is for

This book is for both experienced and novice IT administrators who deploy, configure, secure, and monitor devices. Anyone who wants to take the MD-100 exam should have a working knowledge of managing identity, access, policies, updates, and apps. Although not necessary, experience with Microsoft 365 workloads, Windows 10 devices, and non-Windows devices will be helpful.

What this book covers

Chapter 1, *Deploying Windows 10*, describes the different methodologies of installing and deploying Windows 10 on a device. You will explore Windows 10 and learn how it operates across a plethora of devices. Understanding which edition is required for the enterprise is important because each edition comes with its own unique features.

Chapter 2, *Upgrading Windows 10*, describes the different processes for upgrading from an earlier version of Windows to the current Windows 10. You will explore how to configure language packs, troubleshoot activation problems, and migrate user data.

Chapter 3, *Customizing and Configuring Windows 10*, explains how to customize different Windows 10 features and configure startup options. You will explore concepts such as configuring desktop settings, Start menus, and color schemes.

Chapter 4, *Managing Local Users, Groups, and Devices*, shows you how to manage local users and groups. You will subsequently explore how devices are managed in a Workgroup.

Chapter 5, *Configuring Permissions and File Access*, discusses the different file systems in Windows 10 and explains how to configure NTFS and share permissions on folders and file access.

Chapter 6, *Configuring and Implementing Local Policies*, explains how to configure local policies and how to implement them in Windows 10. We can set different policies to users or to devices.

Chapter 7, *Securing Data and Applications*, discusses User Account Control, how to configure Threat Protection and AppLocker, and how to implement disk encryption.

Chapter 8, *Configuring Various Networks*, explains the fundamentals of how to configure different options to create formidable connections such as LAN, Wi-Fi, and mobile connectivity.

Chapter 9, *Configuring Remote Connectivity*, discusses remote management via PowerShell to a Windows 10 device. You will learn how to connect to a Windows 10 desktop via Remote Desktop access.

Chapter 10, *Understanding Troubleshooting and Recovery*, discusses errors in Windows 10 that can be dealt with in several ways. You will learn these different ways, such as file recovery and recovering a complete Windows 10 installation or application. We will look at troubleshooting during the startup/boot process of Windows 10.

Chapter 11, *Managing Updates*, discusses several key strategies for keeping Windows 10 up to date, as it is common knowledge that it is important to keep Windows 10 and your applications up to date.

Chapter 12, Managing Log Files, explores different log files that are built in to Windows 10 and how to read those files.

Chapter 13, Mock Exam A and B, contains mock exams for the reader to test the knowledge they have gained from the book.

Assessments, contains the answers to the questions asked in the chapters.

To get the most out of this book

You should know the basics of Windows 10, **Azure Active Directory** (**Azure AD**) and **Microsoft Endpoint Manager** (**Microsoft Intune**) before you can proceed with the book.

Software covered in the book	OS Requirements
Enterprise Mode Site List Manager (schema v.2)	Windows
Hyper-V, or VMware or similar for installing or upgrading the Windows operating system	Windows

Before starting with this book, you should join the **Microsoft 365 Developer Program** to set up and configure an **Azure AD Developer** tenant. More information about this program can be found at `https://docs.microsoft.com/en-us/office/ developer-program/microsoft-365-developer-program`.

If you already own an Azure AD tenant for testing purposes, then you can use that.

If you are using the digital version of this book, we advise you to type the code yourself or access the code via the GitHub repository (link available in the next section). Doing so will help you avoid any potential errors related to copy/pasting of code.

Download the example code files

You can download the example code files for this book from your account at `www. packt.com`. If you purchased this book elsewhere, you can visit `www.packtpub.com/ support` and register to have the files emailed directly to you.

You can download the code files by following these steps:

1. Log in or register at `www.packt.com`.

2. Select the **Support** tab.

3. Click on **Code Downloads**.

4. Enter the name of the book in the **Search** box and follow the onscreen instructions.

Once the file is downloaded, please make sure that you unzip or extract the folder using the latest version of:

- WinRAR/7-Zip for Windows

- Zipeg/iZip/UnRarX for Mac

- 7-Zip/PeaZip for Linux

The code bundle for the book is also hosted on GitHub at `https://github.com/PacktPublishing/Microsoft-Exam-MD-100-Windows-10-Certification-Guide`. In case there's an update to the code, it will be updated on the existing GitHub repository.

We also have other code bundles from our rich catalog of books and videos available at `https://github.com/PacktPublishing/`. Check them out!

Code in Action

Code in Action videos for this book can be viewed at (`https://bit.ly/2LsQDqD`).

Download the color images

We also provide a PDF file that has color images of the screenshots/diagrams used in this book. You can download it here: `https://static.packt-cdn.com/downloads/9781838822187_ColorImages.pdf`.

Conventions used

There are a number of text conventions used throughout this book.

`Code in text`: Indicates code words in text, database table names, folder names, filenames, file extensions, pathnames, dummy URLs, user input, and Twitter handles. Here is an example: "Replace `<KBnumber>` with the actual KB number in the command if you wish to uninstall the update."

Any command-line input or output is written as follows:

```
wmic qfe list brief /format:table
```

Bold: Indicates a new term, an important word, or words that you see onscreen. For example, words in menus or dialog boxes appear in the text like this. Here is an example: "Open **Settings | Update & Security | Windows Update** option."

> **Tips or important notes**
> Appear like this.

Get in touch

Feedback from our readers is always welcome.

General feedback: If you have questions about any aspect of this book, mention the book title in the subject of your message and email us at customercare@packtpub.com.

Errata: Although we have taken every care to ensure the accuracy of our content, mistakes do happen. If you have found a mistake in this book, we would be grateful if you would report this to us. Please visit www.packtpub.com/support/errata, selecting your book, clicking on the Errata Submission Form link, and entering the details.

Piracy: If you come across any illegal copies of our works in any form on the Internet, we would be grateful if you would provide us with the location address or website name. Please contact us at copyright@packt.com with a link to the material.

If you are interested in becoming an author: If there is a topic that you have expertise in and you are interested in either writing or contributing to a book, please visit authors.packtpub.com.

Reviews

Please leave a review. Once you have read and used this book, why not leave a review on the site that you purchased it from? Potential readers can then see and use your unbiased opinion to make purchase decisions, we at Packt can understand what you think about our products, and our authors can see your feedback on their book. Thank you!

For more information about Packt, please visit packt.com.

Section 1 : Deploying Windows

Windows 10 is Microsoft's latest version of its OS and the most widely adopted version in use today. Unlike previous Windows OS versions, Windows 10 is continuously updated with new features and capabilities and offers new methods of deployment, management, and integration with today's cloud technologies.

This section will help you develop an understanding of which edition is required for your enterprise. Also, you will learn how to customize different Windows 10 features, as well as how to install and deploy Windows 10 on any device.

This section comprises the following chapters:

- *Chapter 1, Deploying Windows 10*
- *Chapter 2, Upgrading Windows 10*
- *Chapter 3, Customizing and Configuring Windows 10*

1
Deploying Windows 10

Windows 10 is Microsoft's latest version of its **Operating System (OS)** and the most widely adopted version in use today. Unlike previous Windows OS versions, Windows 10 is continuously updated with new features and capabilities, and offers new methods of deployment, management, and integration with today's cloud technologies.

The first chapter of this book will introduce the first objective, which is deploying Windows 10. This chapter will begin to prepare you for the **MD-100** (Windows 10) exam, which is part the **Microsoft 365 Certified: Modern Desktop Administrator Associate** certification.

The following topics will be covered in this chapter:

- Understanding Windows 10 editions and capabilities
- Performing a clean installation

In this chapter, we will focus on the different Windows 10 editions and their capabilities. This chapter will also provide you with the necessary skills to perform a clean installation of Windows 10.

Technical requirements

In this chapter, you will learn step-by-step how a clean installation of Windows 10 works. These steps that you will follow have also been recorded. You can find these videos at `https://bit.ly/2LsQDqD`.

Understanding Windows 10 editions and capabilities

Microsoft has different Windows 10 editions available for home users, enterprise users, and education users.

Before you deploy Windows 10 in your environment, you must select the most suitable edition for your environment. The different Windows 10 editions address the needs of your environment and your end users. In this section, we will look at the different features of each edition, as well as the difference between the 32-bit and 64-bit versions. Let's start by looking at what Windows 10 editions are available.

Learning about Windows 10 editions

In this section, we will learn about the different Windows 10 editions that you can install in your organization. In the following screenshot, you can see the different Windows 10 editions that are available when you are installing from an installation media, such as **Digital Video Disc (DVD)** or **Universal Serial Bus (USB)**:

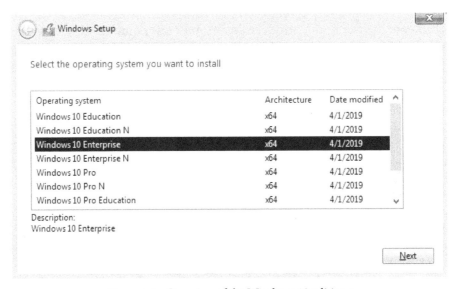

Figure 1.1 - Overview of the Windows 10 editions

Before you can install Windows 10, you must select the most suitable edition for your organization. In the following table, you can see the different Windows 10 editions and their consumers, ranging from individuals to large enterprises:

Edition	Consumer	Availability
Windows 10 Home	Individual/home use	Everybody
Windows 10 Pro	Small and medium-sized businesses, advanced users	Everybody
Windows 10 Enterprise	Large enterprises	Only available to Volume Licensing customers
Windows 10 Enterprise LTSB	Large enterprises	Only available to Volume Licensing customers
Windows 10 Education	School staff, administrators, teachers, and students	Only available through academic Volume Licensing

Table 1.1 - Various Windows editions

You can buy the Windows 10 Home and Windows 10 Pro editions via a computer shop or online. If you want to use the Windows 10 Enterprise or Windows 10 Education editions, then you must get a **Volume Licensing contract** via a software broker or directly from Microsoft.

In the next section, we will look at the different capabilities of each Windows edition.

Understanding Windows 10 capabilities

There are different features for each Windows 10 edition. So, if you were to install and use any one of the Windows OS editions, then you would need to have pretty decent knowledge of these features. We will list what these main different features are in each Windows 10 edition.

Windows 10 Home

Windows 10 Home edition is a consumer-oriented desktop edition of Windows 10. Windows 10 Home is pre-installed on consumer **Personal Computers (PCs)**, tablets, and hybrid laptop/tablets. The new features of Windows 10 Home are as follows:

- **Cortana**
- **Microsoft Edge**
- Tablet mode for touch devices
- **Windows Hello**

- Virtual desktops
- **Windows Sandbox**
- Built-in universal Windows apps such as Photos, Maps, Mail, and so on
- New updates and features are received automatically
- Support for Windows Information Protection through **Mobile Application Management** (**MAM**) via **Intune**

Windows 10 Pro

Windows 10 Pro edition has the same features as Windows 10 Home, but with many extra features to meet the needs of small- and medium-sized businesses. Some of these features are as follows:

- **BitLocker**
- **Virtualization**
- **Windows Autopilot**
- **Windows Update for Business**
- Active Directory domain join
- Ability to join **Azure Active Directory** (**Azure AD**)
- Group policy management
- **Remote Desktop**
- **Windows Store for Business**
- Enterprise Data Protection
- Granular User Experience Control

Windows 10 Enterprise

Windows 10 Enterprise edition has the same features mentioned earlier, but with more features, such as the following:

- **Always on VPN**, also known as **DirectAccess**. This feature is supported on all Windows 10 editions that have at the **Windows 10 version 1607 (Anniversary Edition)** installed.
- **Windows to Go Creator**.
- **AppLocker**.

- Start Screen Control with Group Policy.
- **Windows Defender Credential Guard**.
- **Windows Defender Application Control**.
- **Windows Defender Application Guard**.

Windows 10 Enterprise LTSB

Windows 10 Enterprise **Long-Term Servicing Branch** (**LTSB**) is a special edition that Microsoft will not update with any new features. This version only gets security updates and other important updates. *Why only security updates and not any feature updates?* Because you can install Windows 10 Enterprise LTSB on devices that run on specialized systems, such as PCs that control medical equipment, **Automated Teller Machines** (**ATMs**), **Point Of Sale** (**POS**) systems, and many other *critical* systems.

The Windows 10 Enterprise LTSB has fewer features than the Windows 10 Enterprise edition. These include the following:

- Many built-in universal Windows apps are missing
- No Cortana
- No Windows Store
- No **Microsoft Edge** browser

Windows 10 Education

Windows 10 Education edition offers the same features as the Windows 10 Enterprise edition. This edition is only available through **Academic Volume Licensing** and is suitable for teachers, students, administrators, and school staff.

Learning about 32-bit versus 64-bit Windows 10 editions

All the previously mentioned Windows 10 editions, as shown in the *Table 1.1*, are available in both 32-bit and 64-bit versions. The 64-bit versions are similar to the 32-bit versions, but they offer several advantages, such as the following:

- Improved performance
- Enhanced memory
- Improved security
- Support for the **Hyper-V** feature

Keep in mind that the 64-bit editions of Windows 10 do not support the 16-bit **Windows on Win32 (WoW)** environment. If your environment requires 16-bit application versions, consider deploying those applications in a separate way. This is because Windows 10 64-bit editions will refuse to run those applications.

> **Important Note**
> All 32-bit Operating Systems are limited to 4 GB of addressable memory, while the 64-bit OS can address more than 4 GB. The 64-bit version of Windows 10 Home will not support the Hyper-V feature.

Performing a clean installation

There are different methods for carrying out a Windows 10 installation. In this section, we will focus on a clean installation.

Making a new deployment of any kind of Windows 10 edition consists of nothing more than carrying out a clean installation of your hardware. For example, imagine a situation in which you buy yourself a self-customized gaming PC with different hardware components because you want the best of the best. However, this gaming PC is then delivered without an operating system. In cases like this, you would carry out a clean installation.

However, there a few different approaches to carrying out a clean installation of Windows 10. Some examples are as follows:

- **Installation media**: When you buy a self-customized gaming PC with different hardware components, you will use a DVD or USB with a **Windows 10 ISO** file on it and boot the computer from your installation media.

- **System image**: A system image also refers to a golden image. It is typically a file that contains a snapshot, which can be referred as a capture image, of a generic computer with the OS installed, including drivers, specific configurations, and perhaps some applications, such as **Microsoft Office** and **Adobe Reader**.

  There are various tools available for creating and deploying images, such as **System Center Configuration Manager (SCCM)** and **Microsoft Deployment Toolkit (MDT)**. A system image is the preferred method and is used for medium- and large-sized enterprise organizations. These kinds of deployments are faster and more automated than installing from a DVD or USB.

- **Windows Autopilot**: If the computer already has Windows 10 pre-installed, then Windows Autopilot can be used to carry out a new deployment. Windows Autopilot allows administrators to apply organization-specific configurations and some types of applications.

This can be done with Intune, for example, as most computers nowadays come with Windows 10 pre-installed and enable organizations to come to the same result, without needing to deploy system images over the corporate network. Windows Autopilot will not be discussed in this exam guide, because this topic belongs to **MD-101**.

Understanding the clean installation process

This section will cover step-by-step instructions on how to install Windows 10 on a new or existing device through a clean installation (so no in-place upgrades or migration paths). Let's make a start:

1. Insert your Windows 10 installation media, start the computer, and boot from the installation media:

```
Press any key to boot from CD or DVD....
```

Figure 1.2 - Press any key screen for Windows 10 installation

2. On the **Windows Setup** screen, choose the appropriate language, **Time and currency format**, and **Keyboard or input method** and click **Next**:

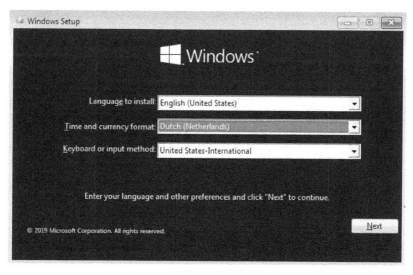

Figure 1.3 - Language and preferences Windows Setup window

3. After that, on the **Windows Setup** window, click **Install Now**:

Figure 1.4 - Install now Windows Setup window

4. Then, on the **Select the operating system you want to install** window, choose your appropriate Windows 10 edition and click **Next**:

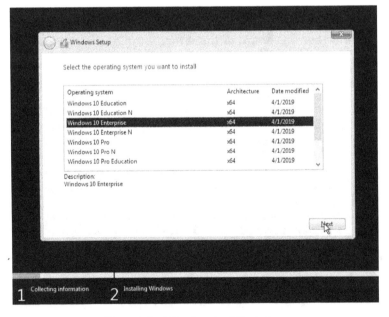

Figure 1.5 - Selecting the OS window

5. Then, on the **Applicable notices and license term** window, accept the license terms and click **Next**:

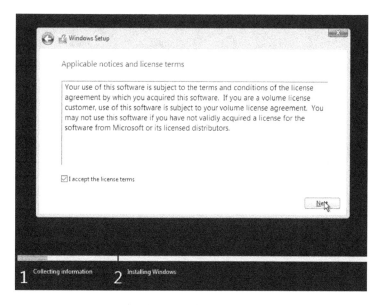

Figure 1.6 - Accepting license terms window

6. After that, on the **Which type of installation do you want?** window, choose the **Custom: Install Windows only (advanced)** option:

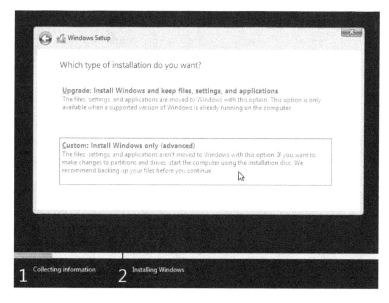

Figure 1.7 - Selecting the type of installation

7. Then, on the **Where do you want to install Windows?** window, select **Drive 0 Unallocated Space** and click **Next**:

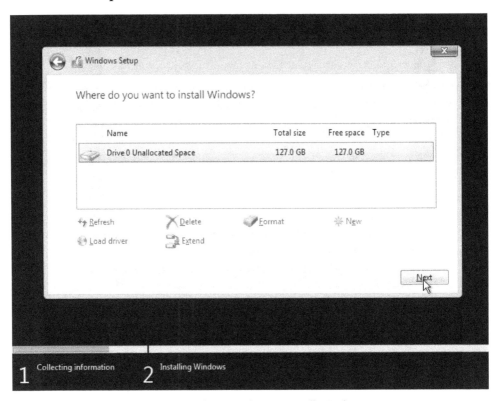

Figure 1.8 - Selecting where to install Windows

> **Important Note**
> For a clean installation of Windows 10 on a device that already has an OS installed on it, erase all the partitions by formatting or deleting any partitions during the setup process.

So, now, the installation begins. After a few minutes, you will need to choose the appropriate settings, such as keyboards, regions, and more. Follow these steps to finish the installation of Windows 10:

1. On the **Let's start with region. Is this right?** window, select your region and click **Yes**:

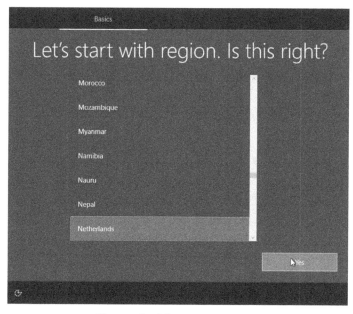

Figure 1.9 - Selecting your region

2. Then, on the **Is this the right keyboard layout?** window, choose your respective keyboard layout and click **Yes**:

Figure 1.10 - Selecting the right keyboard layout

3. After that, on the **Want to add a second keyboard layout?** window, click **Skip**:

Figure 1.11 - Adding a second keyboard layout

4. Then, on the **Sign in with Microsoft** page, click on **Domain join instead** to add a local account:

Figure 1.12 - Sign in with Microsoft account window

5. After that, on the **Who's going to use this PC?** window, fill in a name and click **Next**:

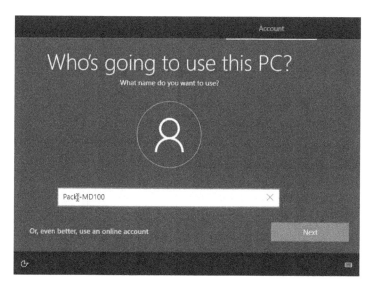

Figure 1.13 - Adding a name to the PC account

6. On the **Create a super memorable password** page, enter a password and click **Next**:

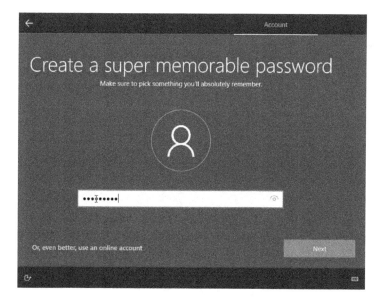

Figure 1.14 - Creating a password

7. After that, on the **Confirm your password** page, again, fill in the same password from the previous page and click **Next**:

Figure 1.15 - Confirming your password

8. After that, on the **Create security questions for this account** page, choose three questions, fill in their corresponding answers, and click **Next**:

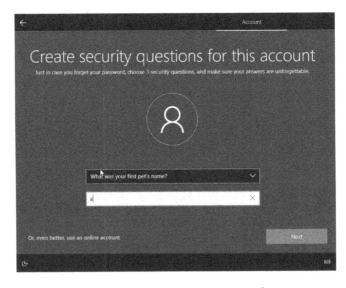

Figure 1.16 - Creating security questions and answers

9. Then, on the **Do more across devices with activity history** page, click on the option of your choice. For now, we will choose **No**:

Figure 1.17 - Activating an account's activity history

10. On the **Do more with your voice** page, select the option of your choice and select **Accept**:

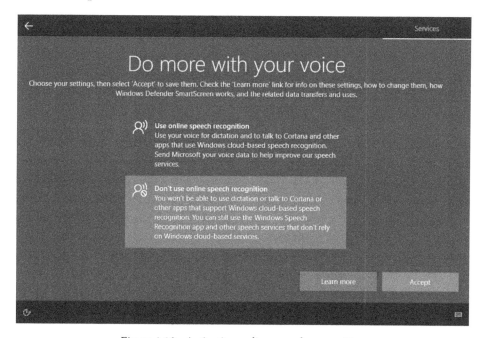

Figure 1.18 - Activating online speech recognition

11. The, on the **Let Microsoft and apps use your location** page, select the option of your choice and select **Accept**:

Figure 1.19 - Selecting to use your location

12. Then, on the **Find my device** page, select the option of your choice and select **Accept**:

Figure 1.20 - Choosing to turn on Find my device

13. After that, on the **Send diagnostic data to Microsoft** page, select the option of your choice and select **Accept**:

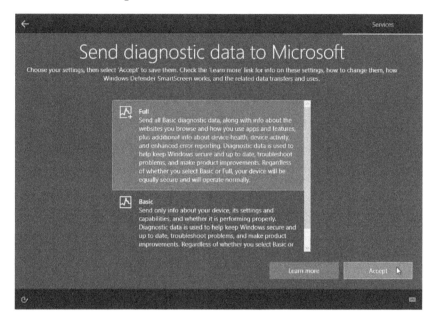

Figure 1.21 - Choosing to Send diagnostic data to Microsoft

14. Then, on the **Improve inking & typing** page, select the option of your choice and select **Accept**:

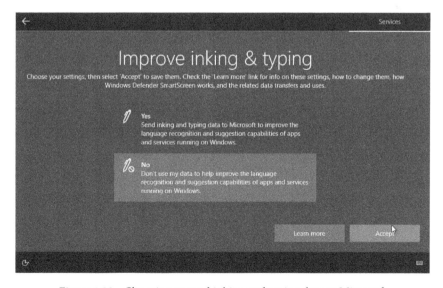

Figure 1.22 - Choosing to send inking and typing data to Microsoft

15. After that, on the **Get tailored experiences with diagnostic data** page, select the option of your choice and select **Accept**:

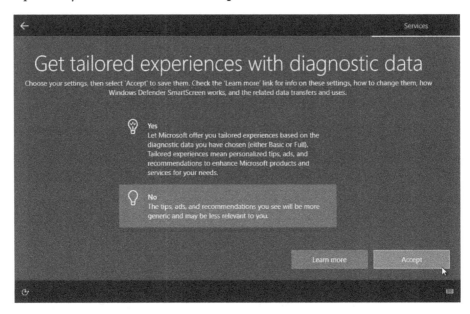

Figure 1.23 - Choosing to let Microsoft offer you more relevant tips

16. Then, on the **Let apps use advertising ID** page, select the option of your choice and select **Accept**:

Figure 1.24 - Choosing to let apps use advertising ID

17. After a while, the installation of Windows 10 will be finished, and you will see the desktop environment. With that, you have successfully installed Windows 10 through a clean installation method.

At this point, you have performed a clean installation of Windows 10 on a computer. Such an installation, as you did in the previous steps, will only occur if you've bought a new computer without an OS, or if you want to reinstall Windows 10 completely on your computer.

Summary

In this chapter, we learned about the various aspects and troubleshooting methods of Windows 10. You learned about the different Windows 10 editions and their capabilities, as well as how to perform a clean installation of Windows 10.

After completing this chapter, you have the skills to install and boot the Windows 10 OS successfully.

In the next chapter, you are going to learn how to do an in-place upgrade from, for example, Windows 8.1 to Windows 10. You will also learn how to troubleshoot activation issues and how to migrate user data.

Questions

1. You want to deploy **Applocker** and **Windows Defender Credential Guard** on your school's network. Can you install the Windows 10 Education version?

2. Can you buy Windows 10 Enterprise in a computer store?

3. You have a 32-bit version of Windows 10. Is it possible to install the Hyper-V feature?

4. Is it possible to boot and install Windows 10 from a DVD?

Further reading

- **What is the difference between a 32-bit and 64-bit CPU?**: https://www.computerhope.com/issues/ch001498.htm

- **Introducing Windows 10 Editions**: https://blogs.windows.com/windowsexperience/2015/05/13/introducing-windows-10-editions/

2
Upgrading Windows 10

In the previous chapter, you learned about the different editions of Windows 10 and how to perform a clean installation. Besides doing a clean installation, you need to learn how to perform an in-place upgrade of Windows 10.

In this chapter, we will focus on how to upgrade Windows 10 from an earlier edition. We will also learn about different installation methods, as well as how to configure language packs. In addition to this, we will learn how to migrate user data and how to troubleshoot activation methods.

This chapter will provide you with the necessary skills that will help you successfully upgrade earlier Windows **Operating System** (**OS**) editions to Windows 10.

The following topics will be covered in this chapter:

- Performing an in-place upgrade
- Configuring language packs
- Migrating user data
- Troubleshooting activation issues

Technical requirements

In this chapter, you will learn, step by step, how an in-place upgrade to Windows 10 works. These steps that you will follow have also been recorded. You can find these videos at `https://bit.ly/2LsQDqD`.

Performing an in-place upgrade

In this section, we will look at the in-place upgrade method. An in-place upgrade is also known as an upgrade. For example, you may have several **Windows 7** desktops or laptops and you want to upgrade these desktop machines to Windows 10.

During an in-place upgrade, all user applications, hardware device settings, data, files, and other configuration information are retained. An in-place upgrade consists of four phases that occur throughout the upgrade process:

1. System check
2. Installing Windows 10 with **Windows Preinstallation Environment** (**WinPE**)
3. First startup
4. Installing the OS and a second startup

> **Important Note**
> During the upgrade installation, you can rollback in any of these four phases. However, always back up any important data before doing the upgrade.

You can upgrade any Windows 7 or Windows 8.1 edition to a Windows 10 edition. If you want to upgrade from Windows 8 to Windows 10, then you must install the Windows 8.1 update.

The following table shows some of the upgrade paths to Windows 10:

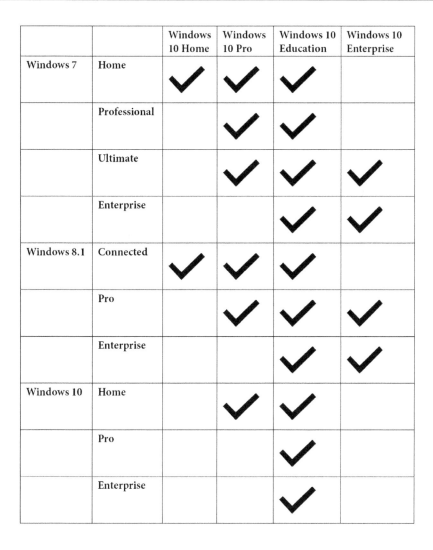

		Windows 10 Home	Windows 10 Pro	Windows 10 Education	Windows 10 Enterprise
Windows 7	Home	✓	✓	✓	
	Professional		✓	✓	
	Ultimate		✓	✓	✓
	Enterprise			✓	✓
Windows 8.1	Connected	✓	✓	✓	
	Pro		✓	✓	✓
	Enterprise			✓	✓
Windows 10	Home		✓	✓	
	Pro			✓	
	Enterprise			✓	

Table 2.1 - Upgrade paths to Windows 10

In the preceding table, you can see which upgrade paths are supported for Windows 10. For example, Windows 8.1 Pro can seamlessly upgrade to Windows 10 Enterprise.

Selecting the right tools for upgrading

You can use different tools to perform an in-place upgrade. In this section, we will choose the appropriate method for this and highlight a few of them.

The following diagram shows four of the different methods that are available for carrying out an in-place upgrade:

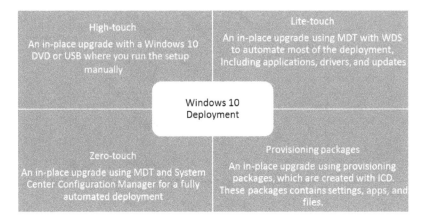

Figure 2.1 - Windows 10 upgrade options

We'll look at the four methods shown in the preceding diagram, one by one, in the following sections. This will allow us to understand why one method may be more suitable than another in certain projects.

Understanding the High-touch deployment method

This type of deployment strategy is time-consuming. However, it can be ideal for small organizations with less than 100 computers and no IT staff. For this, you need to go to each computer and manually start the Windows 10 installation from a **Digital Video Disc (DVD)** or **Universal Serial Bus (USB)**, which requires you to provide an answer for each prompt during the setup stage.

Learning about the lite-touch deployment method

This type of deployment strategy is ideal for medium-sized organizations with between 200 and 500 computers. In most cases, this deployment type uses the **Microsoft Deployment Toolkit (MDT)** in combination with **Windows Deployment Services (WDS)**. MDT automates most of the installation of Windows 10 together with installing applications, device drivers, and updates.

Important Note

Windows Assessment and Deployment Kit (Windows ADK) must be installed on the MDT server before you can install the Microsoft Deployment Toolkit.

Understanding the Zero-touch deployment method

This type of deployment strategy is ideal for large organizations with more than 500 computers. This strategy uses the **Microsoft Deployment Toolkit** (**MDT**) in combination with **System Center Configuration Manager** (**SCCM**) for a more streamlined and fully automated deployment without any user intervention. In some organizations, you will see that they have SCCM without MDT. That also works perfectly because many options that you can configure in MDT can also be configured in SCCM with Task Sequences.

Learning about provisioning packages

With the Windows **Imaging and Configuration Designer** (**ICD**) tool, you can create provisioning packages, which you can use to deploy to computers via email, network share, or removable media.

These packages modify a Windows 10 installation and configure it without reinstalling the Windows OS. This type of provisioning eases the installation process and helps reduce the costs of deploying Windows 10 installations.

You can install the Windows ICD tool from the **Windows Assessment and Deployment Kit** (**Windows ADK**). The following screenshot shows the **Windows Configuration Designer** application, along with an example setting that can be changed:

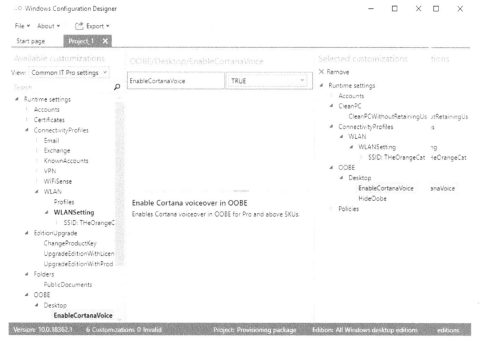

Figure 2.2 - Windows Configuration Designer

In the preceding example application, we can see that we set the **EnableCortanaVoice** setting to **True**. Provisioning packages contain many rules for customizing a Windows 10 installation. These include the following:

- Change edition upgrade
- Configure settings (such as computer name, domain, local users, Start Menu customization, and so on)
- Add or remove Universal Apps
- Deploy drivers, applications, and execute scripts
- Configure VPN and/or Wi-Fi profiles

In this section, you learned about the different tools you can use to do an in-place upgrade. Choose the right solution for your organization to save time and effort. In the next section, we will take a closer look at why you should do an in-place upgrade or a migration scenario.

Learning about High-touch in-place upgrades

Since there are several in-place upgrade methods, we will look at this topic as a step-by-step guide to performing a High-touch in-place upgrade. Before you do the in-place upgrade on any computer, the recommendation is to create a backup first, before proceeding with the upgrade. In this example, we have a running Windows 8.1 Enterprise edition and we will do an in-place upgrade to Windows 10 Enterprise edition:

1. Run the `setup.exe` program from the root of the Windows 10 installation media:

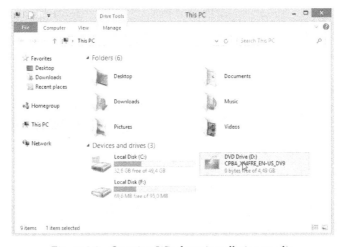

Figure 2.3 - Opening Windows installation media

2. On the **User Account Control** window, click **Yes** to allow the program to make changes:

Figure 2.4 - User Account Control window

3. Then, on the **Install Windows 10** page, click **Next**:

Figure 2.5 - Install Windows 10 screen

4. On the **Select Image** page, choose the appropriate Windows 10 edition and click **Next**:

Figure 2.6 - Select Image screen

5.   On the **Applicable notices and license terms** page, click **Accept**:

Figure 2.7 - Accepting license terms screen

6.   Then, on the **Ready to install** page, adjust the **Change what to keep** setting so that it's relevant to you and click **Install**:

Figure 2.8 - Ready to install screen

The in-place upgrade will now start, and your computer will restart several times. This might take some time:

Figure 2.9 - Working on updates blue screen

After the setup is finished, you can log in with your account and proceed with finishing the upgrade.

7. Now, on the **Do more with your voice** page, select the option of your choice and select **Accept**:

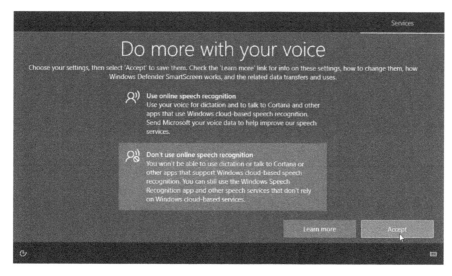

Figure 2.10 - Activating online speech recognition

8. Then, on the **Let Microsoft and apps use your location** page, select the option of your choice and select **Accept**:

Figure 2.11 - Selecting to use your location

9. After that, on the **Find my device** page, select the option of your choice and select **Accept**:

Figure 2.12 - Choosing to turn on the Find my device option

10. Then, on the **Send diagnostic data to Microsoft** page, select the option of your choice and select **Accept**:

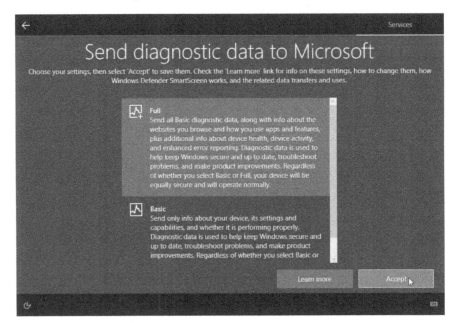

Figure 2.13 - Choosing to Send diagnostic data to Microsoft

11. After that, on the **Improve inking & typing** page, select the option of your choice and select **Accept**:

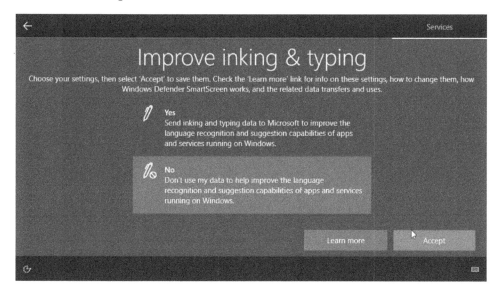

Figure 2.14 - Choosing to send inking and typing data to Microsoft

12. Then, on the **Get tailored experiences with diagnostic data** page, select the option of your choice and select **Accept**:

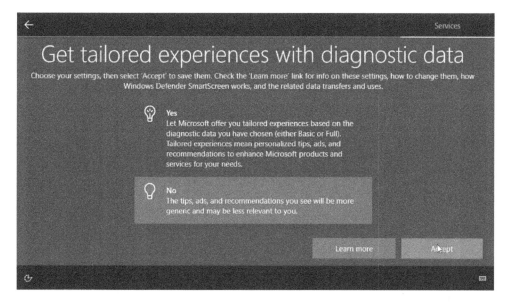

Figure 2.15 - Choosing to let Microsoft offer you more relevant tips

13. After that, on the **Let apps use advertising ID** page, select the option of your choice and select **Accept**:

Figure 2.16 - Choosing to let apps use advertising ID

After the last step, you will see your desktop. With this, your computer has been successfully upgraded from Windows 8.1 Enterprise to Windows 10 Enterprise.

Choosing between an in-place upgrade and migration

In this (and the previous) section, you will learn about the difference between an in-place upgrade and a migration of Windows 10. Each upgrade project is a different upgrade, especially in larger organizations. The following tables show some of the advantages and disadvantages of the two scenarios for in-place upgrade:

Advantages	Disadvantages
Retains user and application settings and files.	No ability to start fresh with a default Windows 10 OS.
Preserves installed application, typically without the need to reinstall them.	Preserved installed applications may not work after upgrading from an older Windows version.
Additional storage is not required for migration files.	Files or settings from an in-place upgrade can lead to performance and security issues.
User interaction is minimal.	Does not allow changes to the edition of Windows 10.
A simpler setup process.	Is only available on supported Operating Systems
Rollback is possible in case of a problem.	Computers need to have the minimum hardware requirements.

Table 2.2 - In-place upgrade comparison

The in-place upgrade is the recommended way to move from an existing Windows OS to Windows 10. You perform an in-place upgrade when you want to retain all user applications, files, and settings. During an in-place upgrade, the installation program will do this automatically for you.

The following table shows the advantages and disadvantages of a migration scenario:

Advantages	Disadvantages
Offers a fresh start for existing computers. More stable and secure.	You need to use migration tools such as User State Migration Tool (USMT) to capture and restore user data and settings.
Allows installation of any kind of Windows 10 edition.	Reinstallation of applications is necessary.
You can reconfigure hardware-level settings, such as disk partitioning.	Requires additional storage for migrated user's data, settings, and files.
Malicious software, viruses, and malware are eliminated on the computer.	Can have an impact on user productivity because of reconfiguring applications and their settings.

Table 2.3 - Migration comparison

You can perform a migration when you have a computer already running the Windows OS and you need to move files and settings to a new Windows 10-based computer. You can perform the migration as follows:

1. Back up the user's settings and data.

2. Perform a clean installation.

3. Reinstall the necessary applications.

4. Restore the user's settings and data.

Now, we will move on to the next section about configuring language packs.

Configuring language packs

With a language pack for Windows 10, you can set different **User Interface** (**UI**) elements to the language you want, such as dialog boxes, (Start) menu items, and help files.

There are different ways to add a language pack to your Windows 10 installation. In this section, we will highlight a few.

Important Note

You can add language packs and regional support to any kind of Windows 10 edition, except for the **Windows 10 Home Single Language** and **Windows 10 Home Country-Specific** editions.

In the following screenshot, you can see the **Language** settings page:

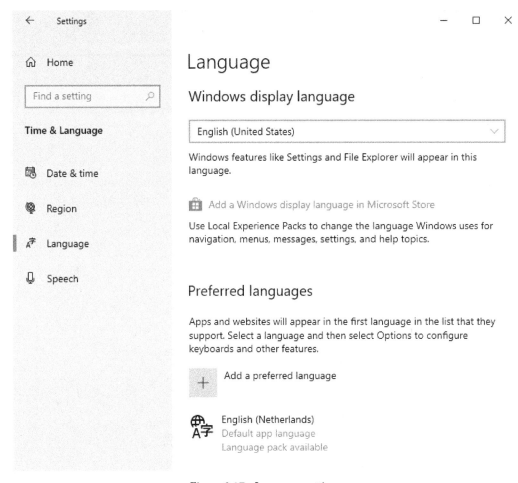

Figure 2.17 - Language settings

As shown in the previous screenshot, on this page, you can add and remove additional languages.

Windows 10 installations start with at least one language pack and its components. You can add the following packs:

- **Language packs**: **Language packs (LPs)** are localization packages that are delivered as .cab files. These .cab files includes UI elements such as dialog boxes, (Start) menu items, and help files. These are delivered as a .cab file.

- **Features on Demand**: **Features on Demand (FOD)** packs includes language basics, such as spelling check, fonts, handwriting, character recognition, text-to-speech, and speech recognition. These are delivered as a .cab file.

- **Language Interface Packs**: **Language Interface Packs (LIPs)** are partially localized language packs. These LIPs require a base language pack. From **Windows 10 1809**, these packs are delivered as **Local Experience Packs (LXP)** and they have a .appx file extension. For previous versions of Windows 10, these files are delivered as .cab files.

As you can see, there are three different language packs that you can add in Windows 10. You can manually add language packs and FOD packs. LIPs are designed for regional markets that do not have a fully localized version of Windows 10.

How to get and install language packs

You can add language packs after Windows 10 has been installed by selecting **Settings | Time & Language | Language**.

In the following example, we will add the **Dutch (Nederlands)** language pack and the **Features on Demand** options to the Windows 10 installation. We will do this like so:

1. Click on the **Settings | Time & Language | Language** option.

2. Click on **Add a preferred language**, as shown in the following screenshot:

Preferred languages

Apps and websites will appear in the first language in the list that they
support. Select a language and then select Options to configure
keyboards and other features.

 Add a preferred language

Figure 2.18 - Preferred languages page

3. Type in the name of the language that you want to add and click **Next**. On this
    window, you can select what you want to add and then click on **Install**:

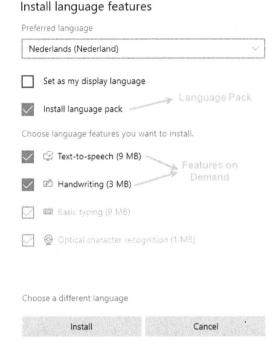

Figure 2.19 - Install language features page

4. After clicking **Install**, your selected language will be installed (the time this will
    take will depend on the size of your language pack), including the features you have
    selected:

Figure 2.20 - Selecting the desired language pack

5. If you want to change the language pack options or completely remove the language
    pack, click on the corresponding buttons:

Figure 2.21 - Language pack options

In this section, you learned how to add a language pack and features on demand to a Windows 10 installation. In the next section, we will take a look at how to migrate user data.

Migrating user data

If your company does not use roaming profiles or any other kind of user experience management, you can use Microsoft **User State Migration Tool** (**USMT**) to migrate user state and data during large deployments of Windows 10 in an organization.

> **Important Note**
>
> USMT can be installed when setting up the **Windows Assessment and Deployment Kit** (**Windows ADK**).

USMT captures user accounts, user files, OS settings, and application settings before migration and migrates these settings to your new Windows 10 installation. This can be used for computer replacement and computer migrations. You will need to set up a file server or a removal media to store the computer settings and user settings during the migration process. To migrate user settings, you need to know the following commands: `scanstate.exe` and `loadstate.exe`.

Understanding the scanstate.exe command

The `scanstate` command is used to scan the source computer, collect files and settings, and write them to a file share or a removable media.

The syntax of this command is as follows:

```
scanstate.exe \\server\share\folder\ /i:migapp.xml /i:miguser.
xml
```

Here, `scanstate.exe` is the command we use to back up the user's data and applications; `\\server\share\folder` is the path to your shared folder or removable media where you put the backup file; and `/i:migapp.xml` and `/i:miguser.xml` are the files that are required in order to migrate supported application settings and user settings.

We can execute the `scanstate.exe` command like so:

```
scanstate.exe X:\Migration\ /i:migapp.xml /i:miguser.xml
```

In the following screenshot, you can see the output of the previous command:

Figure 2.22 - Output from the scanstate.exe command

In the preceding screenshot, if you look at the file path that you used in the command, you will see a USMT.MIG file:

Home	Share	View

This PC > USB drive (X:) > Migration > USMT

Name	Date modified	Type	Size
USMT.MIG	14/10/2019 14:27	MIG File	367.301 KB

Figure 2.23 - The scanstate.exe migration file

This .mig file contains all the user's files, OS settings, and application settings. As you can see, this file is nearly 370 MB in size.

Understanding the loadstate.exe command

Now that you've used the scanstate command and the migration to Windows 10 is ready, you can use the loadstate command to restore the .mig file you created earlier, which contains all the user files, OS settings, and application settings, we will restore the file to the new installed computer so that the user can start using their new computer straight away.

The syntax of this command is as follows:

```
loadstate.exe \\server\share\folder\ /i:migapp.xml /i:miguser.
xml
```

Here, `loadstate.exe` is the command we use to migrate the user's data and applications; `\\server\share\folder` is the path to your shared folder or removable media where the backup file has been placed; and the `/i:migapp.xml` and `/i:miguser.xml` files are required to restore the application settings and user settings.

We can execute the `loadstate.exe` command like so:

```
loadstate.exe X:\Migration\ /i:migapp.xml /i:miguser.xml
```

In the following screenshot, you can see the output of the previous command:

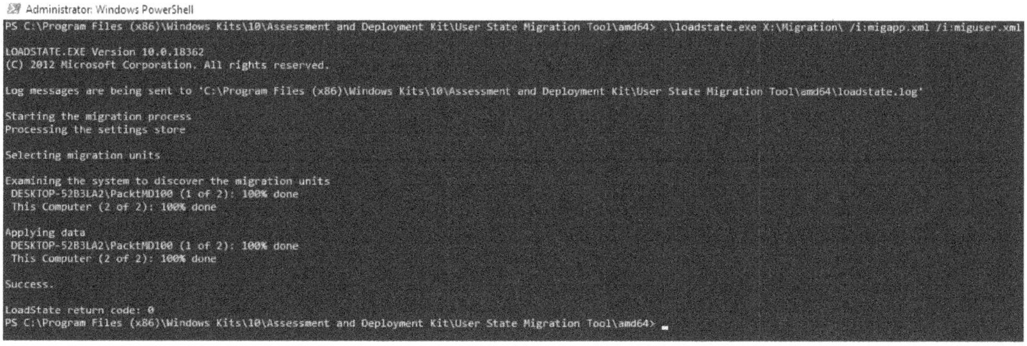

Figure 2.24 - Output from the loadstate.exe command

In the preceding screenshot, you can see that all the user's files, OS settings, and application settings have been migrated to the new computer.

Now, let's move on to troubleshooting activation issues.

Troubleshooting activation issues

Since the release of **Windows XP** back in 2001, we have needed to activate our Windows installation. **Windows Product Activation** is used to protect users against illegal copies of a Windows 10 installation. The combination of your hardware and your Windows 10 license is crucial. If you change your hardware frequently, you'll need to activate your installation again.

Since Windows 10, there has been an enormous difference regarding product distribution. For existing Windows 7, Windows 8, and Windows 8.1 users, Windows 10 is free for the first year. However, you still need to activate the product after that time. Windows 10 does not have a grace period, which was possible with Windows 7. Instead, you must activate Windows 10 after the installation is finished. If you do not activate it, then it is not possible to make any customizations.

Learning about activation methods

As we discussed, it is important to activate the Windows OS to make optimal use of its features. There are three different methods for activating your Windows 10 installation. These methods are as follows:

- **Retail activation**: If you buy a new Windows 10 product in a retail store, it comes with a unique product key that you can use during the product installation process.

- **OEM activation**: If you buy new hardware with Windows 10 pre-installed, then you can associate the new hardware with the OS. Normally, this will be done automatically during the installation of Windows 10.

- **Microsoft Volume Licensing**: This type of licensing is mostly tailored to the size of your organization. This is a special agreement between your organization and Microsoft. These agreements include more benefits, such as **Software Assurance**, support, upgrade benefits, **FastTrack** options, and so on. You use the **Volume Activation Services** role to assist with the activation process via the **Key Management Service** (**KMS**). You can also use the **Multiple Activation Key** (**MAK**) models. The main difference between these activation methods is that KMS uses a **Licensing Server** in your network, while MAK will contact Microsoft's activation service directly.

Now that you have understood the different activation methods, let's understand the different methods we can use to troubleshoot activation issues.

Understanding troubleshooting methods

Before you start troubleshooting to find out why your version of Windows 10 hasn't been activated, please check if you have a working internet connection. After you have confirmed that the internet is working, you can view the activation status of your version of Windows 10 by opening **Start** | **Settings** | **Update & Security** | **Activation**. This activation page is shown in the following screenshot:

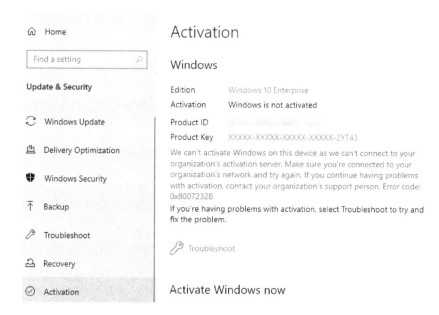

Figure 2.25 - Settings app activation status

Alternatively, you can view the activation status of Windows 10 by running the following command in the Command Prompt:

```
slmgr.vbs -dli
```

When you run the `slmgr.vbs -dli` command and press *Enter*, you will see a pop-up that displays the current activation status:

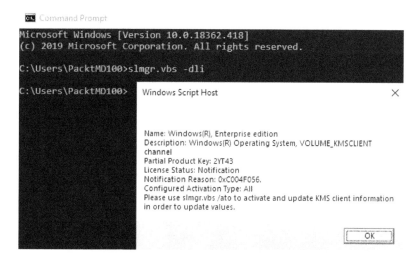

Figure 2.26 - Current activation status pop-up

As shown in the previous screenshot, my Windows 10 installation hasn't been activated because there are some problems with finding the KMS server. However, I can use a MAK key to activate my Windows 10 installation.

You can do this by using the **Windows 10 Activation troubleshooter**. To open it, click **Start | Settings | Update & Security | Activation | Troubleshoot**. If Windows 10 still cannot find any KMS server, then you can choose **Change product key**. We can do this as follows:

1. Enter your product key and press **Next** to continue:

Figure 2.27 - Enter a product key window

2. On the next window, click **Activate**:

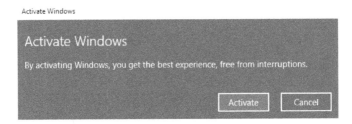

Figure 2.28 - Activate Windows window

3. After a few seconds, you will see that this copy of **Windows is activated**. Click **Close** to close this window:

Figure 2.29 - Windows is activated window

4. After you have closed this window, you will see a confirmation message, stating that the specified version of Windows has been activated:

Activation

Windows

Edition	Windows 10 Enterprise
Activation	Windows is activated with a digital license
	Learn more

Figure 2.30 - Confirmation of activation window

Instead of activating your version of Windows 10 through the **Settings** app, you can also use the Command Prompt. To do this, follow these steps:

1. Open the Command Prompt as an Administrator.

2. Type the following command and press *Enter*:

```
slmgr.vbs -ipk <productkey>
```

In the following screenshot, you can see the output of the preceding command and that the product key has been successfully installed:

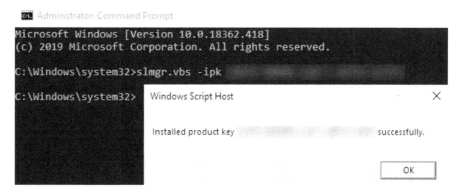

Figure 2.31 - Product key installed successfully

3. Now, you need to run the following command and press *Enter*:

```
slmgr.vbs -ato
```

4. The following screenshot shows the output of the preceding command and that the product has been successfully activated:

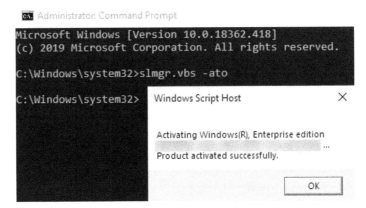

Figure 2.32 - Product activated successfully

After this, your Windows 10 installation will be activated, and all the features and customization options will be available. You can now interact with all the features of Windows 10.

Summary

In this chapter, you learned how to perform an in-place upgrade with various tools. You also learned about the various kinds of language packs, FOD packs, and LIPs that are available, as well as how to install them. You also learned how to migrate user data and how to troubleshoot activation problems.

After reading this chapter, you have the skills to perform an upgrade of Windows 10. You can also troubleshoot the problems that you might face while activating a Windows 10 OS.

In the next chapter, you will learn how to customize different Windows 10 features, such as the Start menu, Edge settings, and configure startup options.

Questions

1. Can you upgrade from Windows 8 Pro to Windows 10 Pro in just one step?

2. If you want to add **Text-to-speech** and **Handwriting** to your Windows 10 OS, can you install the language pack for this?

3. Is it possible to upgrade from **Windows 8.1 Connected** edition to a **Windows 10 Education** edition?

Further reading

- **Install the Windows 8.1 Update (KB 2919355)**: `https://support.microsoft.com/en-us/help/15356/windows-8-install-update-kb-2919355`

- **Windows Configuration Designer provisioning settings (reference)**: `https://docs.microsoft.com/en-us/windows/configuration/wcd/wcd?redirectedfrom=MSDN`

- **Windows 10 upgrade paths**: `https://docs.microsoft.com/en-us/windows/deployment/upgrade/windows-10-upgrade-paths`

- **ScanState syntax**: `https://docs.microsoft.com/en-us/windows/deployment/usmt/usmt-scanstate-syntax`

- **LoadState syntax**: `https://docs.microsoft.com/en-us/windows/deployment/usmt/usmt-loadstate-syntax`

- **Understanding Volume Activation Services**: `https://secureinfra.blog/2019/01/13/understanding-volume-activation-services-part-1-kms-and-mak/`

- **Switch between languages using the Language bar**: `https://support.office.com/en-us/article/switch-between-languages-using-the-language-bar-1c2242c0-fe15-4bc3-99bc-535de6f4f258`

3
Customizing and Configuring Windows 10

Windows 10 is Microsoft's latest version of its **Operating System** (**OS**) and is the most widely adopted version in use today. Unlike previous Windows OS versions, Windows 10 is continuously updated with new features and capabilities and offers new methods of deployment, management, and integration with today's cloud technologies.

This chapter introduces the second objective of this book, which is learning about customizing and configuring Windows 10. We will focus on how to configure **Edge** and **Internet Explorer** (**IE**) and their different sign-in options. Furthermore, we will learn how to customize the desktop and the Start menu. Of course, we will also cover working with **PowerShell**.

The following topics will be covered in this chapter:

- Configuring Edge and IE
- Configuring the sign-in options
- Configuring the mobility options
- Customizing the Windows desktop
- Customizing the Windows Start menu
- Working with PowerShell

By providing you with the necessary skills to use Windows 10, this chapter will help you to prepare for the **MD-100** (Windows 10) exam, which is part of the **Microsoft 365 Certified: Modern Desktop Administrator Associate** certification.

Technical requirements

In this chapter, you will see us use PowerShell code. This code is available at the following GitHub page: `https://github.com/PacktPublishing/Microsoft-Exam-MD-100-Windows-10-Certification-Guide/tree/master/Chapter03`

Configuring Edge and IE

With the introduction of Windows 10, Edge is the new default browser on Windows 10. So, you might expect Edge to replace **IE 11**, but this isn't the case. Windows 10 still has IE 11, but it's there for legacy purposes, such as for web applications that use **ActiveX** components.

But how different are Edge and IE? Let's explore this in the upcoming sections.

Understanding Edge

Edge is built to be highly compatible as it has modern web standards, such as **HTML5**, and provides a consistent interface across different Windows 10 devices. Edge's interface is simple and touch-friendly, and it offers a safe and fast browsing experience. Edge is also available on **Android** and **iOS** devices.

One of the benefits of the integration between Windows 10 and Edge is the ability to customize Edge for your organization. You can configure these settings through **Group Policy** or **Microsoft Intune**. We are not going to look at every setting in this chapter, but we have provided links to these settings at the end of this chapter.

Some of the best features of Edge are as follows:

- **Reading View**: This presents an attractive, distraction-free layout so that you can concentrate on the page's text.

- **Web Notes**: This is a feature that allows you to send web pages to OneNote, as well as to make any notations on the page or highlight text.

- **Cortana integration**: This brings Microsoft's digital assistant to your desktop.

- **Pinned tabs**: In Microsoft Edge, you can pin tabs to the tab row. They reappear when you close and reopen Microsoft Edge.

- **Paste and go**: If you copy a link to the clipboard, you can right-click in the address bar and then click **Paste and go**. This takes Microsoft Edge directly to the site.

Edge is updated through Windows Update, which installs security fixes, product features, group policies, and **Mobile Device Management** (**MDM**) settings.

Learning about IE 11

IE 11 is included on Windows 10 to provide backward compatibility for websites that require features that are currently not supported on Edge. IE supports ActiveX, **Silverlight**, **Visual Basic scripting**, and older versions of HTML. IE 11 also supports many extensions.

Internet Explorer 11 continues to receive security updates. Bugs are evaluated by Microsoft on a case-by-case basis. Microsoft recommends Microsoft Edge as the default browser and IE 11 for backward compatibility. In the next section, we will look at the **Enterprise Mode** function of Internet Explorer 11 and Edge. With this functionality, you can configure backward compatibility on Edge and IE 11.

Understanding Enterprise Mode Site Lists

If you have enterprise web apps that use older techniques such as ActiveX, you can use Enterprise Mode. Enterprise Mode redirects websites from Edge to IE 11 so that the user can still use the older web apps.

Enterprise Mode helps you run legacy web applications with better backward compatibility. You can configure Edge and IE 11 to use the same Enterprise Mode site list to switch seamlessly between the two browsers to support both modern and legacy web apps. You can configure the Enterprise Mode site list through Group Policy or Microsoft Intune:

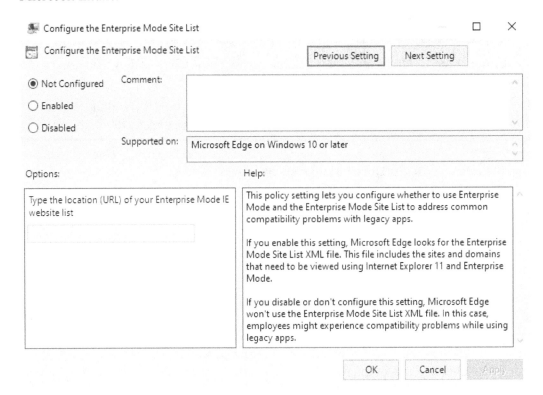

Figure 3.1 - The Enterprise Mode site list settings window in a Group Policy Object

You can find this settings page by going to **Group Policy editor | Administrative Templates | Microsoft Edge | Configure the Enterprise Mode Site List**.

To configure the Enterprise Mode Site List in Microsoft Intune, take the following steps:

1. Go to the **Microsoft Endpoint Manager admin center** at `https://endpoint.microsoft.com`.

2. Click on the **Devices | Configuration profiles | Create a Profile** option.

3. Then, choose the **Windows 10 or later** option.

4. After that, choose **Device Restrictions** for **Profile type** and click **Create**.

5. Give the **Device Restrictions** policy a name and click **Next**.

6. Then, click on **Settings | Microsoft Edge Browser | Start Experience** option.

If you scroll down on the **Start experience** settings page, you will see the **Enterprise mode site list location (Desktop only)** setting, where you can fill in the path to the exported .xml file, as shown in the following screenshot:

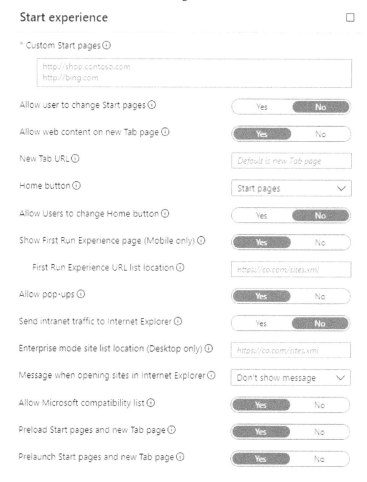

Figure 3.2 - The Enterprise Mode Site List settings in Microsoft Intune policy

As you can see in the previous screenshot, you need to type in a location for the website list, which either takes the form of a .xml file in a file location or a **Uniform Resource Locator** (URL). To generate this .xml file, you need to download and install the **Enterprise Mode Site List Manager** tool for Windows 10. You can download the tool from https://www.microsoft.com/en-us/download/details.aspx?id=49974.

In the next section, we will install this tool and create a .xml file that contains links to the web apps we require to run in Enterprise Mode.

Installing Enterprise Mode Site List Manager

As we saw, we need to generate a .xml file by using the Enterprise Mode Site List Manager tool. So, after downloading the tool (.msi file), install it by following these steps:

1. Run the .msi file and click **Next**:

Figure 3.3 - Welcome window of Enterprise Mode Site List Manager

2. Now, accept the terms of the license agreement and click **Next**:

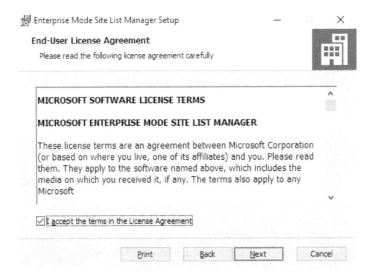

Figure 3.4 - End User License Agreement window

3. Choose your destination folder and click **Next**:

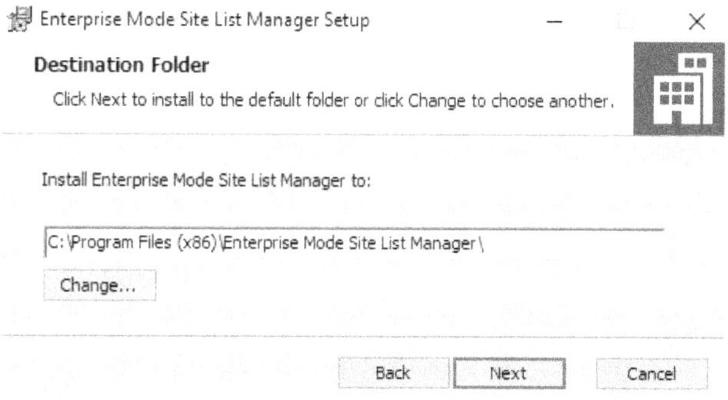

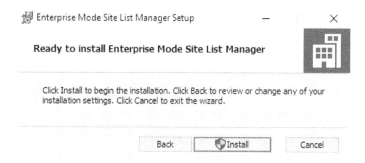

Figure 3.5 - Destination Folder window

4. After that, click **Install** on the ready to install page of the setup:

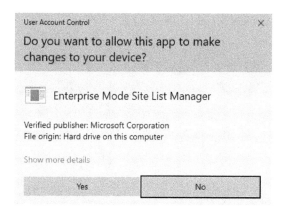

Figure 3.6 - Ready to install page

5. If the **User Account Control** (**UAC**) prompts you to run this as an **administrator**, click **Yes**:

Figure 3.7 - User Account Control prompt window

6. Now, click **Finish**:

Figure 3.8 - Finish button on the last page of the setup

Now that you have installed the Enterprise Mode Site List Manager tool, we can learn how to use it to create a list of compatible web apps.

Using Enterprise Mode Site List Manager

In this section, you will create a `.xml` file that is populated with individual website domains and domain paths for web apps. We will also specify whether the web app renders using Enterprise Mode or the default mode.

Let's start by launching Enterprise Mode Site List Manager by clicking on the icon on the desktop. Then, follow these steps:

1. After the tool's window opens, click **Add** to add a website:

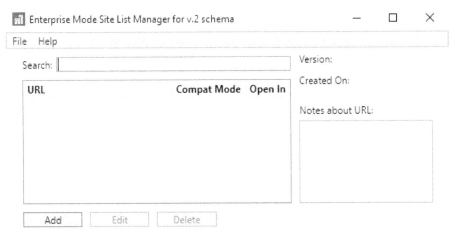

Figure 3.9 - Enterprise Mode Site List Manager main page

2. In the **URL** box, type in the URL for the desired website (do not include `http://` or `https://`):

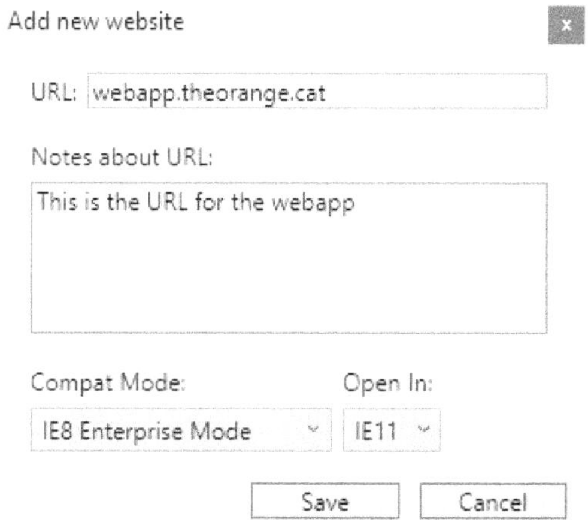

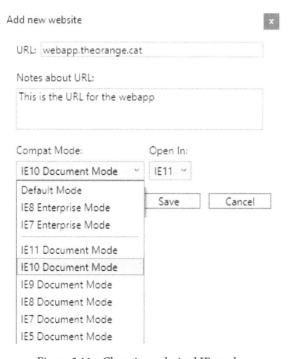

Figure 3.10 - Adding a new URL

3. In the **Compat Mode** drop-down list, choose your desired IE mode and click **Save**:

Figure 3.11 - Choosing a desired IE mode

4. After you have added all the necessary websites, your settings page should look like this:

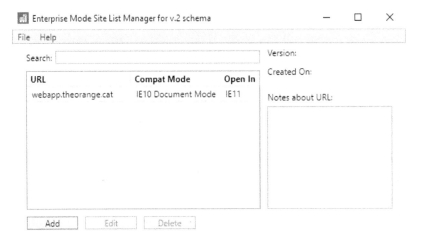

Figure 3.12 - URLs added on the main page

5. When you are ready, click on **File**, then click on **Save to XML** and save it to a central location:

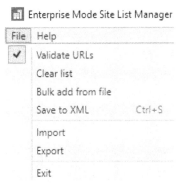

Figure 3.13 - File menu to save to XML

6. Now, you can use the link to the central location from the .xml file and paste it into Group Policy or the corresponding setting in Microsoft Intune.

You now know the difference between Edge and IE 11, as well as how these browsers are used in an organization. You also know how you can create an Enterprise Mode site list with the correct tooling. In the next section, we will learn how to configure several types of login for Windows 10, including **biometrical**, **Windows Hello for Business**, and local accounts.

Configuring the sign-in options

During the installation of Windows 10, if you have a working internet connection, you will be prompted to specify your **Microsoft account**. If you don't have a Microsoft account, then you can create one or create a local account to use with Windows 10. If you create a local account, then you can create a Microsoft account afterward and link it to the local account or to an **Active Directory Domain Services (AD DS)** account.

Microsoft accounts are primarily intended for consumers. With a Microsoft account, you can do the following:

- Access and share photos, documents, and other files, including on **OneDrive** and **Outlook**
- Download and install **Microsoft Store** apps
- Sync Microsoft Store apps with user-specific settings
- Sync apps between your devices

In this section, we will look at several different sign-in options for Windows 10. On the sign-in page, you will see the following methods that are available for Windows 10:

- **Windows Hello face recognition**
- **Windows Hello fingerprint reader**
- **Windows Hello PIN**
- **Security key**
- **Password**
- **Picture password**

> Important Note
>
> You can browse Microsoft Store even if you don't have a Microsoft account. However, you can't install apps without a Microsoft account.

Whichever method you choose from the preceding options depends on which hardware you have Windows 10 installed on. To access your sign-in options, go to **Start** | **Settings** | **Accounts** | **Sign-in options**. Let's take a look at these sign-in options individually.

Using Windows Hello

Windows Hello is a two-factor biometrical authentication mechanism that is built into Windows 10. It lets you sign in to your devices, apps, online services, and networks. This is done using your **face, iris, fingerprint**, or a **PIN**. Even if your Windows 10 device can use Windows Hello biometrics, you don't have to set it up. When you set up Windows Hello, it's important to know that the info that identifies your face, iris, or fingerprint never leaves your device—Windows does not store pictures of them anywhere.

Windows Hello for Business is the enterprise implementation of Windows Hello that allows users to authenticate to an **Active Directory** or an **Azure Active Directory** (**Azure AD**) account. Administrators can configure Windows Hello for Business by using Group Policy or Microsoft Intune as an MDM policy.

Some benefits of Windows Hello are as follows:

- It helps strengthen your protections against credential theft. If your computer is stolen, an attacker must have both the device and the biometric info or PIN, so it's much more difficult to gain access without the owner's knowledge.

- Users use a simple authentication method (with a PIN as backup) that's always with them, so there's no risk of forgetting their password.

To turn on Windows Hello, go to **Start** | **Settings** | **Accounts** | **Sign-in options**, then select the Windows Hello method that you want to set up and select **Set up**. As mentioned earlier, the methods that are available depend on the hardware of your computer.

To remove Windows Hello and the associated biometric identification data from a device, go to **Start** | **Settings** | **Accounts** | **Sign-in options**. Select the Windows Hello method you want to remove and then select **Remove**.

Now, let's move on to the next section, where we will figure out Windows Hello face recognition.

Configuring Windows Hello face recognition

I assume that you are already on the sign-in options page ready to start with the configuration of Windows Hello, so let's get started.

To configure Windows Hello face recognition, follow these steps:

1. Go to **Windows Hello Face** | **Set up** | **Get Started**.

2. Enter your PIN or password to verify your identity.

3. Allow Windows Hello to capture your facial features.

4. Once complete, you are presented with an **All Set!** message, which you can close.

Now, let's see how to configure our fingerprints with Windows.

Configuring a Windows Hello fingerprint

We will follow the same steps as in the previous section to configure the Windows Hello fingerprint reader:

1. Click on the **Windows Hello Fingerprint | Set up | Get Started** option.

2. Enter your PIN or password to verify your identity.

3. Scan your finger on the fingerprint reader. You must do this multiple times to give the scanner a good picture of your fingerprints.

4. Once complete, you are presented with an **All Set!** message, which you can close. Alternatively, you can add another fingerprint by clicking on **Add Another**.

Let's now move on to adding a Windows Hello PIN.

Configuring a Windows Hello PIN

Up to now, we have seen configuration using your face and fingerprints. We will now configure a Windows Hello PIN.

To configure a Windows Hello PIN, follow these steps:

1. Click on the **Windows Hello PIN | Add | Next** option.

2. Enter your password to verify your identity and click the **Sign in** button.

3. Create a PIN that you want to use instead of your password.

4. Once complete, click the **OK** button.

In the next section, we will look at a security key device that uses your fingerprint or PIN for security purposes on Windows 10.

Understanding the security key device

A **security key** is a **hardware** device that you can use instead of your username and password to sign in on the web. Since it's used in addition to a fingerprint or PIN, even if someone has your security key, they won't be able to sign in to the device without the PIN or fingerprint that you added. Security keys are generally available for purchase from retailers that sell computer accessories.

To set up a security key, go to **Start | Settings | Accounts | Sign-in options** and then follow these steps:

1. Click on the **Security Key | Manage** option. You will have to insert your security key device.

2. Then, after that, you will have to touch your security key device.

3. Click on **Add** under **Security Key PIN**.

4. Fill in the PIN code you want.

5. Click on **OK**.

To reset your security key, go to **Start | Settings | Accounts | Sign-in options**. From here, you should follow these steps:

1. Click on the **Security Key | Manage** option.

2. You will have to insert your security key device.

3. Then after that, you will have to touch your security key device.

4. Click on **Reset** under **Reset Security Key**.

5. Click on **Proceed**.

6. Then, you'll have to reinsert the security key device.

7. And then touch the device twice within 10 seconds for authentication. When you see the **Reset Complete** message, it means the security key has been removed.

Changing your Windows password

If you think your password has been compromised or your organization's policy requires you to change your password after a certain period of time, you may need to change your password. To change your password, follow these steps:

1. Click on **Start | Settings | Accounts | Sign-in options**.

2. Click on **Change**.

3. Follow the simple instructions on the screen to reset your password.

> **Important Note**
> To change your password on a domain, press *Ctrl+Alt+Delete*, then select **Change a Password**.

Configuring a picture password

The **picture password** option is one of the many new features offered by Windows 10 to sign in. It is a handy feature for people who may have difficulty typing in letters or numbers on a keyboard, or for those who just want to try something different. To use a picture password on a touchscreen device, a Windows 10 user draws right over a photo with their finger on the screen. On a normal **Personal Computer** (**PC**) (that is, not a touchscreen device), the user draws with their mouse.

To set up a picture password, go to **Start | Settings | Accounts | Sign-in options** and follow these steps:

1. Click on **Picture Password**.
2. Click on **Add**.
3. Fill in your password and click **OK**.
4. Click on **Choose picture** and browse to the picture you want to use, then click on **Open**.
5. Drag your picture to position it the way you want.
6. Click on **Use this picture**.
7. Draw three lines over the picture.
8. Draw the three lines again.
9. On the **Congratulations!** window, click on **Finish**.

Now, to change the picture for your picture password, go to **Start | Settings | Accounts | Sign-in options** and then follow these steps:

1. Click on **Picture Password**.
2. Click on **Change**.
3. Fill in your password and click **OK**.
4. Click on **Choose picture** and browse to the picture you want to use, then click on **Open**.
5. Drag your picture to position it the way you want.
6. Click on **Use this picture**.
7. Draw three lines over the picture.
8. Draw the three lines again.
9. On the **Congratulations!** window, click on **Finish**.

Now, if you want to remove the picture password, follow these steps:

1. Go to **Start | Settings | Accounts | Sign-in options**

2. Click on **Picture Password**.

3. Click on **Remove**.

Now, let's look at another new sign-in feature of Windows 10 in the next section.

Configuring a Dynamic lock

Another new feature of Windows 10 is using a **Dynamic lock**. If you are away from your computer and you forgot to lock it, Windows can use the devices that are paired with your computer to automatically lock it shortly after the paired device is out of the **Bluetooth** range of your computer. To set this up, you will need to use Bluetooth to pair your phone with your computer.

To make use of the Dynamic lock feature, you have to make sure that your device is paired with your computer. We can pair devices with our computer using Bluetooth communication. Follow these steps to do so:

1. Go to **Settings | Devices | Bluetooth & other devices**.

2. Turn on Bluetooth using the toggle switch on your computer. Also, make sure you turn on Bluetooth on your phone.

3. Next, click on the + button under **Add Bluetooth or other device**.

4. In the **Add a device** pop-up window, click on **Bluetooth**, then choose your device from the list that appears.

5. Prompts should appear on both your computer and phone. Accept them in order to pair the devices.

Now that we have paired our devices, we can activate the Dynamic lock feature on our computer by following these steps:

1. Go to **Start | Settings | Accounts | Sign-in options**.

2. Scroll down to **Dynamic Lock**.

3. Check the **Allow Windows to automatically lock your device when you're away** box. Dynamic lock is now activated.

We now know that Windows 10 has many sign-in options, with the important ones being the Windows Hello features. Deploying Windows Hello for Business is the first step toward a password-less environment. Now that we're familiar with how to set up a security key and picture password, as well as how to activate the Dynamic lock feature, we will look at configuring the mobility settings.

Configuring the mobility settings

Computers play an important part in people's daily lives. The ability to carry out computing tasks at any time and in any place has become a necessity for most users. Mobile computers are portable devices that you can use for work. They include the following devices:

- Laptops and notebooks
- Tablets

Computing devices need electrical power, regardless of whether they are in use. A priority for users of these kinds of hardware is to be able to conserve battery life. If users are on the road or in a remote location, it is important for them to know how to configure the power settings in Windows 10 to meet their needs.

In this section, we will talk about how to configure the basic power options, power plans, and presentation settings.

Understanding the basic power plans

By default, there are three preconfigured power plans:

- **Balanced**
- **Power saver**
- **High performance**

You can adjust and save any of these power plans or create your own power plan. The following table provides details about each plan:

Power plan	Energy usage	Screen brightness	System activity
Balanced	Medium	Can turn off the display after a specified amount of time.	Measures ongoing activity and, when in use, continues to provide full power to all system components.
Power saver	Least	By default, after 5 minutes of inactivity, the display powers off.	Saves energy by reducing system performance whenever possible.
High performance	Highest	Sets the screen at its highest brightness.	Keeps the system's disk drive, memory, and processor continuously supplied with power.

Table 3.1 - Basic power plan types

Now that you understand the different basic power plans, we will move on to configuring them.

Configuring the power plans

To open the **Power & sleep** page, go to **Start | Settings | System | Power & sleep**.

There are different options available on the **Power & sleep** page. The options that are available on your device depend on the device's hardware configuration. For example, on a laptop or other mobile device, you will have the following configurable options, with a drop-down list to set various minutes and hours (from **1 minute** to **5 hours**). You can also choose **Never** to disable a setting:

- The **Screen** setting: You can choose time intervals under the **On battery power, turn off after** option. You can also do the same for the **When plugged in, turn off after** option.

- The **Sleep** setting: You will see various time options under the **On battery power, PC goes to sleep after** option. You also have the same options for the **When plugged in, PC goes to sleep after** option.

- The **Network connection** setting: You will only find one option here, which is **When my PC is asleep and on battery power, disconnect from the network**.

> **Important Note**
> The **Network connection** power setting is only available on laptops and tablets.

You can also click on the **Additional power settings** hyperlink, which you will find on the right-hand side of the **Power & sleep** page under **Related settings**.

To view more power settings, open the **Power Options** configuration page in the **Hardware and Sound** section of the **Control Panel**. The **Power Options** configuration page includes many options, including the following:

- The **Choose what the power button does** setting
- The **Choose what closing the lid does** setting
- The **Create a power plan** setting
- The **Change when the computer sleeps** setting

> **Important Note**
>
> Not all devices have the settings mentioned in the previous list. Several of these settings apply to particular hardware that may not be present on all devices.

The **Power Options** screen also lists the default and custom power plans. When you click **Change plan settings** and access a power plan, the **Change advanced power settings** option becomes available. This opens the **Power Options** window, providing a list of options that you can expand and individually select. These options include the settings for the battery and the hard disk and the graphics, multimedia, and USB settings.

Let's now move on to a different mobility setting.

Configuring the Presentation Settings

Windows 10 includes a utility called **Windows Mobility Center**. This utility can be used to configure various mobility settings. One of them is the presentation settings.

If you are presenting a **PowerPoint** presentation in a meeting or during an event, then you probably want to turn on the presentation settings on your Windows 10 device. When you enable the presentation settings, the following settings are applied temporarily:

- Pop-ups and notifications area pop-ups are disabled.
- Windows 10 is prevented from going into sleep mode.
- Windows 10 is prevented from turning the screen off.
- The display background and volume settings that are defined in the presentation settings are used.

You can access Windows Mobility Center by following these steps:

1. Right-click on the Start menu or press the *Win + X* shortcut keys.

2. Click on **Mobility Center**.

3. Under **Presentation Settings**, click **Turn on** to enable presentation mode.

4. To customize the Presentation Mode settings, double-click on the tray icon:

Figure 3.14 - The Presentation Settings tray icon

5. The **Presentation Settings** window then opens:

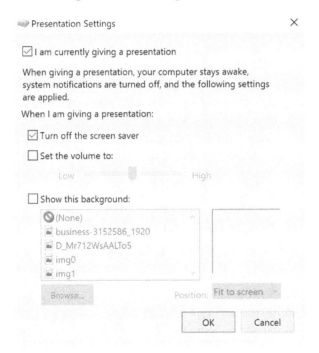

Figure 3.15 - Presentation Settings window

Here, you can turn on presentation mode and tweak other settings, such as turning off the screen saver, setting the volume, and showing another background.

In this section, you have learned about basic power plans and how to configure custom power plans. You also learned how you can use the Presentation Settings during a presentation and how to open Windows Mobility Center. Now, let's look at how to customize the Windows desktop.

Customizing the Windows desktop

After you have installed Windows 10, you can customize the user interface and personalize Windows. The user interface of Windows 10 is similar to other versions of Windows, such as **Windows 7**, as it has a Start menu, a desktop, and a taskbar.

To configure the desktop, click on the **Start | Settings | Personalization** option.

From the **Personalization** page, we can personalize the following options:

- **Background**: You can select and configure the desktop background color or image, or you can select a slideshow of images.

- **Colors**: You can choose a color scheme, enable transparency effects, change the accent colors on the Start menu, change the taskbar color, go to **Action Center**, and change the title bars and window borders. You can also choose between the light and dark default app modes.

- **Lock Screen**: You can select and configure a background image to display when your device is locked. **Windows Spotlight** displays different background images on the lock screen each day. You can also set the screen timeout time and the screensaver settings. If you want, you can also choose to show detailed info or a quick status from certain apps on the lock screen.

- **Themes**: With Themes, you can configure and apply the theme settings. You can change the background, color, sound, mouse cursor, and the desktop icons. You can download and install dozens of themes that are available for free via Microsoft Store.

- **Fonts**: With Fonts, you can install a wide range of fonts from Microsoft Store or from the internet.

- **Start**: You can configure your Start menu to show more tiles, recently added apps, or your most-used apps, or set the Start menu to fullscreen.

- **Taskbar**: You can lock the taskbar, automatically hide the taskbar, use small icons, and replace Command Prompt with Windows PowerShell in this menu. Also, you can set where the location of the taskbar should be, such as on the right-hand side of your screen. You can also configure the notification area to show or hide icons.

We now know how to customize numerous aspects of the Windows desktop, such as the taskbar, background, and lock screen. Now, let's explore how to customize the Start menu and how to export a default Start menu to an enterprise environment.

Customizing the Windows Start menu

Just as in earlier Windows versions, you can customize the Start menu of Windows 10. For users who have never worked with Windows 10 before, the appearance of the Start menu may be significantly different than what they were previously used to. You can configure the Start menu from the **Settings** app, as explained in the last section.

You can customize the application tiles that appear on the Start menu and how those tiles look and behave. When a tile is pinned to the Start menu, you can configure it from the context menu. The context menu appears when you right-click on the pinned tile:

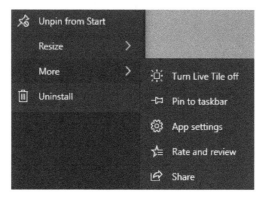

Figure 3.16 - Context menu

The options in the context menu, shown in the previous screenshot, are as follows:

- **Unpin from Start**: This unpins the tile from the Start menu.
- **Resize**: Choose from **Small**, **Medium**, **Large**, and **Wide**. This is dependent on the app.
- **More**: You have several options, which are also dependent on the type of app you're using. For example, you may have the **Turn Live Tile off**, **Pin to taskbar**, **App settings**, **Rate and review**, and **Share** options.
- **Uninstall**: You will see this option for installed desktop applications.

Let's look at how to export the Start menu in the next section.

Exporting the Start menu layout

It is possible to manually customize the Start menu, but when using devices in an organization, this is not practical. In a corporate environment, you can control the Start menu layout by creating a customized Start menu on a computer and then exporting the layout to other computers.

There are two different layout export options:

- **The full Start menu layout**: With this layout, your end users cannot pin, unpin, or uninstall apps from the Start menu.

- **The partial Start menu layout**: With this layout, your end users can create and customize their own groups. Specified groups cannot be changed, such as your enterprise line-of-business apps.

The Start menu layout is exported as a .xml file, which can be deployed with the following:

- Group Policy

- The Windows Configuration Designer provisioning package

- Microsoft Intune

Once you have configured the desired Start menu layout, you can use the Export-StartLayout PowerShell command to export the Start menu layout to a .xml file using the following procedure:

1. Open **Windows PowerShell**.

2. On a device running Windows 10 versions **1607**, **1703**, or **1803**, run the Export-StartLayout command with the following syntax:

```
Export-StartLayout -path <path><filename>.xml
```

For our example, Export-Startlayout is the command, -path is the path variable, and <path><filename>.xml is the folder and filename to save with:

```
Export-StartLayout -Path X:\StartMenuLayout.xml
```

3. On a device running Windows 10 version **1809** or higher, run the Export-StartLayout command with the -UseDesktopApplicationID switch:

```
Export-StartLayout -UseDesktopApplicationID -Path X:\
StartMenuLayout.xml
```

4.   Now that you've run this, your Start menu should look as follows:

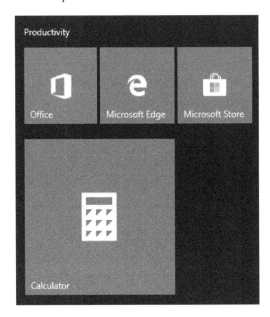

Figure 3.17 - Exported Start menu layout

In addition, the `.xml` file from your exported Start menu is as follows:

```
<LayoutModificationTemplate xmlns:defaultlayout="http://
schemas.microsoft.com/Start/2014/FullDefaultLayout"
xmlns:start="http://schemas.microsoft.com/Start/2014/
StartLayout" Version="1" xmlns="http://schemas.microsoft.com/
Start/2014/LayoutModification">
  <LayoutOptions StartTileGroupCellWidth="6" />
  <DefaultLayoutOverride>
    <StartLayoutCollection>
      <defaultlayout:StartLayout GroupCellWidth="6">
        <start:Group Name="Productivity">
          <start:Tile Size="2x2" Column="2"
Row="0" AppUserModelID="Microsoft.
MicrosoftEdge_8wekyb3d8bbwe!MicrosoftEdge" />
          <start:Tile Size="2x2" Column="0"
Row="0" AppUserModelID="Microsoft.
MicrosoftOfficeHub_8wekyb3d8bbwe!Microsoft.MicrosoftOfficeHub"
/>
          <start:Tile Size="2x2" Column="4" Row="0"
```

```
AppUserModelID="Microsoft.WindowsStore_8wekyb3d8bbwe!App" />
        </start:Group>
        <start:Group Name="Calculator">
          <start:Tile Size="4x4" Column="0" Row="0"
AppUserModelID="Microsoft.WindowsCalculator_8wekyb3d8bbwe!App"
/>
        </start:Group>
      </defaultlayout:StartLayout>
    </StartLayoutCollection>
  </DefaultLayoutOverride>
</LayoutModificationTemplate>
```

https://github.com/PacktPublishing/Microsoft-Exam-MD-100-Windows-10-Certification-Guide/blob/master/Chapter03/StartMenuLayout.xml

To configure a partial Start menu layout, you should export the Start menu layout and then open the .xml file. There is a <DefaultLayoutOverride> element in the exported .xml file. Add LayoutCustomizationRestrictionType="OnlySpecifiedGroups" to this element by following these steps:

1. Copy the exported file to a shared folder.

2. Deploy the exported .xml file using any of the deployment methods.

You have now successfully created and exported a Start menu as a .xml file. The next step is to deploy this Start menu.

Deploying the Start menu with Group Policy

If you plan to use Group Policy, you must specify the .xml file in Group Policy. In the following steps, we will add the exported .xml file to a Group Policy setting:

1. On a computer, press the *Windows* key and type gpedit and then select **Edit Group Policy**.

2. Click on **User Configuration** or click on the **Computer Configuration | Administrative Templates | Start menu and Taskbar** option.

3. Right-click on **Start Layout** and click **Edit**.

4. Select the **Enabled** option.

5. Fill in the path that specifies the location of the .xml file and click **OK**.

If you followed the previous steps, then the resulting page will look as in the following screenshot:

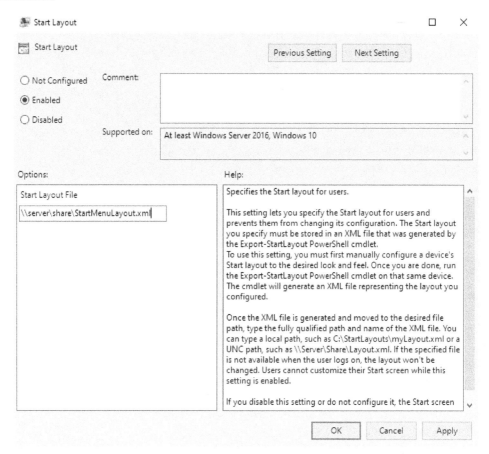

Figure 3.18 - Start menu policy settings in Group Policy

Now, let's move on to deploying the Start menu with Microsoft Intune.

Deploying the Start menu with Microsoft Intune

If you plan on using Microsoft Intune, you need to upload the .xml file to a **device restrictions policy**. In the following steps, we will upload the exported .xml file to a device restrictions policy:

1. In the Microsoft Azure portal, go to **Intune**.

2. Click on the **Device configuration | Profiles | Create profile** option.

3. Then, enter a friendly name.

4. After that, select **Windows 10 and later**.

5. Then, select **Device restriction** for the profile type.

6. Select **Start**.

7. In the Start menu, browse to the .xml file and select it.

8. Then, click **OK**.

9. After that, click **OK** again.

10. Lastly, click **Create**.

The result of the previous steps should be as follows:

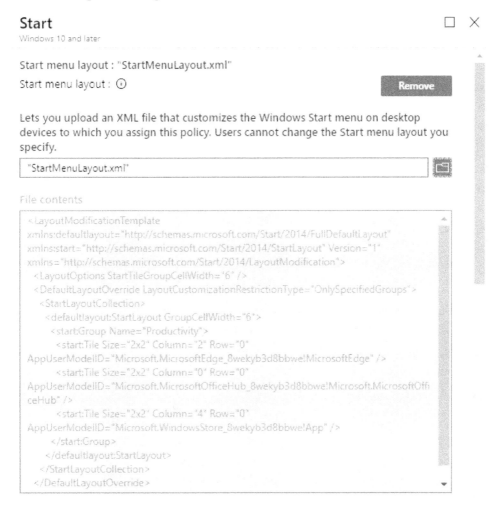

Figure 3.19 - Start menu policy settings in Microsoft Intune

We now know how to customize the Start menu for our own Windows 10 computer. We have also learned how to customize it in an organization environment and how to deploy it with Group Policy and Microsoft Intune. You can design the Start menu to be entirely what you or your business want it to be.

Next, we will look at working with PowerShell. As an administrator, your daily work will mostly involve working with PowerShell.

Working with PowerShell

Windows PowerShell is a powerful tool that you can use to configure a Windows 10 device using the **Command-Line Interface** (**CLI**). PowerShell allows desktop support staff and administrators to create reusable scripts to make more complex configuration changes quickly or apply changes to multiple devices.

Windows PowerShell is an integrated shell environment that enables scriptable, flexible, and comprehensive management of Windows 10:

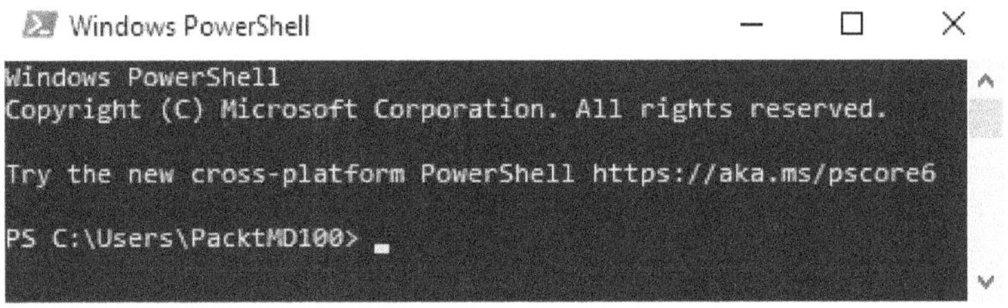

Figure 3.20 - The Windows PowerShell command line window

Windows PowerShell has several features that make it ideal for the local and remote management of one or more Windows 10 devices. These features are as follows:

- **Windows OS integration**: This is a built-in feature in Windows 10 and other earlier Windows versions, such as **Windows 7** and **Windows Server 2016**.

- **Remote management capability**: You can use PowerShell to manage remote computers.

- **Script-based execution**: You can use PowerShell scripts to build automation and complex logic into tasks.

You can use PowerShell to run individual **cmdlets** (pronounced **command-lets**) that perform actions or to run scripts that use cmdlets. Using PowerShell is much simpler than using other scripting languages, such as **Visual Basic Script** (**VBScript**).

PowerShell uses Windows PowerShell drives to provide access to data stores. These drives present data in formats such as a file system. Some common Windows PowerShell drives are as follows:

- The **C drive** is the local file system's C drive.
- The **cert drive** is the local certificate store.
- The **Env drive** contains the environmental variables that are stored in memory.
- The **HKCU drive** is the HKEY_CURRENT_USER portion of the registry.
- The **HKLM drive** is the HKEY_LOCAL_MACHINE portion of the registry.
- The **Variable drive** contains the variables that are stored in memory.

Let's move on to the next section, where we will look at the CLI.

Using the Command-line interface

Commands are PowerShell's main functionality. There are several types of commands, including cmdlets, functions, and workflows. These commands are building blocks, designed for piecing together and implementing complex and customized processes and procedures. PowerShell provides a CLI that you can use to enter cmdlets interactively.

Using the Graphical User Interface

PowerShell is not restricted to the command line. For example, the **Active Directory Administrative Center** in **Windows Server 2012 R2** and **Windows Server 2016** is a **Graphical User Interface** (**GUI**) that uses Windows PowerShell to perform all of its tasks.

Windows PowerShell ISE

There is another PowerShell app in the same app area called Windows PowerShell **Integrated Scripting Environment** (**ISE**), which allows you to see all the available commands and the parameters that you can use with these commands. You also can use a scripting window to construct and save PowerShell scripts.

The ability to view cmdlet parameters ensures that you are aware of the full functionality of each cmdlet and can create the correct PowerShell commands. Windows PowerShell ISE provides color-coded cmdlets to assist you with troubleshooting. Windows PowerShell ISE also provides debugging tools that you can use to debug simple and complex PowerShell scripts. You can use Windows PowerShell ISE to view the available cmdlets by module, as shown in the following screenshot:

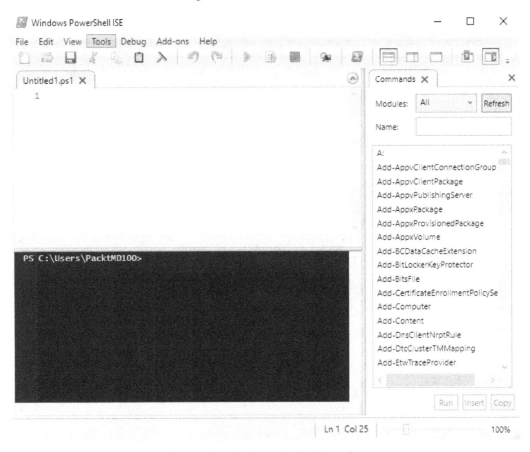

Figure 3.21 - The PowerShell ISE window

Let's look at cmdlets in a bit more detail in the next section.

Understanding cmdlets

Cmdlets use a naming convention of a verb or action followed by a noun or a subject. For example, to retrieve a list of services, you would use the `Get-Service` cmdlet. This standardization makes it easier to learn how to accomplish administrative tasks. Some common cmdlet verbs are as follows:

- `Get`: This retrieves data.

- `Set`: This establishes or modifies data.

- `New`: This creates a new object.

Each cmdlet has options called parameters. Some parameters are required while others are optional. The parameters vary for each cmdlet. The following example shows how to start the `Application Identity` service by using the `Name` parameter:

```
Start-Service -Name "Application Identity"
```

> **Important Note**
> The cmdlets that are available for use on a computer system vary depending on its Windows PowerShell version and the snap-ins with the cmdlets that are installed.

Let's move on to understanding the compatibility with command-line tools.

Understanding compatibility with command-line tools

You can run batch and executable files in Windows PowerShell. For example, you can run `ipconfig.exe` in Windows PowerShell and it behaves exactly as if would if you ran it from the Command Prompt. This allows you to start using Windows PowerShell as your default command-line environment for administration. Note that there are also equivalent cmdlets that return similar values as older executables. For example, the cmdlet alternative to `ipconfig.exe /all` is `Get-NetIPAddress`, which returns a somewhat similar dataset.

In some cases, commands or options for commands contain reserved words or characters for Windows PowerShell. In these cases, you can enclose the command in single quotation marks to prevent Windows PowerShell from evaluating the reserved word or combination of words. You can also use the *grave accent* (`) character to prevent the evaluation of a single character.

In some rare cases, an executable file will not run correctly in Windows PowerShell. You should test batch files to ensure that they work properly in Windows PowerShell.

Getting help with using Windows PowerShell

You can use several cmdlets to help you use Windows PowerShell. One of the key cmdlets to get help is the Get-Help cmdlet. Using Get-Help followed by the name of the cmdlet you need help with will give you a brief but detailed guide on that cmdlet, including the parameters that you can use.

For example, we can run the following command:

```
PS C:\Users\PacktMD100> Get-Help Get-NetIPAddress
```

It returns the following result:

```
NAME
Get-NetIPAddress
SYNTAX
Get-NetIPAddress [[-IPAddress] <string[]>] [-InterfaceIndex
<uint32[]>] [-InterfaceAlias <string[]>]
[-AddressFamily {IPv4 | IPv6}] [-Type {Unicast | Anycast}]
[-PrefixLength <byte[]>] [-PrefixOrigin {Other | Manual
| WellKnown | Dhcp | RouterAdvertisement}] [-SuffixOrigin
{Other | Manual | WellKnown | Dhcp | Link | Random}]
[-AddressState {Invalid | Tentative | Duplicate | Deprecated |
Preferred}] [-ValidLifetime <timespan[]>]
[-PreferredLifetime <timespan[]>] [-SkipAsSource <bool[]>]
[-AssociatedIPInterface
<CimInstance#MSFT_NetIPInterface>] [-PolicyStore <string>]
[-IncludeAllCompartments] [-CimSession <CimSession[]>]
[-ThrottleLimit <int>] [-AsJob]   [<CommonParameters>]
ALIASES
None
REMARKS
Get-Help cannot find the Help files for this cmdlet on this
computer. It is displaying only partial help.
-- To download and install Help files for the module that
includes this cmdlet, use Update-Help.
```

Another useful cmdlet is Get-Command. This cmdlet shows a list of all the cmdlets, aliases, functions, workflows, filters, scripts, and applications installed on your version of Windows PowerShell.

Summary

In this chapter, you learned the differences between the new Microsoft Edge browser and IE 11, how you can configure Enterprise Mode site lists to allow selected websites to open in IE 11 for web app and website compatibility, and how you can deploy this through Group Policy or Microsoft Intune. This will help you to understand how to configure browser settings in Edge and IE 11.

In addition to this, you learned how to configure different sign-in options, such as Windows Hello face recognition, Windows Hello fingerprint reader, a Windows Hello PIN, Dynamic lock, and a picture password, as well as signing in with a security key. All the different sign-in options use a two-factor biometric authentication mechanism. Understanding these Windows security components will help you keep your devices safe and secure from potential hackers.

You also learned how to customize the Windows desktop and the Windows Start menu with manual interaction or by deploying an exported Start menu template with Group Policy or Microsoft Intune. Finally, you learned how powerful Windows PowerShell is as a scripting tool or as a replacement for the Command Prompt. Knowing all of this will also help you get started with PowerShell. These skills will enable you to handle and operate the Windows 10 OS with efficiency and will also help you navigate the subsequent chapters of this book.

In the next chapter, we will look at managing local users, groups, and devices.

Questions

1. Can we open legacy web applications in Microsoft Edge?
2. To export the Start menu to a `.xml` file, is the following command correct?

```
Export-StartLayout -Path \\server\share\folder\StartMenuLayout.xml
```

3. Can you use Command Prompt commands in PowerShell?
4. If you need help with using a PowerShell command, is `Get-Help <PowerShell cmdlet>` the correct command to use?

Further reading

Microsoft Edge group policies: `https://docs.microsoft.com/en-us/microsoft-edge/deploy/group-policies/`

Enterprise Mode Site List Manager (schema v.2): `https://www.microsoft.com/en-us/download/details.aspx?id=49974`

Passwordless Strategy: `https://docs.microsoft.com/en-us/windows/security/identity-protection/hello-for-business/passwordless-strategy`

Customize and export Start: `Layout https://docs.microsoft.com/en-us/windows/configuration/customize-and-export-start-layout`

Windows 10 and Windows Server 2016: `PowerShell https://docs.microsoft.com/en-us/powershell/windows/get-started?view=win10-ps`

The Windows Hello biometric requirements: `https://docs.microsoft.com/en-us/windows-hardware/design/device-experiences/windows-hello-biometric-requirements`

Section 2 : Managing Devices and Data

In this section, you will learn how to manage devices and users, configure access to data, implement policies, and manage the security of your device.

This section comprises the following chapters:

- *Chapter 4, Managing Local Users, Groups, and Devices*
- *Chapter 5, Configuring Permissions and File Access*
- *Chapter 6, Configuring and Implementing Local Policies*
- *Chapter 7, Securing Data and Applications*

4
Managing Local Users, Groups, and Devices

If you want to log on to Windows 10, you must have a user account. With this user account, the user can access resources on the local computer or on network computers, such as file servers. User accounts are, in most cases, members of a local group. Giving file access rights to a local group is much easier than giving access rights to individual user accounts.

The following topics will be covered in this chapter:

- Managing local users
- Managing local groups
- Managing devices

In this chapter, you will learn about the differences between authentication and authorization. You will learn about the various logon accounts and how you can customize them. This is important as users need to have access to data that is stored on file servers and on other network connected devices. We will focus on how to manage Windows 10 devices in **Azure Active Directory** (**Azure AD**) and how to manage local users and local groups.

With the previously mentioned skills under your belt, you will be able to prepare for the **MD-100** (Windows 10) exam, which is part of the **Microsoft 365 Certified: Modern Desktop Administrator Associate** certification.

Technical requirements

This chapter will use PowerShell code. This code is available in this book's GitHub repository at `https://github.com/PacktPublishing/Microsoft-Exam-MD-100-Windows-10-Certification-Guide/tree/master/Chapter04`.

In the *Managing devices* section, you will learn about joining and registering devices in **Azure AD**. The steps that you will follow have also been recorded. You can find the videos for these here: `https://bit.ly/2LsQDqD`

Managing local users

In this section, we will look at the local users in Windows 10. If you have experience with an earlier edition of Windows, you might be familiar with configuring local users since this has remained unchanged over the years.

Before you log into Windows 10, you must create a user account during the initial setup. There are three types of accounts you can use to do this:

- Local account
- Domain account
- Microsoft account

In this chapter, we will focus on the local account, because this will appear in the MD-100 exam.

As described previously, a user account is required to log on in Windows 10. To secure it, the user account should have a password. While installing Windows 10, user accounts that are automatically created. We will look at this shortly.

Configuring local accounts

As the name suggests, a local user account resides on the local device only. It does not allow a user to access resources on other Windows 10 computers. Typically, you use local user accounts for workgroup environments in which you have networked only a few computers, and in which users typically work with resources attached to their own devices.

Choose a local account if you are not connecting to a network domain. You will be able to log in, change your settings, install software, and keep your user area separate from others on the system. However, local users will not be able to access features made available by Microsoft Accounts.

Default local accounts

While installing Windows 10, three accounts are created automatically:

- **Administrator**
- **DefaultAccount**
- **Guest**

Local user accounts, including the three default accounts, are stored in the **Security Accounts Manager** (**SAM**) database in the registry.

The default administrator account cannot be deleted or locked out, but you can rename or disable it. When the default administrator account is enabled, it will require a strong password. By default, the administrator account is disabled.

You can create additional local user accounts and give these accounts any name you want, but keep in mind that the username must fulfil the following requirements:

- It must be 1 to 20 characters in length.
- It must be unique among all the other accounts and group names.
- It cannot contain the following characters: \, /, ", [,], :, |, <, >, +, =, ;, ,, ?, *, @ .

The initial user account that's created while you install Windows 10 is automatically a member of the local Administrators group and can perform local management tasks on the device.

Creating a local user

To create another account on your **Personal Computer** (**PC**) for someone else who does not have a Microsoft account, follow these steps:

1. Right-click the **Start** menu or press *Win + X* and click on **Computer Management**.

2. The **Computer Management** console will open.

3. Expand **System Tools**.

4. Expand **Local Users and Groups**.

5. Click on **Users**:

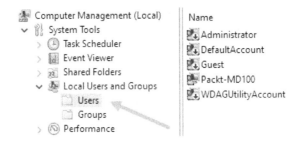

Figure 4.1 - Users folder in Computer Management console

6. Right-click somewhere in the middle pane.

7. Click on **New User…**.

8. The **New User** window will open:

Figure 4.2 - Adding details for New User

9. Fill in the empty fields for a new user, click **Create**, and then click **Close**. The new local user account has now been created.

After you have created the new local user account, you can modify more properties by double-clicking the user account. This will open the **Properties** window of the user account. Here, you will see three tabs: the **General** tab, the **Member Of** tab, and the **Profile** tab. The **General** tab is shown in the following screenshot:

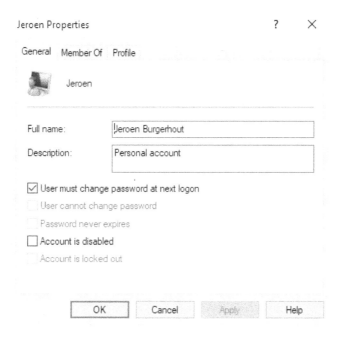

Figure 4.3 - The user's Properties window general tab

In the **Member Of** tab, you can add the user to one or more local groups or remove the user from one or more groups on the computer. In the **Profile** tab, you can modify the following properties:

- **Profile Path**: This is the path to the location of a user's profile. The profile stores the user's settings, such as the color scheme, wallpaper, and app settings. By default, each profile will be stored in the C:\Users\Username folder.

- **Logon Script**: Here, you can type in the path to a script that will run while the user logs in. Typically, this type of script is a .cmd or .bat file.

- **Home Folder**: This is the personal storage location for the user where they can store their personal documents. By default, it is the `C:\Users\Username` folder, but you can specify an alternate location by using **Local Path** or the **Connect** field. **Local Path** is a different path that's local on the computer, for example, `D:\Users\Username`. Using the **Connect** field, you can set up a network location as the default user's folder with a specified drive letter; for example, `H:\Users\Username`.

The preceding settings can be seen in the following screenshot:

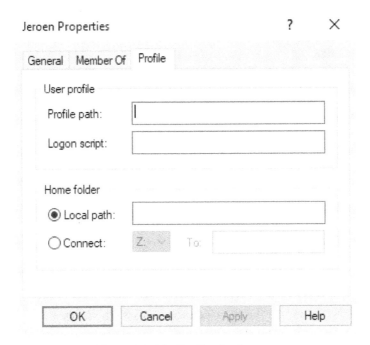

Figure 4.4 - The Profile tab of a user

Let's move on and learn how to use Windows PowerShell.

Using Windows PowerShell

You can use **Windows PowerShell** to view, add, modify, or delete a local user account. You need to run the cmdlets with elevated rights.

To manage local users with PowerShell, you can use the following cmdlets:

- `Disable-LocalUser`: This cmdlet disables local user accounts.

- `Enable-LocalUser`: This cmdlet enables local user accounts.

- `Get-LocalUser`: This cmdlet gets local user accounts.
- `New-LocalUser`: This cmdlet creates a local user account.
- `Remove-LocalUser`: This cmdlet deletes local user accounts.
- `Rename-LocalUser`: This cmdlet renames a local user account.
- `Set-LocalUser`: This cmdlet alters or modifies a local user account.

For example, to add a new local user with a password, run the following cmdlets:

```
$Password = Read-Host -AsSecureString
New-LocalUser -Name Jeroen -Password $Password -Description
"Personal account" -FullName "Jeroen Burgerhout"
```

Now, you're aware of how the three default local user accounts are created while Windows 10 is being installed. You also know how to create a local user account with the Computer Management console, how to create a local user account with PowerShell, and how to modify the properties of a user account with (for example) a different profile location or home folder.

Now, let's look at how we can manage and create local groups.

Managing local groups

In the previous section, you learned that there are built-in local user accounts. There are also a few built-in local groups in Windows 10 that provide users with an easier way to delegate the same permissions and rights as other group members. Assigning permissions to groups is much more efficient than applying these rights to individual user accounts.

If you open the **Users** group or the **Administrators** group, then you should see members that you recognize. Administrators have complete and unrestricted access to the computer. Users are unable to make system-wide changes, but they can run most applications that have already been installed on the computer.

Default local groups

In the `Groups` folder, which you can find in the Computer Management console, you can create local groups, change group memberships, rename groups, and delete groups. Microsoft's best practice is to use the default local groups wherever possible. The built-in groups already have the appropriate permissions.

While Windows 10 is being installed, these built-in groups are created, just like the default local user accounts. In the following screenshot, you can see the built-in local groups in the **Name** column:

Figure 4.5 - The built-in local groups

You can create additional local groups and give these groups any name you want, but keep in mind that the group name should have the following properties:

- It can be up to 256 characters in length.

- It must be unique among all the other accounts and group names.

- It cannot contain the following characters: \, /, ", [,], :, |, <, >, +, =, ;, ,, ?, *, @ .

The default local groups are also stored in the SAM database in the registry.

Creating local groups

If you want to create an additional local group on a computer, follow these steps:

1. Right-click the **Start** menu or press *Win* + *X* and click on **Computer Management**.

2. The **Computer Management** console will open.

3. Expand **System Tools**.

4. Expand **Local Users and Groups**.

5. Click on **Groups**:

Figure 4.6 - Computer Management console window

6. Right-click somewhere in the middle pane.

7. Click on **New Group…**.

8. The **New Group** window will open:

Figure 4.7 - New Group window

9. Fill in the empty fields for the new group.

10. Click the **Add…** button to add existing local users to this group.

11. Click **Create** and then **Close**. The new local group will be created.

> **Important Note**
> Only members of the Administrators group can manage users and groups.

After you have created the new local group, you can add or remove users from the group by double-clicking the local group.

Using Windows PowerShell

You can use Windows PowerShell to view, add, modify, or delete a local user account. In order to do this, you need to run the cmdlets with elevated rights.

To manage local users with PowerShell, you can use the following cmdlets:

- `Get-LocalGroup`
- `New-LocalGroup`
- `Remove-LocalGroup`
- `Rename-LocalGroup`
- `Set-LocalGroup`
- `Add-LocalGroupMember`
- `Get-LocalGroupMember`
- `Remove-LocalGroupMember`

For example, to create a new local group and add an existing local user to this group, run the following cmdlets:

```
New-LocalGroup -Name W10NewLocalGroup
Add-LocalGroupMember -Member Jeroen -Name W10NewLocalGroup
```

Now, you know that there are built-in local groups that are created while Windows 10 is being installed. You also know how to create a local group with the Computer Management console and how to create a local group with PowerShell.

Now, let's look at how we can manage devices.

Managing devices

Windows 10 was designed to be managed using cloud-based tools such as **Microsoft Intune** and **Microsoft Endpoint Manager**. Nowadays, more businesses are moving away from on-premises domain environments to the cloud.

In this section, you will learn how to register a device in Azure AD with a work or school account using cloud-based services. We will also look at how to enable device registration and the process of joining devices to Azure AD.

Azure AD is Microsoft's cloud-based identity authentication and access management authorization service that enables your users to benefit from **Single Sign-On** (**SSO**) for cloud-based applications, such as **Microsoft Office 365** and many other **Software as a Service** (**SaaS**) applications. Azure AD join also enables **Windows Hello**, as well as access to the **Microsoft Store** for Business. Users can easily join their devices to your organization's Azure AD tenant.

When joining devices to an on-premises domain environment, the types of devices that you can join are quite restrictive; for example, devices must be running a supported **Operating System** (**OS**). However, Azure AD is less restrictive. With Azure AD, you can join different device types such as tablets, laptops, smartphones, and desktop computers to Azure AD.

Devices can be managed by Azure AD using two methods:

- Joining a device to Azure AD
- Registering a device to Azure AD

We'll look at these methods in detail in the next section.

Joining a device to Azure AD

Joining a device to Azure AD is intended for organizations that want to be cloud-first or cloud-only. Azure AD join works well in a hybrid environment that enables the user to have access to both cloud and on-premises resources. Organizations of any size can deploy Azure AD join devices. Azure AD joined devices are signed into using an organizational Azure AD account.

IT Administrators can secure and further control Azure AD joined devices using **Mobile Device Management** (**MDM**) tools such as Microsoft Intune or in co-management using **System Center Configuration Manager**. With these tools, you can provide organizations with the required configurations, such as encrypted storage, password complexity, software installations, and software updates. You can also make applications available using Microsoft Intune, System Center Configuration Manager, and the **Microsoft Store for Business**.

Registering a device to Azure AD

Registering a device to Azure AD is a method that's used to provide your users with support for **Bring Your Own Device** (**BYOD**) or mobile scenarios. The user can access your organization's Azure AD resources using a personal device such as **Windows 10**, **Android**, **iOS**, or **macOS**.

All corporate data and apps will be kept separate from personal data and apps on the user's device. If the user's device does not meet your corporate security standards and compliances (for example, the device is jailbroken or has an unsupported OS version), then access to the resource will be denied.

The main reasons to implement device registration are as follows:

- To enable access to corporate resources from non-domain joined or personally owned devices
- To enable SSO for specific resources that are managed by Azure AD

Configuring device management

The Azure portal provides a cloud-based location where you can manage your devices. Device management requires configuration to ensure that your users can register their device to Azure AD. By default, this setting is enabled and allows all supported Windows 10 devices (or other devices that provide a valid credential) to be managed by Azure AD.

To allow devices to be registered to Azure AD, follow these steps:

1. Go to the **Azure** portal at `https://portal.azure.com`.
2. **Sign in** as an administrator.
3. On the left navigation bar, click **Azure Active Directory**.
4. In the **Manage** section, click **Devices**.

5. Click **Device Settings**.

6. Make sure that the **Users may join devices to Azure AD** setting is configured to **All**.

7. Click **Save**.

In the following screenshot, you can see part of the Azure portal where you can configure this setting:

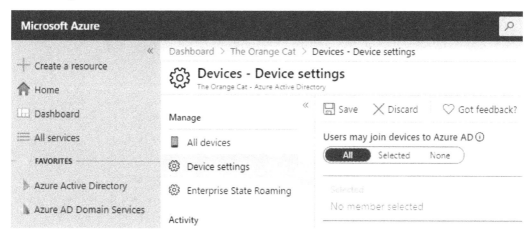

Figure 4.8 - Azure AD device registration settings

As you can see, you have two more options regarding how and which users can join devices: **Selected** and **None**.

If you select **None**, then nobody can join their device to your Azure AD. With the **Selected** option, you can define a group of users or individual users who are able to join their devices to your Azure AD.

Managing device tasks

Once devices have been registered or joined to Azure AD, they will appear in a list within the **All Devices** section of the Azure AD blade, as shown in the following screenshot:

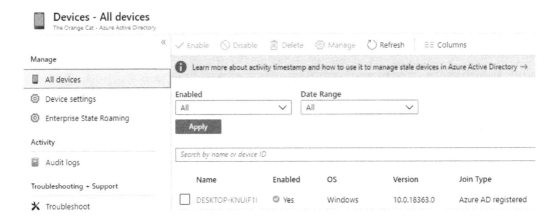

Figure 4.9 - List of all registered and joined devices in Azure AD

You can also see that devices managed by Microsoft Intune are also listed in this view. To locate a device, you can search using the device's name or by device ID. Once you have located a device and double-clicked on it, you can perform some device management tasks, such as the following:

- Managing the device
- Enabling the device
- Disabling the device
- Deleting the device

In this overview, you will see the properties of the selected device and also see **the BitLocker Key ID**, as shown in the following screenshot:

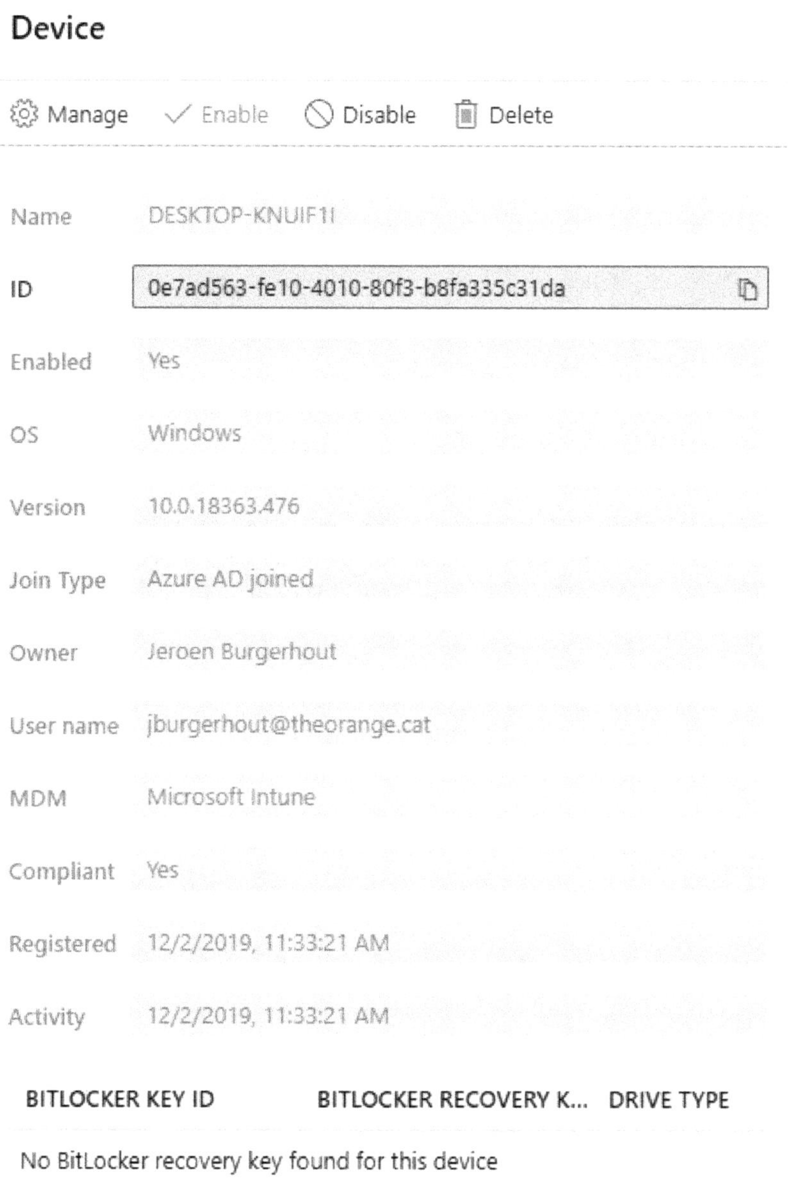

Device

⚙ Manage   ✓ Enable   ⊘ Disable   🗑 Delete

Name	DESKTOP-KNUIF1I
ID	0e7ad563-fe10-4010-80f3-b8fa335c31da 📋
Enabled	Yes
OS	Windows
Version	10.0.18363.476
Join Type	Azure AD joined
Owner	Jeroen Burgerhout
User name	jburgerhout@theorange.cat
MDM	Microsoft Intune
Compliant	Yes
Registered	12/2/2019, 11:33:21 AM
Activity	12/2/2019, 11:33:21 AM

BITLOCKER KEY ID	BITLOCKER RECOVERY K...	DRIVE TYPE

No BitLocker recovery key found for this device

Figure 4.10 - The Azure AD Device Properties blade

As you can see, you will find a lot information about a specific device, such as the name of the device, registration date, last activity date, owner name, OS and OS version, and the method by which they joined Azure AD.

Connecting devices to Azure AD

After you have configured the prerequisites to allow device registration, you will be able to connect devices to Azure AD. There are three ways to do this:

- Joining a new Windows 10 device to Azure AD
- Joining an existing Windows 10 device to Azure AD
- Registering a Windows 10 device to Azure AD

In this section, you will learn about the required steps for each method in order to connect a Windows 10 device to Azure AD.

Joining a new Windows 10 device

In this section, we will take a new Windows 10 device and join it to Azure AD during the first-run experience. If the device is running Windows 10 Professional edition or Windows 10 Enterprise edition, then the first-run experience will present the setup process. To join a new Windows 10 device to Azure AD during this first-run experience, follow these steps:

1. Start the new device and start the setup process.

2. On the **Let's start with region. Is this right?** page, choose your region and click **Yes**.

3. On the **Is this the right keyboard layout?** page, choose your preferred keyboard layout and click **Yes**.

4. On the **Want to add a second keyboard layout?** page, click **Skip**.

5. On the **Sign in with Microsoft** page, enter your work or school account and click **Next**.

6. On the **Enter your password** page, enter your password and click **Next**.

7. *This step is optional and depends on the configuration of your Azure AD tenant.* On the **Help us protect your account** page, **confirm** the Authenticator notification.

8. On the **Do more with your voice** page, select the option of your choice and select **Accept**.

9. On the **Let Microsoft and apps use your location** page, select the option of your choice and select **Accept**.

10. On the **Find my device** page, select the option of your choice and select **Accept**.

11. On the **Send diagnostic data to Microsoft** page, select the option of your choice and select **Accept**.

12. On the **Improve inking & typing** page, select the option of your choice and select **Accept**.

13. On the **Get tailored experiences with diagnostic data** page, select the option of your choice and select **Accept**.

14. On the **Let apps use advertising ID** page, select the option of your choice and select **Accept**.

> Important Note
> *Step 15* and *16* are optional steps and depend on the configuration of your Azure AD tenant.

15. On the **Your organization requires Windows Hello** page, click on **Set up PIN**.

16. In the **Windows Security popup**, add a new PIN code (you'll need to do this twice for verification purposes) and click **OK**.

17. On the **All set!** page, click **OK**.

Now, you will be logged in to an Azure AD joined Windows 10 device. To verify that the device is registered in organization's Azure AD, follow these steps:

1. Open the **Azure** portal at `https://portal.azure.com`.

2. Sign in as an administrator.

3. On the left navigation bar, click **Azure Active Directory**.

4. In the **Manage** section, click **Devices**.

5. Under **All devices**, you will see the Azure AD joined device in the right pane, as shown in the following screenshot:

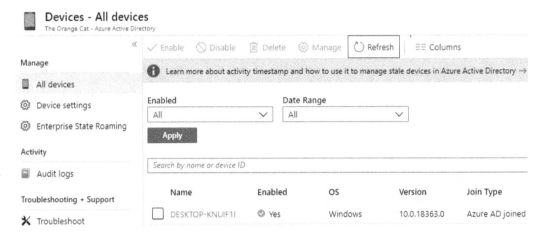

Figure 4.11 - Device is Azure AD joined

With that, you have successfully joined a new Windows 10 device to Azure AD. In the next section, we are going to join an existing Windows 10 device to Azure AD.

Joining an existing Windows 10 device

In this section, we are going to take an existing Windows 10 device and join it to Azure AD. You can join a Windows 10 device to Azure AD at any time. Just follow these steps to join Azure AD:

1. Open the **Settings** app.

2. Click **Accounts**.

3. Click **Access work or school**.

4. Click on **Connect**.

5. Under **Alternate actions**, click **Join this device to Azure Active Directory**.

6. Log in with your work or school account and follow the wizard.

7. In the **Make sure this is your organization window**, review it and click **Join**.

8. If everything goes well, you will see your email address, as shown in the following screenshot:

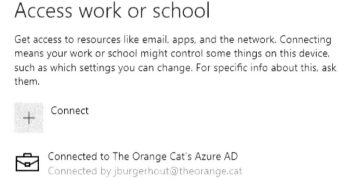

Figure 4.12 - Connecting an existing Windows 10 device to Azure AD

To verify that the device is registered in the organization's Azure AD, follow these steps:

1. Open the **Azure portal**.

2. Sign in as an administrator.

3. On the left navigation bar, click **Azure Active Directory**.

4. In the **Manage** section, click **Devices**.

5. Under **All devices**, you will see the Azure AD joined device in the right pane, as shown in the following screenshot:

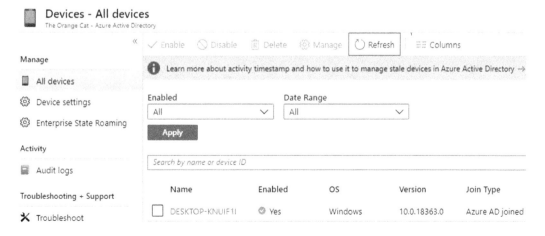

Figure 4.13 - Device is Azure AD joined

With that, you have successfully joined an existing Windows 10 device to Azure AD. In the next section, we are going to register a Windows 10 device to Azure AD.

Registering a Windows 10 device

Personally owned devices, such as a mobile phone or a personal Windows 10 laptop, can connect you to Azure AD using the **Add Work or School Account** feature in the **Settings** app. Device registration is used to allow devices to be known by Azure AD and Microsoft Intune. In this section, we will take an existing Windows 10 device and register it to Azure AD. To do this, follow these steps:

1. Open the **Settings** app.

2. Click **Accounts**.

3. Click **Access work or school**.

4. Click on **Connect**.

5. In the **Microsoft account** window, fill in your **work or school account** email address and click **Next**.

6. Follow the wizard to complete this process.

7. If everything goes well, you will see your email address, as shown in the following screenshot:

Figure 4.14 - Registering a Windows 10 device to Azure AD

To verify that the device is registered in the organization's Azure AD, follow these steps:

1. Open the **Azure portal**.

2. Sign in as an administrator.

3. On the left navigation bar, click **Azure Active Directory**.

4. In the **Manage** section, click **Devices**.

5. Under **All devices**, you will see the Azure AD device you just registered in the right pane, as shown in the following screenshot:

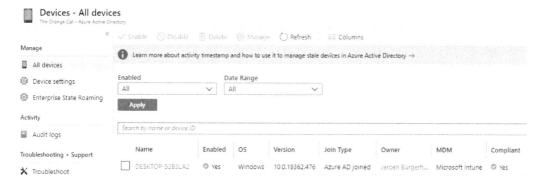

Figure 4.15 - Device is Azure AD joined

With that, you have successfully registered a Windows 10 device in Azure AD.

Important Note

You can register personally owned devices with Azure AD using the preceding steps. Personal devices are then known in Azure AD but are not fully managed by your organization.

Summary

You have learned a lot in this chapter, including the difference between the three sorts of user accounts that can be logged into with Windows 10. In addition to that, you learned know how to create, modify, and delete local user accounts via Computer Management and PowerShell.

You saw which user accounts are created during the initial setup of Windows 10. We also covered local groups in this chapter, and you learned how to create, modify, delete, and rename local groups via Computer Management or PowerShell. As well as doing this, you are now familiar with which built-in local groups are created during the installation of Windows 10 and where these local users and local groups are stored on a computer. This will help you understand how you can administer local users and local groups.

Furthermore, we covered how to manage Windows 10 devices via Azure AD. Here, you configured Azure AD so that users can enroll their Windows 10, Android, or iOS devices into Azure AD. You then used different methods to connect a Windows 10 device to Azure AD, such as by registering and joining your organizational Azure AD tenant.

Once these devices are known in Azure AD, you can manage them via the Azure portal by disabling or deleting a device from Azure AD. This has helped you understand how you can connect and manage devices in Azure AD.

In the next chapter, we will learn how to configure NTFS permissions, share permissions, and configure file access.

Questions

1. Can you fully manage a registered Windows 10 device in Azure Active Directory?
2. Is the local Administrator account enabled by default?
3. Can you register a smartphone to Azure Active Directory?
4. What is the correct PowerShell cmdlet to use to create a new local group?

Further reading

- **What is Azure Active Directory?**: https://docs.microsoft.com/en-us/azure/active-directory/fundamentals/active-directory-whatis

- **Azure AD registered devices**: https://docs.microsoft.com/en-us/azure/active-directory/devices/concept-azure-ad-register

- **Azure AD joined devices**: https://docs.microsoft.com/en-us/azure/active-directory/devices/concept-azure-ad-join

- **What is a device identity?**: https://github.com/MicrosoftDocs/azure-docs/blob/master/articles/active-directory/devices/overview.md?

5
Configuring Permissions and File Access

When users connect to a shared folder over a network, they can access the folders and files that the shared folder contains. Shared folders can contain applications, public data, or a user's personal data. This chapter will discuss the various methods of sharing folders, along with the effect that these methods will have on file and folder permissions when you create shared folders on a **New Technology File System** (**NTFS**) formatted partition.

This chapter will also talk about managing and configuring NTFS and sharing permissions on folders and files.

The following topics will be covered in this chapter:

- Overviewing different types of file systems
- Configuring and managing file access
- Understanding shared folder permissions
- Configuring and managing shared folders

In this chapter, you will learn about the different file systems that you can use in Windows 10. Furthermore, you will learn about the configuration that's available for the NTFS file system and shared folders. You will also learn how to manage file access. This chapter will help you prepare for the **MD-100** (Windows 10) exam, which is part of the **Microsoft 365 Certified: Modern Desktop Administrator Associate** certification.

Technical requirements

In this chapter, you will see various pieces of PowerShell code. These codes are available in this book's GitHub repository: `https://github.com/PacktPublishing/Microsoft-Exam-MD-100-Windows-10-Certification-Guide/tree/master/Chapter05`

In the *Understanding permission inheritance* section, you will learn about the difference between permission inheritances. The steps that you will follow have also been recorded. You can find these videos here: `https://bit.ly/2LsQDqD`

Overviewing different types of file systems

Before you can store data on a volume, you must format it. To format a volume, you must select the file system that the volume should use. Windows 10 supports different file systems, including **file allocation table (FAT)**, **FAT32**, and **extended file allocation table (exFAT)**; the NTFS file system and the **Resilient File System (ReFS)**.

There is also the **Compact Disc File System (CDFS)** and the **Universal Disk Format (UDF)**, which are used on optical and read-only media. These two file types are out of the scope of this exam guide.

In this section, you will learn about the differences and benefits of the file systems that Windows 10 supports. Let's learn about all these file systems in detail.

FAT

FAT is the oldest file system that Windows 10 supports. It has a low overhead but many limitations compared to newer file systems. However, enterprises often use it because nearly every operating system supports it. For example, you would use FAT on removable media, such as a USB drive, when you need to transfer data between Windows 10 and a non-Microsoft operating system or on a local hard drive if you have a PC with dual-boot configuration.

Windows 10 supports three versions of FAT, which are **FAT**, **FAT32**, and **exFAT**. The main differences between these three versions are as follows:

- The size of the largest supported volume

- The default cluster size

- The maximum number of files and folders that you can create on the volume

The following table lists the differences between the three FAT versions:

Attribute	FAT	FAT32	exFAT
Maximum partition size	32 GB	2 TB	232 – 1 clusters
Maximum file size	4 GB	4 GB	16 exabytes (EB)
Maximum files per volume	65,536 files	4,194,304 files	Nearly unlimited

Table 5.1 - Difference between FAT versions

> **Important Note**
> A cluster is the smallest unit of disk space that you can allocate to store a file.
> For example, if a volume cluster is 4 **kilobytes** (**KB**) and you store a file that's
> 100 bytes in size on that volume, it will use one cluster, which is 4 KB.
> The exFAT file system supports clusters that ranges from 512 bytes to 32
> **megabytes** (**MB**).

When you must choose between the FAT or NTFS file system to format a volume, you will have to compare the file systems. You will find that many NTFS features are not available with FAT, such as the following:

- **Security**: You cannot configure file permissions and limit user actions on a FAT volume.

- **Auditing**: You cannot audit user actions on the FAT file system.

- **Compression**: The FAT file system does not support compression and each file uses its full original size, rounded to the closest cluster size.

- **Encryption**: **Encrypting File System** (**EFS**) is not supported, and you cannot use it on exFAT volumes.

- **Disk quota**: The FAT file system does not support quotas. This means that you cannot limit the disk space that users can use on a FAT volume.

After you have formatted a volume, you cannot change the file system or cluster size. You can only perform a backup and reformat the volume. The only exception is that you can convert FAT or FAT32 file system volumes into NTFS file system format.

Now, let's learn about the NTFS system.

NTFS

This type of file system is the default file system in Windows 10. The NTFS provides better performance, reliability, and advanced features that are not available in any version of FAT.

The NTFS file system provides the following:

- **Reliability**: The NTFS file system uses log file and checkpoint information to restore the consistency of the file system when the computer restarts. In the event of a bad sector error, the NTFS file system dynamically remaps the cluster that contains the bad sector, and it allocates a new cluster for the data. The NTFS file system also marks that cluster as bad and does not use it again.

- **Security**: You can set permissions on a file, folder, or the entire NTFS volume, which enables you to control which users, groups, or computers can read, modify, or delete data. You also can enable auditing to log activities on the NTFS volume

- **Data confidentially**: The NTFS file system supports the EFS in order to protect file content. If you have EFS enabled, you can encrypt files and folders for one user. Only this user can access these encrypted files. Other users can't access these files.

- **Limit storage growth**: The NTFS file system supports the use of disk quotas. With this feature, you enable the amount of disk space that is available to a user. When disk quotas are enabled, you can configure whether to allow users to exceed their limits.

- **Additional space**: The NTFS file system allows you to create extra disk space by compressing files, folders, or whole drives. You also can extend an NTFS volume by mounting an additional volume to an empty folder.

- **Support for large volumes**: You can format a volume up to 256 **terabytes** (TB) in size by using the NTFS file system with a 64 KB cluster size. The NTFS file system supports larger files and supports a larger number of files per volume compared to any FAT version. The NTFS file system also manages disk space efficiently by using smaller cluster sizes. For example, a 30 GB NTFS volume uses 4 KB clusters. The same volume formatted with FAT32 uses 16 KB clusters. Using smaller clusters reduces space wastage on hard disks.

- **Advanced features**: The NTFS file system includes multiple advanced features, such as distributed link tracking, sparse files, and multiple data streams.

In Windows 10, there is a utility called `Convert.exe` that you can use to convert FAT or FAT32 file systems into the NTFS file system type on data volumes. The benefit of using this utility is that you will not have downtime or data loss.

We will not go too deep into `Convert.exe` as it is beyond the scope of this book, but in the following example, you will see that the `convert` command is used to convert the volume on drive F into `ntfs` with messages during the conversion process:

```
convert F: /fs:ntfs /v
```

As mentioned earlier in this chapter, you cannot convert NTFS into FAT. First, you must backup your data, reformat the volume by using the NTFS file system, and then restore the data.

Next, we will look at the ReFS system.

ReFS

Resilient File System (ReFS) was introduced in **Windows Server 2012**. It is also available in **Windows 8.1**, **Windows Server 2012 R2**, and in all newer Microsoft operating systems, including Windows 10. ReFS is built on top of the NTFS file system and is designed to provide the highest level of resiliency, integrity, and scalability, regardless of software or hardware failures.

ReFS includes only some of the NTFS features, such as security and auditing, but does not support others, such as quota, compression, and EFS. ReFS is especially useful for data volumes in **multi-terabyte (TB)** file servers and for cluster-shared volumes in failover clusters.

The ReFS file system has the following benefits:

- ReFS is designed to provide the highest level of protection for data from common errors that can cause corruption, such as unexpected loss of power or disk failure.

- The ReFS system periodically scans volumes. If it detects corruption within volumes, ReFS tries to correct the corruption automatically. If it cannot repair the corruption automatically, ReFS localizes the salvaging process to the corruption area.

- ReFS supports extremely large volumes, even larger than the NTFS file system, without impacting performance. ReFS volumes can contain petabytes of data with ease.

Windows 10 provides limited support for ReFS. You can use it only with two-way or three-way storage spaces. You cannot format ReFS for non-mirrored storage spaces, such as simple or parity storage spaces.

In this section, you learned about the three most common file systems for Windows 10. In the next section, we will look at how you can configure and manage file access and NTFS permissions.

Configuring and managing file access

You can control user access to files by configuring file and folder permissions. If file permissions are supported by the file system, such as the NTFS or ReFS file systems, you can configure permissions at the volume (root folder), folder, and file levels. You can also assign permissions explicitly or you can inherit them from the higher levels.

Understanding tools for managing files and folders

You can store data as files on local storage or remote storage. To manage these files, you can use several tools in Windows 10, such as File Explorer, Command Prompt, and PowerShell. Let's learn about each of them in the following sections.

File Explorer

File Explorer is a tool that you typically use to manage files and folders. In the previous editions of Windows, File Explorer was called Windows Explorer. File Explorer provides a simple interface that is familiar to most Windows users. By using File Explorer, you can perform several functions, some of which are as follows:

- Creating files and folders
- Accessing files and folders
- Managing the properties of files and folders
- Searching for content in files and folders
- Previewing content of files and folders

If you need to manage file permissions in File Explorer, right-click the object and then select **Properties**. You can configure permissions on the **Security** tab of the **Properties** dialog box.

Now, we'll move on to the **Command Prompt** tool.

Command Prompt

You can use the Command Prompt to access files and folders. To open the Command Prompt, click on the **Start** menu icon and start typing cmd.

Some common commands for managing files and folders are as follows:

- cd: Changes the parent directory
- md: Creates a directory
- del: Deletes one or more files
- move: Moves one or multiple files
- dir: Displays a list of files and subdirectories in a directory
- icacls: Displays or modifies permissions by using **access control lists** (**ACLs**)

Now, let's learn about the PowerShell tool.

PowerShell

You can use PowerShell to access and manage files and folders. To open PowerShell, click on the **Start** menu icon and start typing PowerShell. PowerShell provides many cmdlets that you can use to manage files and folders, as follows:

- Get-Childitem: This displays a directory's list of files and subdirectories.
- Set-Location: This changes the parent directory.
- Get-Alias: This is used to view a list of all aliases.

It also includes many aliases, which are the same as the familiar tools in the Command Prompt, such as dir and cd, and you can use them instead of the PowerShell cmdlets.

To manage file permissions, you can use the Get-ACL and Set-ACL cmdlets. For example, to see the current ACL on the C:\Windows\regedit.exe file with the output in list format, run the following command:

```
Get-ACL C:\Windows\regedit.exe | Format-List
```

To modify a file or folder's ACL, use the Set-ACL cmdlet. You also can use the Get-ACL cmdlet in conjunction with the Set-ACL cmdlet. You can use the Get-ACL cmdlet to provide the input by getting the object that represents the file or folder's ACL, and then using the Set-ACL cmdlet to change the ACL of the target file or folder so that it matches with the values that the Get-ACL cmdlet provides.

For example, to set the ACL on the `C:\Temporary` folder so that it's the same as the permissions on `C:\Windows`, including inheritance settings, you would run the following command:

```
Get-ACL C:\Windows | Set-ACL C:\Temporary
```

With that, you've learned how to see and change the ACL via PowerShell and Command Prompt. In the next section, you will learn how to set file and folder permissions and what types of permissions there are.

Configuring file and folder permissions

You can only configure file and folder permissions on NTFS and ReFS volumes. Permissions are rules that determine which specific users can perform on a file or a folder. A file or folder's owner can grant or deny permissions to it, just like anyone with **Full Control** permissions can, which grants that person rights to modify permissions for that file or folder.

You assign permissions to files and folders by granting or denying a specific permission level. Typically, you assign them in groups to minimize administrative overhead. If you assign permissions to a group, every group member has the assigned permission. You can also assign permissions to individual users and computers. If you assign permissions to a group and to individual group members, they are cumulative. This means that a user has the permissions that you assign to him or her, in addition to those you assign to the group.

You can configure two types of permissions for files and folders, namely **basic** and **advanced**. The difference between these types is as follows:

- **Basic permissions**: This type of permission is used the most. You must work with basic permissions often and assign them to groups and users.

- **Advanced permissions**: This type of permission provides a finer degree of control. However, advanced permissions are more complex to document and manage than basic permissions.

You can choose which permission you want to allow or to deny on a file or folder. The basic file and folder permissions are as follows:

- **Full Control**: This provides complete control of the file or folder and control of permissions.

- **Modify**: This allows you to read a file, write changes to it, and modify permissions.

- **Read & execute**: This allows you to see folder content, read files, and start programs.

- **Read**: This allows you to read a file, but not make any changes to it.

- **Write**: This allows you to change folder and file content.

- **Special permissions**: This is a custom configuration.

> **Important Note**
> Groups or users that have the **Full Control** permission on a folder can delete any files in that folder, regardless of the permissions that protect the file.

You must have the Full Control permission for a folder or file to modify the permissions, except for the file and folder owners. The owner can always modify the permissions and administrators can always take ownership of files and folders to configure permissions.

The next section will be about inheritance of permissions. Permission inheritance is all about permissions that will be applied automatically to files and subfolders in a root folder.

Understanding permission inheritance

Permission inheritance allows the permissions that you set on a folder to be applied automatically to files that users create in that folder and its subfolders. This means that you can set permissions for an entire folder structure at a single point. If you must modify permissions, then you must perform the change at that single point itself.

For example, when you create a folder called `Folder1`, all subfolders and files created within `Folder1` automatically inherit that folder's permissions. Therefore, `Folder1` has explicit permissions, while all the subfolders and files within it have inherited permissions.

Permissions on a file are a combination of inherited and explicit permissions. For example, if you assign `Group1` **Read permissions** on a folder and **Write permissions** on a file in the folder, the members of `Group1` can read and write in the file. If inherited and explicit permissions collide with each other, explicit permissions take precedence.

As mentioned earlier, you have two types of permissions. These types are as follows:

- **Explicit permissions**: When you set permissions directly on a file or a folder, the permissions are applied explicitly. You can assign permissions to the object directly by modifying the security settings in the object's properties dialog box.

- **Inherited permissions**: Files and folders are typically arranged in a nested structure, where a folder contains subfolders and files, and those subfolders contain files and folders. Permission inheritance allows for child objects to inherit the parent object's permissions settings.

This allows you to assign explicit permissions to a parent folder and have inheritance pass those permissions settings down to the parent folder's subfolders and files. By doing this, you can control inheritance behavior. Inherited permissions ease the task of managing permissions, and they ensure the consistency of permissions among all a container's objects.

Now that you know about the inheritance of permissions, you will learn how to configure inheritance for all objects.

Configuring inheritance for all objects

If the **Allow** or **Deny** checkboxes that are associated with each of the permissions appear shaded, then this means a file or folder has inherited permissions from one of its parent folders. There are two ways that you can make changes to inherited permissions, as follows:

- You can make changes to a parent folder that you set permissions for explicitly. The file or folder will inherit these modified permissions.

- You can choose not to inherit permissions from a parent object. You can then make changes to the permissions or remove a user or group from the permissions list of the file or folder.

All the child objects only inherit permissions that they are capable of inheriting. When you set permissions on a parent object, you can decide whether folders, subfolders, and files can inherit permissions. We can perform the following procedure to assign permissions that child objects can inherit:

1. Open **File Explorer**.
2. Right-click on a file or subfolder.
3. Click the **Properties | Security | Advanced** button.
4. In the **Advanced Security Settings** for file or folder dialog box, the **Inherited From** column lists where the permissions are inherited from. The **Applies To** column lists the **folders**, **subfolders**, or **files** that the permissions have been applied to, as shown in the following screenshot:

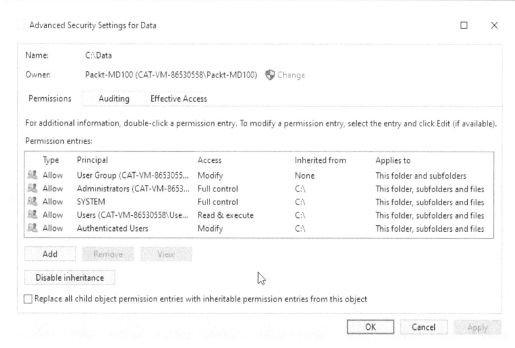

Figure 5.1 - The Advanced Security Settings box

5.   Double-click the user or group that you want to adjust permissions for.

6.   In the **Permissions Entry for name** dialog box, click the **Applies to** drop-down list:

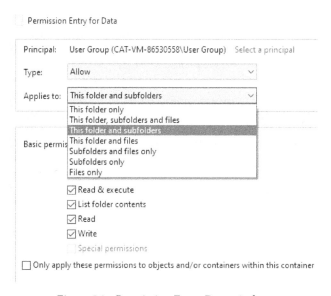

Figure 5.2 - Permission Entry Data window

7. From the previous step, select one of the following options from the **Applies to** drop-down list: **This folder only**, **This folder, subfolders and files**, **This folder and subfolders**, **This folder and files**, **Subfolders and files only**, **Subfolders only**, or **Files only**.

8. Click **OK** in the **Permission Entry for name** dialog box.

9. After that, click **OK** in the **Advanced Security Settings for name** dialog box.

10. Then, click **OK** in the **Properties** dialog box.

> **Important Note**
>
> If the **Special permissions** entry in the **Permissions for User or Group** box is shaded, this does not imply that this permission is inherited. Rather, this means that a special permission has been selected.
>
> If you add permissions for **Creator Owner** at the folder level, those permissions will apply to the user who created the file in the folder.

With that, you've learned how to modify inheritance permissions. We can also prevent inheritance to files and folders. In the next section, you will learn what the consequences of doing this are and how to configure this particular setting.

Preventing inheritance

After you've set permissions on a parent folder, new files and subfolders that users create in the folder inherit these permissions. You can block permission inheritance to restrict access to these files and subfolders. For example, you can assign all Accounting users the **Modify permission** to the Accounting folder. For the Invoices subfolder, you can block inherited permissions and grant only a few specific users' permissions to the folder.

> **Important Note**
>
> When you block permission inheritance, you have the option to convert inherited permissions into explicit permissions, or you can remove all inherited permissions. If you want to restrict a group or user, you can convert inherited permissions into explicit permissions to simplify the configuration.

To prevent a folder or file from inheriting permissions from a parent folder, perform the following procedure:

1. Open **File Explorer**.

2. **Right-click** a file or subfolder.

3. Click the **Properties | Security | Advanced** button.

4. In the **Advanced Security Settings** for file or folder dialog box, click **Disable inheritance**, as shown in the following screenshot:

Figure 5.3 - Advanced properties tab

5. Then, in the **Block Inheritance** dialog box, select one of the following options: **Convert inherited permissions into explicit permissions on this object** or **Remove all inherited permissions from this object**.

The following screenshot shows the previously stated options that will appear in the **Block Inheritance** dialog box:

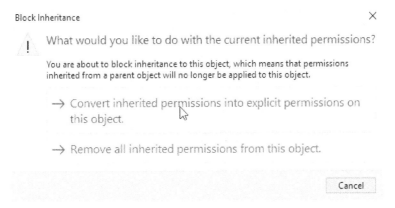

Figure 5.4 - Block Inheritance window

6. Click **OK** in the **Advanced Security Settings for name** dialog box.

7. Click **OK** in the **Properties** dialog box.

In the next section, you will learn about forcing the inheritance of permissions and the effects this has on the permissions of files and folders.

Forcing permission inheritance

The **Advanced Security** dialog box for folders includes a **Replace all child object permission entries** checkbox with inheritable entries from this object. Selecting this checkbox will replace the permissions on all child objects that you can change permissions for, including child objects that had **Block inheritance** configured. This is useful if you need to change permissions on many subfolders and files, especially if you set the original permissions incorrectly.

You might be overwhelmed with inheritance permissions after reading the previous sections, but there is still a feature to check; that is, what the inheritance of permissions will do for a user or a group with the Effective Access feature. In the next section, you will learn what you can do with this feature.

Understanding the Effective Access feature

The **Effective Access** feature determines the permissions a user or group has on an object by calculating the permissions that are granted to the user or group. The calculation considers the group membership permissions and any of the permissions that are inherited from the parent object.

The calculation determines all the domain and local groups that the user or group is a member of.

The Effective Access feature only produces a rough calculation of the permissions that a user has. The actual permissions that a user has might be different, because permissions can be granted or denied based on how a user signs in.

To view the Effective Access permissions, follow the following steps:

1. Open **File Explorer**.
2. **Right-click** on a folder.
3. Click the **Properties | Security | Advanced | Effective Access | Select a user** button.
4. Choose a user and click **OK**.
5. Then, click **View effective access**. The **Effective Access** tab can be seen in the following screenshot:

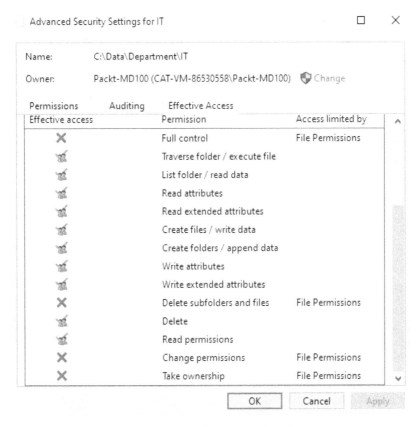

Figure 5.5 - Effective Access dialog box

In the next section, we will take a look at what the behavior of file and folder permissions are when we copy or move the files and folders to a different location (on the same or different volume).

Learning about copying and moving files

When you copy or move a file or folder, the permissions can change, depending on where you move the file or folder. Therefore, when you copy or move files or folders, it is important to understand the impact this has on permissions.

Effects of copying files and folders

When you copy a file or folder from one folder to another folder, or from one volume to another volume, the permissions for the files or folders might change. Copying a file or folder creates new objects with the same content as the original files or folders, which has the following effects on permissions:

- When you copy a file or folder within a **single volume**, the copy of the folder or file will receive the permissions of the destination folder.

- When you copy a file or folder to a **different volume**, the copy of the folder or file will receive the permissions of the destination folder.

When you copy a file or folder to a volume that does not support permissions, such as a FAT file system, the copy of the folder or file loses its permissions. This is because the target volume does not support permissions.

> **Important Note**
> When you copy a file or folder within a single volume or between volumes, you must have the **Read** permission for the source folder and the **Write** permission for the destination folder.

When you are copying or moving files and folders, the copied files and folders will receive the permissions from the folder above (origin folder). *But what are the effects of moving files and folders?* You will learn about that in the next section.

Effects of moving files and folders

When you move a file or folder, permissions might change, depending on the destination folder's permissions. Moving a file or folder has the following effects on permissions:

- If you move a file or folder within the same volume, only the pointers are updated, and data is not moved. Permissions that are inherited at the source location no longer apply and the file or folder that you moved inherits the permissions from the new parent folder. If the file or folder has explicitly assigned permissions, it retains those permissions, in addition to the newly inherited permissions.

- When you move a file or folder to a different volume, the folder or file inherits the destination folder's permissions, but it does not retain the explicitly assigned or inherited permissions from the source location. When you move a folder or file between volumes, Windows 10 copies the folder or file to the new location and deletes the original file from the source location.

- When you move a file or folder to a volume that does not support permissions, the folder or file loses its permissions because the target volume does not support permissions.

> **Important Note**
>
> Most files do not have explicitly assigned permissions. Instead, they inherit permissions from their parent folder. If you move files that only have inherited permissions, they do not retain the inherited permissions during the move.
>
> Also, when you move a file or folder within a volume or between volumes, you must have both the Write permission for the destination folder and the Modify permission for the source file or folder. You need the Modify permission to move a folder or file because Windows 10 deletes the folder or file from the source folder after it has been moved to the destination folder.

The `Copy` command is not aware of the security settings on folders or files. However, commands that are more robust have this awareness, some of which are as follows:

- `Xcopy`: This has the `/o` switch so that it can include ownership and ACL settings.
- `Robocopy`: This has several switches that cause security information to be copied. They are `/Copy:DAT` and `/Sec`. In the `/Copy:DAT` term, D stands for **Data**, A stands for **Attributes**, and T stands for **Timestamps**. You can add the S flag after T, where S stands for **Security**, such as NTFS ACLs. `/Sec` is the equivalent of `/Copy:DATS`.

In this section, you learned how you can configure and maintain file access in a Windows 10 environment. You can do this via the File Explorer, PowerShell, or Command Prompt. You also learned about how to set permissions and what inheritance permissions are, as well as how you can force or prevent this type of permissions. You also learned what will happen when you move or copy files within the same volume or to another volume.

In the next section, you will learn how to configure and maintain shared folders.

Configuring and managing shared folders

The daily administrator's job is to collaborate with your team. Your team might create documents that only team members can share, or you might work with a remote team member who needs access to your team's files. Because of this type of collaboration and the requirements for this, you must understand how to manage shared folders in a network environment.

A user can connect to a shared folder over a network and access the folders and files that are in the shared folder. Shared folders can contain applications, public data, or a user's personal data. By providing a central location for shared folders, you enable the following features:

- Simplification of administrative management
- Ease in backing up data
- Consistent location and availability
- User familiarity

In this section, we will learn about the various methods you can use to share folders, along with the effect this has on file and folder permissions when you create shared folders on an NTFS formatted partition.

When an administrator shares a folder, the administrator makes its content available on the network to multiple users. The administrator can limit who can access the shared folder and what type of shared permissions they have. Additionally, the administrator can limit the number of users who can access the share at the same time and if an offline copy will be created automatically on their computer.

Shared folders maintain a separate set of permissions from the file system permissions, which means that the administrator can set share permissions, even if the administrator shares a folder on the FAT file system. The same share permissions apply to all shared content. This behavior is different from file system permissions, where the administrator can set permissions for each file individually.

The administrator can use these permissions to provide an extra level of security for files and folders that you make available on your network. The administrator can share the same folder multiple times by using a different share name and other share settings for each creation.

After the administrator shares a folder, all users on the network will see the share name. But only the users with Read permissions can view the content inside that share. Windows 10 restricts folder sharing to members of the Administrators group. If a user is not a member of the Administrators group, then the user must provide administrative credentials in the **User Account Control (UAC)** dialog box.

File and printer sharing are disabled by default. When you share the first folder on a Windows 10 device, Windows 10 turns on file and printer sharing automatically. This setting remains turned on, even if you remove all shared folders. You can configure it manually in **Advanced sharing settings** in the **Control Panel**.

Now, let's take a look at shared folder permissions. As you can see, besides files and folder permissions, you can also set permissions on shares. Share permissions are permissions for users or groups so they can access the folder before they can access the files.

Understanding shared folder permissions

When you share a folder, you must configure the permissions that a user or group will have when they connect to the folder through the share. This is called sharing permissions. The following are three options for sharing permissions:

- **Read**: The users can view the content, but they cannot modify or delete it.
- **Change**: The users can also modify, delete, and create content, but they cannot modify permissions. This permission also includes the Read permission.
- **Full Control**: The users can perform all actions, including modifying the permissions. This permission also includes the Change permission.

Besides the previously stated sharing permissions, you also have the basic sharing permissions. These permissions are simplified and can have one of two options, which are given as follows:

- **Read**: The users can open but cannot modify or delete a file.
- **Read/Write**: This is the Full Control option. The users can open, modify, or delete a file and modify permissions.

  Now that you know about the five different shared folder permissions, in the next section, you will learn how you can view which permissions a shared folder has.

Viewing shared folders

Windows 10 creates several shared folders by default. You can view all shared folders in the **Computer Management** console by clicking the **Shared Folders** node. You can also run the following command:

```
net view \\localhost /all
```

We can also run the following command on a PowerShell cmdlet:

```
Get-SmbShare
```

The following screenshot shows the output after executing the **net view \\localhost /all** command:

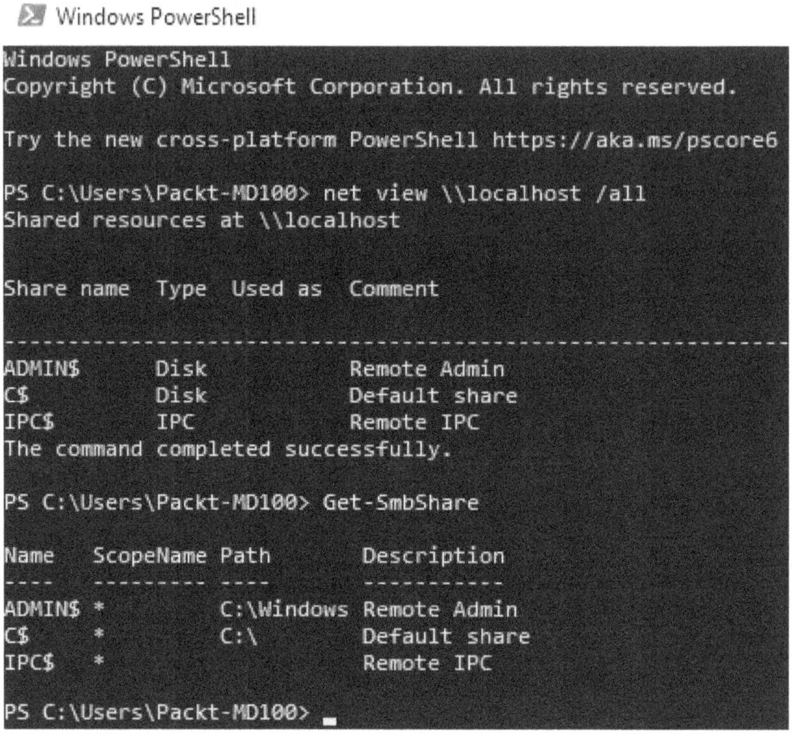

Figure 5.6 - Output of the net view command and Get-SmbShare

In the previous screenshot, you can see the output of both commands. The first output is the command line, while the second output is the PowerShell cmdlet.

> **Important Note**
> In older Windows versions, you could recognize shared folders in File Explorer because there was a different icon for folders that were being shared compared to folders that were not being shared. In File Explorer within Windows 10, the same icon is used, regardless of whether a folder is shared or not.

Now, you know how to view which permissions a shared folder has. In the next section, we will create a shared folder and the tools needed to create such a folder.

Creating shared folders

Users can connect to a shared folder most commonly over the network by using its **Universal Naming Convention** (**UNC**) address. The UNC address contains the name of the computer that is hosting the folder and the shared folder name, separated by a backward slash (\) and preceded by two backward slashes (\\). For example, the UNC name for the `Accounting` shared folder on the **CAT-CL7** computer in the `Theorange.cat` domain would be `\\CAT-CL7.theorange.cat\Accounting`. You can share folders in several ways, as follows:

- Shared Folders snap-in
- File Explorer
- Command Prompt
- PowerShell cmdlets

In the next few sections, you will learn how you can use the previously mentioned ways to share a folder.

Shared Folders snap-in

You can use the Shared Folders snap-in to manage a computer's file shares centrally. You can use this snap-in to create file shares, set permissions, and view and manage open files and the users who can connect to a computer's file shares. Additionally, you can view the properties for the shared folder, which would allow you to perform actions such as specifying file permissions.

Let's create a share and give permissions using the Shared Folders snap-in:

1. Right-click on **Start**.

2. Click **Computer Management | Shared Folders | Shares buttons**. The following screenshot shows the **computer management** window:

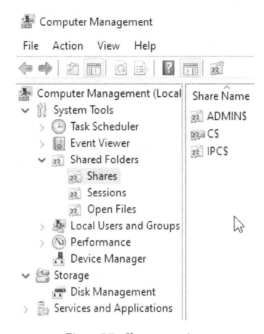

Figure 5.7 - Shares overview

3. **Right-click** in the middle pane, or right-click on **Shares**.

4. Click on **New Share…**.

5.   In the **Create a Shared Folder Wizard**, click **Next**:

Figure 5.8 - The Create a Shared Folder Wizard

6.   Click on **Browse...**, go to the folder you want to share, and click **OK**:

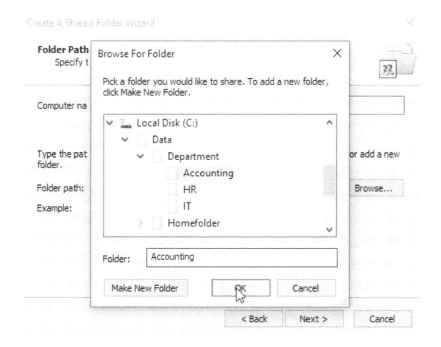

Figure 5.9 - Browse to a folder you want to share

7. Click on **Next**, as shown in the following screenshot:

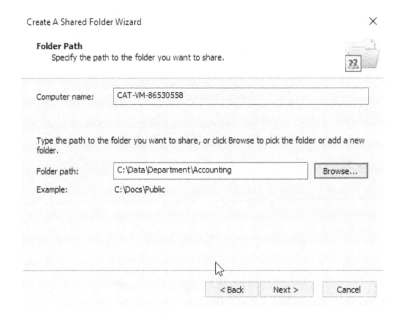

Figure 5.10 - Folder path window

8. Type in the **share name** and **description** and choose the correct **offline settings**:

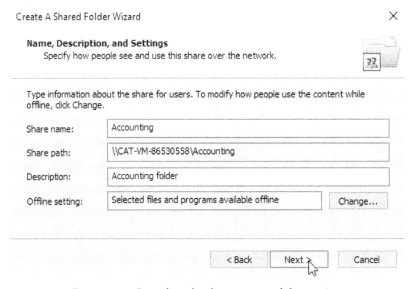

Figure 5.11 - Providing the share name and description

9. Click on **Next**.

10. Choose the correct permissions for the shared folder or customize the permissions by clicking **Customize permissions**:

Figure 5.12 - Shared Folder Permissions window

11. Click on **Finish**.

12. Then, click on the next **Finish** button:

Figure 5.13 - The Sharing was Successful window

With that, you have successfully created a shared folder by using the Shared Folders snap-in:

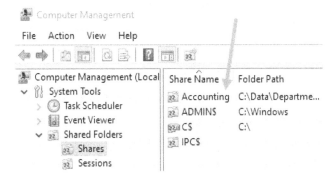

Figure 5.14 - The newly created shared folder

Now that we've created a share via the Shared Folders snap-in, we can do the same via File Explorer.

File Explorer

You can use File Explorer to share a folder using the **Share with** option from the shortcut menu or via the ribbon.

Let's create a shared folder using File Explorer with the **Share with** option:

1. Open **File Explorer** and go to the folder you want to share.

2. Click on the **Share** tab in the ribbon.

3. In the **Share with** box, choose a user:

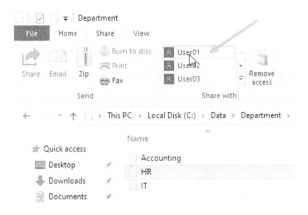

Figure 5.15 - Choosing the user who wants to have access to the share

4. In the **Network access** wizard, click on **Yes, share the items**.

5. If this is your first time doing this, then the **Network discovery and file sharing** dialog box will open. Choose the appropriate option for your environment: **No, make the network that I am connected to a private network** or **Yes, turn on network discovery and file sharing for all public networks**. The **Network discovery and file sharing** window is as follows:

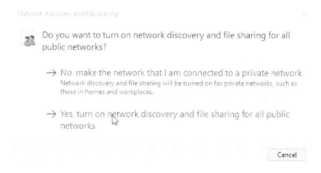

Figure 5.16 - Choosing the appropriate option

6. The folder will now be set up so that it can be shared with the user.

7. To check if the folder is being shared, open the **Properties** dialog box and click on the **Sharing** tab:

Figure 5.17 - Result of your created folder

With that, you have successfully created a share with File Explorer. Next, we will do this with the command line.

Command line

You can share a folder by using the net share command, as shown here:

```
net share IT=C:\Data\Department\IT
```

The previous command will create the IT share, which uses the IT share name, and which grants all users Read permissions. You can specify additional parameters when creating a share, some of which are as follows:

- /Grant:user permission: This allows you to specify Read, Change, or Full share permissions for the specified user.
- /Users:number: This allows you to limit the number of users who can connect to the share.
- /Remark:"text": This allows you to add a comment to the share.
- /Cache:option: This allows you to specify the caching options for the share.
- sharename /Delete: This allows you to remove an existing share.

Besides using Command Prompt, you can use PowerShell as well.

In the following screenshot, you can see an example of how to use the net share command with some optional parameters:

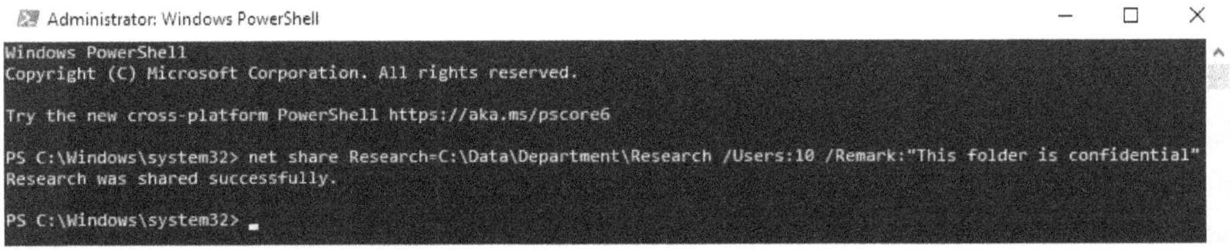

Figure 5.18 - Output of using the net share command with optional parameters

PowerShell

PowerShell includes several cmdlets that you can use to manage shares. The following example illustrates the cmdlet for creating a share:

```
New-SmbShare -Name "Global IT" -Path C:\Data\Department\IT
```

The following points list additional PowerShell commands that you can use to manage shares:

- `Get-SmbShare`: This retrieves a list of the computer's existing shares.
- `Set-SmbShare`: This modifies an existing share.
- `Remove-SmbShare`: This removes an existing share.
- `Get-SmbShareAccess`: This retrieves a share's permissions.
- `Grant-SmbShareAccess`: This sets share permissions.

In the following screenshot, you can see an example of the `New-SmbShare` cmdlet being used with some optional parameters:

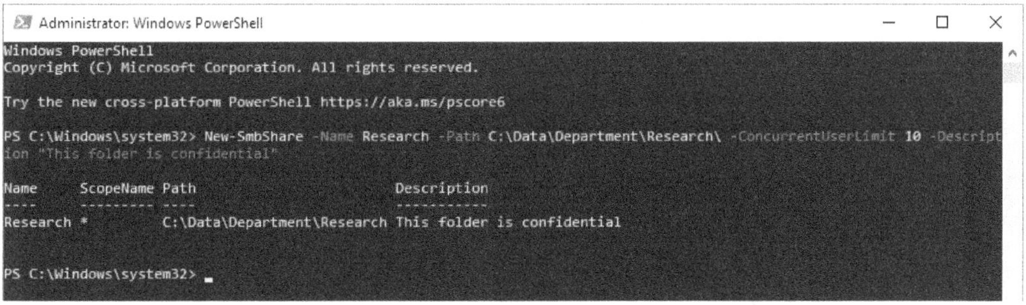

Figure 5.19 - Output of the New-SmbShare cmdlet with additional parameters

With that, you learned how you can create, modify, or delete shares in different ways. Next, you will learn what you can do with this shared folder properties and how you can configure them.

Shared folder properties

You can configure the properties of a shared folder when you create a share or when you modify shared folder properties. The properties that you can configure from a shared folder are as follows:

- The way your users can view and connect to a share
- The number of users that can access a share simultaneously
- Which share permissions will be effective for your users
- The offline settings for the share data

You can configure these three properties in several ways, as follows:

- Advanced Sharing

- The net share command

- The PowerShell cmdlets, namely `New-SmbShare` and `Set-SmbShare`

There are many ways to connect to a shared folder by using the File Explorer, command line, and by using PowerShell. Let's take a look.

Advanced Sharing

From the **Advanced Sharing** option, which you can find in the **Sharing** tab in the **Folder properties** window, you can configure the following parameters: **Share name**, **Number of simultaneous users**, **Caching**, and **Permissions**. The following screenshot shows the **Advanced Sharing** window:

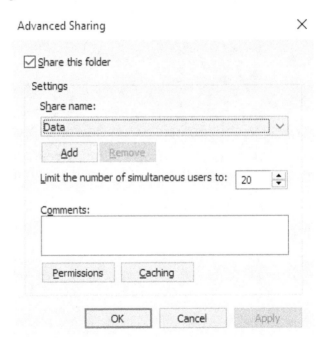

Figure 5.20 - The Advanced Sharing window

From the preceding screenshot, you can see various fields. Let's take a look at them in more detail:

- **Share name**: Each share must have a share name, and it must be unique for each Windows 10-based computer. The share name can be any string that does not contain special characters, and it is part of the UNC path.

  You can share the same folder multiple times and with different properties, but each share name must be unique. If the share name ends with a dollar sign ($), then the share is hidden and not visible on the network. However, you can connect to it if you know the share name and have the appropriate permissions.

- **Number of simultaneous users**: This limits the number of users that can have an open connection to the share. The connection to the share is open when a user accesses the share for the first time, and it closes automatically after a period of inactivity. The default value in Windows 10 is no more than **20** users. However, you can set this to a lower number.

- **Caching**: You can control which of the share's files and programs are available to offline users, or those who do not have network connectivity. You can configure files as follows:

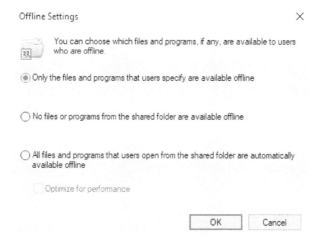

Figure 5.21 - The Offline Settings window

From the previous screenshot, you can see the various options that you can choose from: **Only the files and programs that users specify are available offline**, **No files or programs from the shared folder are available offline**, and **All files and programs that users open from the shared folder are automatically available offline**.

- **Permissions**: You can configure shared folder permissions that Windows uses in conjunction with file system permissions when a user tries to use a shared folder to access data over a network. Shared folder permissions can allow **Read**, **Change**, or **Full control** permissions, as shown in the following screenshot:

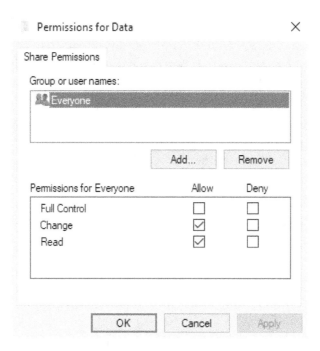

Figure 5.22 - Share Permissions window for a folder

If you try to use a share name that is already in use on the computer, Windows 10 will provide you with an option to stop sharing an old folder and use the share name to share the current folder. If you rename a folder that is being shared currently, you won't receive a warning. However, the folder will no longer be shared.

> **Important Note**
>
> If you share a folder by using **Network File and Folder Sharing**, you can share a folder only once, and you cannot configure its properties manually. The share name is set automatically and is the same as the folder name. The share permissions, number of simultaneous users, and caching properties retain the same value.

We'll look at the command-line option next.

Command line

With the following cmd command, you can view the shared folder properties for a share. In this example, the shared folder is named `Accounting`:

```
net share Accounting
```

The output from this command will be as follows:

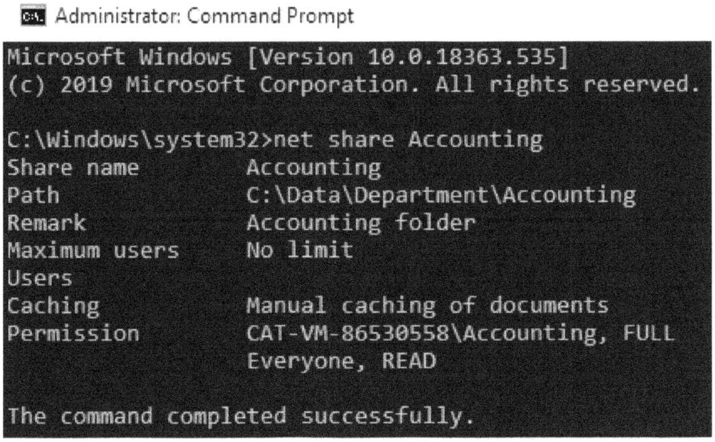

Administrator: Command Prompt

```
Microsoft Windows [Version 10.0.18363.535]
(c) 2019 Microsoft Corporation. All rights reserved.

C:\Windows\system32>net share Accounting
Share name          Accounting
Path                C:\Data\Department\Accounting
Remark              Accounting folder
Maximum users       No limit
Users
Caching             Manual caching of documents
Permission          CAT-VM-86530558\Accounting, FULL
                    Everyone, READ

The command completed successfully.
```

Figure 5.23 - Output of the net share command

As shown in the previous screenshot, not that much information is given about this share, only **Share name**, **Path**, **Remark**, **Maximum users**, **Users**, **Caching**, and **Permission**. When you are using PowerShell, then you will see more information about a share.

PowerShell

With the following PowerShell cmdlet, you can view shared folder properties for a share. In this example, the shared folder is named `Data`:

```
Get-SmbShare -Name Data | Format-List -Property *
```

The output of the preceding command can be seen in the following screenshot:

```
Windows PowerShell

PS C:\Users\burgj1> Get-SmbShare -Name Data | Format-List -Property *


PresetPathAcl             : System.Security.AccessControl.DirectorySecurity
ShareState                : Online
AvailabilityType          : NonClustered
ShareType                 : FileSystemDirectory
FolderEnumerationMode     : Unrestricted
CachingMode               : None
LeasingMode               : Full
SmbInstance               : Default
CATimeout                 : 0
ConcurrentUserLimit       : 43
ContinuouslyAvailable     : False
CurrentUsers              : 2
Description               : Data shared folder
EncryptData               : False
IdentityRemoting          : False
Infrastructure            : False
Name                      : Data
Path                      : C:\Temp\Data
Scoped                    : False
ScopeName                 : *
SecurityDescriptor        : O:BAG:DUD:(A;;0x1301bf;;;WD)
ShadowCopy                : False
Special                   : False
Temporary                 : False
Volume                    : \\?\Volume{58c26e5f-bc7a-40fd-9c82-ccb045ad764d}\
PSComputerName            :
CimClass                  : ROOT/Microsoft/Windows/SMB:MSFT_SmbShare
CimInstanceProperties     : {AvailabilityType, CachingMode, CATimeout, ConcurrentUserLimit...}
CimSystemProperties       : Microsoft.Management.Infrastructure.CimSystemProperties
```

Figure 5.24 - Output window of the Get-SmbShare PowerShell cmdlets

In this section, you learned how you can configure and maintain shared folders in a Windows 10 environment. There are benefits for an administrator to centrally manage shared folders, such as ease of use for backups and simplified management.

You also learned about the different types of shared folder permissions and how you can view shared folders. Then, you learned how to create a shared folder through the Shared Folders snap-in and how to give permissions to users. You can modify the properties from a shared folder by modifying the caching settings, permissions, number of simultaneous connected users, and, of course, the name of the share.

Summary

In this chapter, we have learned a lot of information about file systems, configuring and managing file access, and shared folders and permissions inheritance.

You learned that Windows 10 has three types of file system: FAT, NTFS, and ReFS. However, using FAT/FAT32 as a file system for Windows 10 is not advisable. NTFS is the default file system for Windows 10 and provides better enhancements, such as reliability, security, and support for larger volumes. With the NTFS file system, you can configure and manage file access on local storage or on remote storage, such as on a **Network Attached Storage (NAS)** device. You can configure and manage file access with tools such as File Explorer and PowerShell.

You also learned that there are two types of file and folder permissions: basic permissions and advanced permissions.

Then, you learned about permission inheritance. Permission inheritance allows the permissions that you set on a folder to be applied automatically to files that users create in that folder and its subfolders. You learned how you can configure these permissions on folders or files.

With the Effective Access feature, you can see what a user or group can do or can't do when this user or group has specific access permissions on a specific file or folder. You also learned happens with the file or folder permissions if you are copying or moving files and folders within the same volume or to another volume. Besides this, you learned how to configure and manage shared folders on a NTFS file system.

In the next chapter, you will learn about the Windows 10 local policies, how to configure these policies, and how you can implement them.

Questions

1. Can the FAT file system support a partition size of 1 TB?
2. Does the ReFS file system support the quota feature?
3. With the Read and Execute permissions, is it possible to start programs?
4. When you copy a file within a single volume, will the copy of the file inherit the permissions of the destination folder?
5. Was File Explorer also in older versions of Windows?
6. If you were to remove all shared folders, will Windows 10 automatically delete the firewall rules?
7. Can you use the `net use` command to set the shared folder properties?

Further reading

- **File System Functionality Comparison**: https://docs.microsoft.com/ en-us/windows/win32/fileio/filesystem-functionality- comparison?redirectedfrom=MSDN

- **FAT16 versus FAT32**: https://docs.microsoft.com/en-us/ previous-versions/windows/it-pro/windows-2000-server/ cc940351(v=technet.10)?redirectedfrom=MSDN

- **Resilient File System Overview**: https://docs.microsoft.com/en-us/ previous-versions/windows/it-pro/windows-server-2012-R2- and-2012/hh831724(v=ws.11)?redirectedfrom=MSDN

- **Building a next generation file system for Windows: ReFS**: https://blogs. msdn.microsoft.com/b8/2012/01/16/building-the-next- generation-file-system-for-windows-refs/

- **Icacls**: https://docs.microsoft.com/en-us/previous-versions/ windows/it-pro/windows-server-2012-R2-and-2012/ cc753525(v=ws.11)?redirectedfrom=MSDN

- **Set-Acl**: https://docs.microsoft.com/en-us/powershell/module/ Microsoft.PowerShell.Security/Set-Acl?view=powershell-5.1

- **Get-SmbShare**: https://docs.microsoft.com/en-us/powershell/ module/smbshare/get-smbshare?view=winserver2012r2- ps&redirectedfrom=MSDN

- **Set-SmbShare**: https://docs.microsoft.com/en-us/powershell/ module/smbshare/set-smbshare?view=winserver2012r2- ps&redirectedfrom=MSDN

6
Configuring and Implementing Local Policies

All settings in Windows 10 are stored in the registry. The registry is a database that contains details of all your settings, applications, device drivers, and many more. Without the registry, Windows will not work.

This chapter will introduce how to configure devices by using local policies, configure the local registry, and troubleshoot group policies in Windows 10. **Group policy** is a centrally managed technology that is designed to manage and control Windows 10 devices. The local group policy is the local implementation of these policies, and you need to know how you can configure local settings on a computer using these policies.

The following topics will be covered in this chapter:

- Configuring the local registry
- Configuring local policies
- Implementing account policies
- Troubleshooting group policies

This chapter will provide you with the skills to configure local policies and understand the registry in Windows 10 so that you can configure policies and the registry. This chapter will also help you to prepare for the **MD-100** (Windows 10) exam, which is part of the **Microsoft 365 Certified: Modern Desktop Administrator Associate** certification.

Technical requirements

This chapter will use PowerShell code. This code is available on the GitHub page at `https://github.com/PacktPublishing/Microsoft-Exam-MD-100-Windows-10-Certification-Guide/tree/master/Chapter06`.

In this chapter, you will implement and configure local policies and registry keys. The steps that you will follow are also recorded. You can find these videos here: `https://bit.ly/2LsQDqD`

Configuring the local registry

The **Windows registry** is the heart of the Windows 10 **Operating System (OS)**. All of the settings are stored in the registry. The registry is a database that contains all of the Windows settings, installed software, device drivers, and many more settings. Without this registry, Windows 10 would not work.

You should take care when working with or editing the registry. An incorrect change in the registry can result in an unreliable OS, with a reinstallation of the OS as a solution. You should always create a backup of the registry before editing the registry.

To better handle the registry, we must understand the registry structure first.

Understanding the registry structure

The registry is organized hierarchically. At the top level, there are five registry hives. These five hives are **DEFAULT**, **SAM**, **SECURITY**, **SOFTWARE**, and **SYSTEM**. These five hives are a distinct collection of related settings that are structured as a series of keys, subkeys, and values. You can find the registry in `C:\Windows\System32\Config`. Inside this system folder, you will find several binary files that the registry uses.

The following screenshot will show you the binary files, as mentioned earlier, in the corresponding `C:\Windows\System32\config` folder:

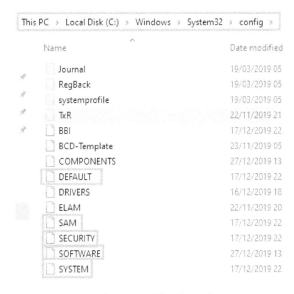

Figure 6.1 - The binary files from the registry

The preceding screenshot shows the binary files and the hives they relate to in the registry, given as follows:

- The **SAM** binary file belongs to the `HKEY_LOCAL_MACHINE\SAM` hive.

- The **SECURITY** binary file belongs to the `HKEY_LOCAL_MACINE\SECURITY` hive.

- The **SOFTWARE** binary file belongs to the `HKEY_LOCAL_MACINE\SOFTWARE` hive.

- The **SYSTEM** binary file belongs to the `HKEY_LOCAL_MACINE\SYSTEM` hive.

- The **DEFAULT** binary file belongs to the `HKEY_USERS\.DEFAULT` hive.

> **Important Note**
> The **SAM** file is used to store the users' passwords. There is also the `USERDIFF` binary file. This file is used only for Windows upgrades and will not be visible on some Windows 10 installations.

The vast majority of changes to the registry are made automatically by Windows whenever you install an application or change a setting inside an application, by using the **Settings** app or the **Control Panel**.

Now that we have understood the registry structure, let's move on to understanding the Registry Editor.

Understanding the Registry Editor

With the built-in Registry Editor, you can view, search, and modify the registry. Some common tasks that you can perform using the Registry Editor are as follows:

- Search the registry for keys and values.
- Create, delete, and modify keys and values.
- Import registry entries from the .REG files.
- Export registry entries into the .REG files.
- Back up the registry.

To open the **Registry Editor**, follow the next steps:

1. Click on the **Start** button.
2. Type registry.
3. Click on **Registry Editor**, as seen in the following screenshot:

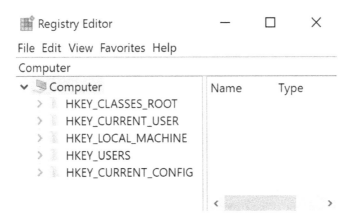

Figure 6.2 - The Registry Editor

We are now going to learn about the previously mentioned five registry hives.

Registry hives

When the Registry Editor is open, you will see five top-level hives. The five top-level hives are given as follows:

- **HKEY_CLASSES_ROOT**: This registry hive contains file association information and defines which application opens when the user double-clicks a file type on the file system.

- **HKEY_CURRENT_USER**: This registry hive contains configuration information for the currently signed-in user. Items such as the users' Windows color scheme and font settings are stored in relevant values in this hive.

- **HKEY_LOCAL_MACHINE**: This registry hive is probably the most important and the one that you likely will make the most edits to. It stores all computer-related configuration settings.

- **HKEY_USERS**: This registry hive contains a collection of all of the configuration information for all users that have signed in locally to the computer, including the currently signed-in user.

- **HKEY_CURRENT_CONFIG**: This registry hive contains information about the current hardware profile that the local computer used during system startup.

Most likely, you will make direct changes only to the values that stored are in the **HKEY_LOCAL_MACHINE** and **HKEY_CURRENT_USER** hives.

Registry keys and subkeys

To maintain structure within the database, similar settings are stored in folders and subfolders known as **keys** and **subkeys**. This makes it easier to reference a registry value. An example of a key is as follows:

```
HKEY_CURRENT_USER\Control Panel\Desktop
```

Let's now understand registry values.

Registry values

Values define the behavior of the OS, and they are stored in keys and subkeys. There are many types of values, depending on the type of data that each store.

In the previous registry path, you can find a value called **Wallpaper**. This value stores the name and location of a user's desktop wallpaper. In the following screenshot, you will see the key, value, and path to the **Wallpaper**:

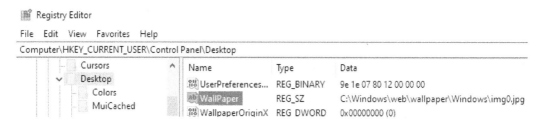

Figure 6.3 - The value of a registry key

In a registry value, you can store text values, numerical data, variables, and similar data. The following table lists the more common types of registry values:

Value type	Data type	Description
REG_BINARY	Binary	It contains/stores raw binary data. These values are usually in a hexadecimal format.
REG_DWORD	DWORD	It contains 4-byte numbers (a 32-bit integer). Many device-driver and service-related values are stored in these values.
REG_SZ	String	It contains a fixed-length text string. These values store the path and filename to the appropriate autostart program.
REG_EXPAND_ SZ	Expandable string	It contains a variable-length text string. The Windows OS uses these values to contain variables.
REG_MULTI_SZ	Multiple strings	It contains multiple string values. This value is typically used when multiple values are stored.

Table 6.1 - Common types of registry values

At this stage, you know what the registry is, how it is built, how it works, and how you can change keys. In the next section, we will look at configuring local policies and especially various security policies.

Configuring local policies

A **group policy** controls the environment of user accounts and computer accounts. A set of group policies is called a **Group Policy Object (GPO)**. And one set of a group policy is called a **Local Group Policy (LGPO)**. The difference between group policy objects and the local group policy is that GPOs are managed centrally and distributed across the Active Directory members, and an LGPO is managed decentrally and is intended for members without Active Directory, for example, standalone computers.

GPOs are processed in the following order:

- Local
- Site
- Domain
- Organizational Unit

Local policies are becoming effective when a user is logging in to a Windows 10 device. In this local policy, you can configure user settings and/or computer settings. For example, you can configure policies that implement auditing, specify user rights, and set security options. These three settings will be handled in the next sections.

Configuring the Audit Policy

The audit policy is used to provide information about basic audit policies of user actions on a Windows 10 device. These actions are recorded as a successor as a failure event. Auditing allows you to create a history of tasks and actions, such as file access and successful login attempts. Auditing can be also used for security violations. To configure the audit policy, three components are involved. These components are as follows:

- Enable auditing for success or failure (or both) for specific actions and events.
- Enable auditing for object access, such as file system files and folders.
- To view the results of auditing in the security log, you can use the **Event Viewer**.

To configure an audit policy to monitor, in this example, account logon events, follow these steps:

1. Click **Start** and type `Secpol.msc`.
2. Click on **Local Security Policy**.
3. In the **Local Security Policy** window, click on the **Local Policies | Audit Policy** tab.

4. Double-click on **Audit account logon events**.

5. In the **Audit account logon events Properties** window, check the **Success** and **Failure** boxes:

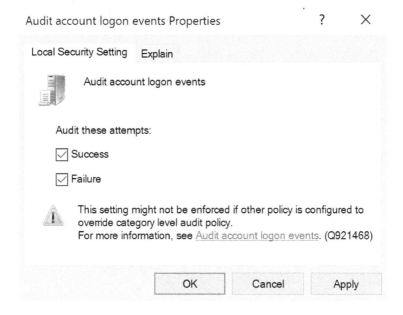

Figure 6.4 - The Audit account logon event Properties window

6. Then, click **OK**.

7. Log off from the device and log back in with an **Administrator** account, but with the wrong password, so you will generate a failure event.

8. Log in again, but now with the correct password.

9. Click **Start** and search for the Event Viewer.

10. Click on **Event Viewer**.

11. In the **Event Viewer**, expand **Windows Logs** and select the **Security log**.

12. You should see an event with an **Event ID** of **4776**.

13. Open this event and note the error message, as shown in the next screenshot:

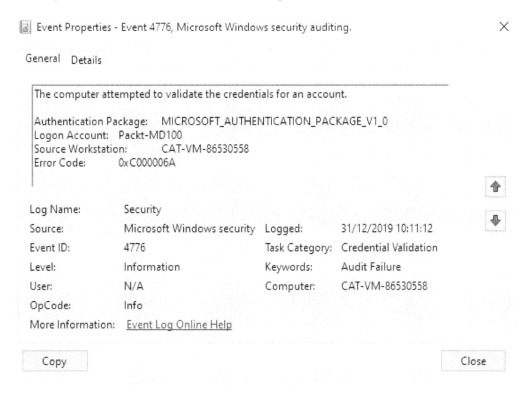

Figure 6.5 - The event log of the logon failure

Now you know how to configure audit account logon events, we can proceed to specify and grant a user the right to perform a volume maintenance task.

Specifying user rights

User rights are used to determine which rights are applied to a user or to a group of users and are applied to the local Windows 10 device. These rights allow users to perform tasks on a Windows 10 device and can override permissions that have been set on specific objects. Some of the activities that you can specify for a user are as follows:

- Adding workstations to domain

- Allowing logon locally

- Allowing logon through Remote Desktop Services

- Backing up files and directories
- Changing the time zone
- Performing volume maintenance tasks
- Taking ownership of files or other objects

In the next steps, we will configure the **Perform volume maintenance** tasks set for a user:

1. Click **Start** and type Secpol.msc.

2. Click on **Local Security Policy**.

3. In the **Local Security Policy** window, click on the **Local Policies | User Rights Assignment** tab.

4. Double-click on the **Perform volume maintenance tasks** user right:

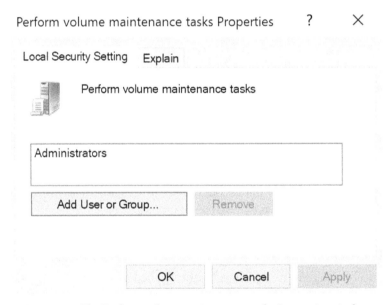

Figure 6.6 - The Perform volume maintenance tasks Properties window

5. Click on **Add User or Group**, and the **Select Users or Groups** dialog box opens.

6. Search for the user you want to give this right to and click twice on **OK**.

7. Now you have selected another user to perform this task, as shown in the next screenshot:

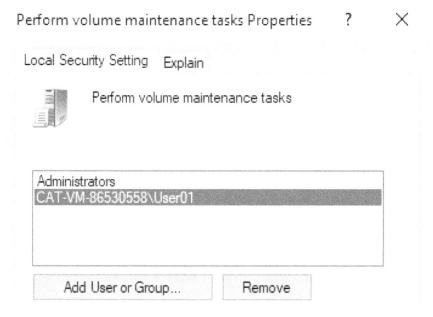

Figure 6.7 - The user is added to perform a task

In the previous steps, you have specified a user right to a user or group. In the next section, we will look at the **Security Options** that you can configure.

Configuring Security Options

There are many options to configure in the **Security Options** section of the Local Security Policy. These options are used to allow or deny activities on a Windows 10 device.

The **Accounts: Block Microsoft accounts**, **Devices: Restrict CD-ROM access to locally logged-on user only**, **User Account Control: Behavior of the elevation prompt for standard users**, and **Shutdown: Clear virtual memory pagefile** settings are a few options that you can configure to allow or deny activities. They describe the best practices for the respective security policy setting.

The following screenshot shows you the **Security Options** settings window:

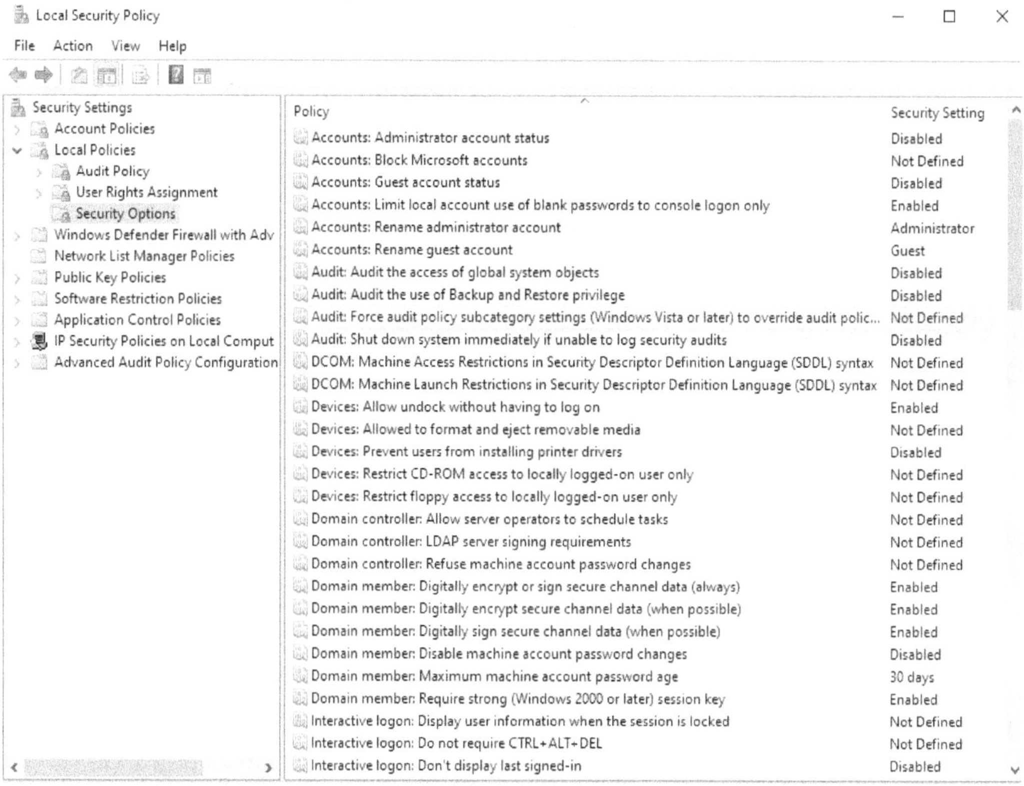

Figure 6.8 - The Security Options policy window

From the previous screenshot, almost all of the **Security Options** settings have their default setting set to **Not Defined**. Once configured, a setting can have the following statuses:

- **Enabled** or **Disabled**
- **Text entry**
- **Value**

My advice is to go through the list of the **Security Options**, so you are aware of what you can configure.

Now, you know how you can configure and understand some local policies; up next, you will learn how to implement the local policies, and you will create some local account policies such as account lockout and password complexity.

Implementing account policies

In the previous section, you learned how you could open the **Local Security Editor** to configure Local Policies to the user or computer. In the Local Security Editor, you can also configure **Account Policies** within this Local Security Editor.

Important Note

These policies only work for local accounts and not for Microsoft accounts.

With the Account Policies, you can configure policies such as **password policies** and **account lockout policies**.

Configuring a Password Policy

If you want to ensure that all users on a local device use secure passwords and these are changed after several days, you can configure a Password Policy. Follow the next steps to configure a Password Policy:

1. Click **Start** and type Secpol.msc.

2. Click on **Local Security Policy**.

3. In the **Local Security Policy** window, click on the **Account Policies | Password Policy** tab:

Figure 6.9 - The password policies settings

4. We first double-click on **Enforce password history**.

5. Change the value to a number that represents the number of unique passwords (that must be used before the user can reuse an old password) and click **OK**:

Figure 6.10 - The Enforce password history Properties window

6. Then, we go back to the **Local Security Policy** window and click on the **Account Policies | Password Policy** tab.

7. Double-click on **Maximum password age**.

8. The default setting is **42 days**. This means that users are required to change their password after 42 days. The best practice for this setting is to set the days between **30** and **90 days**. After you changed this setting, click **OK**:

Figure 6.11 - The Maximum password age Properties window

9. We again go back to the **Local Security Policy** window and then click on the **Account Policies | Password Policy** tab.

10. Double-click on **Minimum password age**.

11. The default setting is **0 days**. This means that users can change their passwords whenever they want. My advice here is to change this setting to, for example, 7 days. After you change this setting, click **OK**:

Figure 6.12 - The Minimum password age Properties window

12. We again go back to the **Local Security Policy** window and click on the **Account Policies | Password Policy** tab.

13. Double-click on **Minimum password length**.

14. The default setting is **0 characters**. To use a more secure password length, change this setting to **8 characters** and click **OK**:

Figure 6.13 - The Minimum password length Properties window

15. Going back again to the **Local Security Policy** window, click on the **Account Policies | Password Policy** tab.

16. Double-click on **Password must meet complexity requirements**.

17. Change this setting to **Enabled** to meet the complexity requirements and click **OK**:

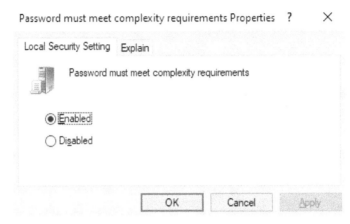

Figure 6.14 - The Password must meet complexity requirements Properties window

18. We again go back to the **Local Security Policy** window and click on the **Account Policies | Password Policy** tab.

19. The last setting you can configure is the **Store passwords using reversible encryption** setting. By default, this setting is **Disabled**. If you **Enabled** this setting, all of the passwords are stored in plaintext, so applications can access these passwords. But this makes them vulnerable to hackers who might access these passwords:

Figure 6.15 - The Store passwords using reversible encryption Properties window

If you followed the previously mentioned steps to configure the Password Policy, then your policy editor window must look like the following screenshot:

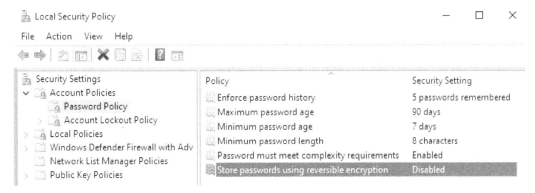

Figure 6.16 - The configured settings of the Password Policy

These settings are applied immediately, but if there are already users logged on, then they can work further with their existing passwords. The next time a user needs to change their password, the new password must comply with the settings you have configured in the **Password Policy**.

If the **Password must meet complexity requirements policy** is **Enabled**, passwords must meet the following minimum requirements:

- They should not contain the user's account name or parts of the user's full name that exceed two consecutive characters.

- They should be at least six characters in length.

- They should contain characters from at least three of the following four categories: English uppercase characters (*A* through *Z*), English lowercase characters (*a* through *z*), base 10 digits (*0* through *9*), and non-alphabetic characters (for example, *!*, *$*, *#*, *%*).

- Complexity requirements are enforced when passwords are changed or created.

In the previous steps, you have successfully configured a Password Policy. In the next section, you will learn to configure the Account Lockout Policy.

Configuring the Account Lockout Policy

When you implement a secure Password Policy, it is recommended to configure an **Account Lockout Policy** as well. An **Account Lockout Policy** is used by administrators to lock an account after several failed login attempts. This prevents malicious users from breaking into your computer systems. You can configure Windows devices to respond to this type of potential attack by disabling the account for some time.

Follow the next steps to configure an **Account Lockout Policy**:

1. Click **Start** and type `Secpol.msc`.
2. Click on **Local Security Policy**.
3. In the **Local Security Policy** windows, click on the **Account Policies | Account Lockout Policy** tab.
4. Double-click on **Account lockout threshold**.
5. Fill in a value, for example, 4, and press **OK**:

Figure 6.17 - The Account lockout threshold

6. When the previous steps are completed, Windows 10 will suggest the two other settings: **Account Lockout Duration** and **Reset account lockout counter after**.

    Account Lockout Duration determines the number of minutes that a locked-out account remains locked out for before automatically becoming unlocked.

    Reset account lockout counter after determines the number of minutes that must elapse after a failed login attempt occurs before the failed login attempt counter is reset to 0 bad login attempts.

The following screenshot shows you the **Suggested Value Changes** window:

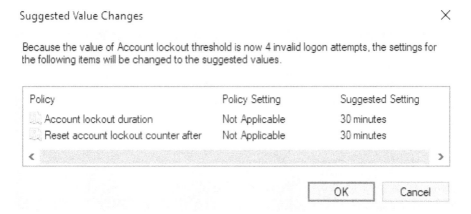

Figure 6.18 - Suggested Value Changes window

7. Click **OK** to close the **Suggested Value Changes** window.

8. Now the other two settings have the suggested values, the **Account Lockout Policy** will look something like the next screenshot:

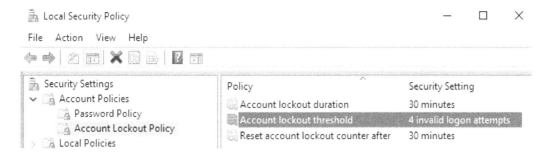

Figure 6.19 - The Account Lockout Policy with the configured settings

In this section, you learned how to configure a Password Policy and an Account Lockout Policy. In the next section, we will learn how we can troubleshoot group policies.

Troubleshooting group policies

You should now be able to understand how to perform basic troubleshooting of Group group policies in Windows 10. We are not going to deep dive into every Group Policy because that is too much to cover in this book.

In general, when we refer to Group Policy, we are referring to **Group Policy Objects** (**GPO**) that contain Group Policy settings that are created by you as an IT administrator and are deployed to devices in a domain environment. **Local Group Policy** refers to policy settings that are locally administered and configured. A Group Policy can fail when applied to a Windows 10 device and there can be many reasons for this, such as incorrect GPO settings or a poor network connection.

Before you start investigating failed group policies, you can do a preliminary check in the following areas:

- **Group Policy Client Service**: Check whether this service has the status **Running** or **Automatic** in the `Services.msc` utility.

- **Network Connection**: Verify the network connection.

- **Time**: The time difference between the client and the server needs to be within five minutes of the time on the server.

To investigate these issues, you can use different tools, such as the **Resultant Set of Policy** (`RsoP.msc`) tool and the **Group Policy Result (GPResult)** tool from the command line.

Resultant Set of Policy

The **Resultant Set of Policy** tool is a diagnostic tool that is built into Windows 10 and is used to check and troubleshoot group policy settings. With this tool, you can view which group policy is being applied to the computer and user, and you can identify which source the policy is coming from. Besides this, you can use the tool to simulate new or modified group policy objects for planning purposes.

There are two modes that the tool can be run in; these modes are as follows:

- **Logging Mode**: It generates a report of policy settings for users and computers.

- **Planning Mode**: It can be used for *what-if* scenarios.

For running the tool to determine the applied user and computer policy settings, follow the next steps:

1. Click **Start**, then type and select `rsop.msc`.

2. The **Resultant Set of Policy** window will open; it runs straight away and generates a report for the user and computer policy settings.

3. In the **Resultant Set of Policy** window, you can view the applied settings for your user account and your computer account:

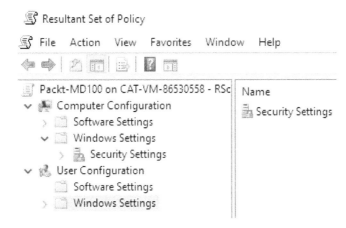

Figure 6.20 - The RSoP output window

4. To simulate group policy object settings, you can use the planning mode of the **Resultant Set of Policy** tool. You must open an empty **Microsoft Management Console (MMC)** and add the **Resultant Set of Policy** snap-in. In the MMC, select the **Resultant Set of Policy** and select the **Generate Rsop Data** from the **Action** menu. In the **Resultant Set of Policy wizard**, choose **Planning mode** and finish the wizard:

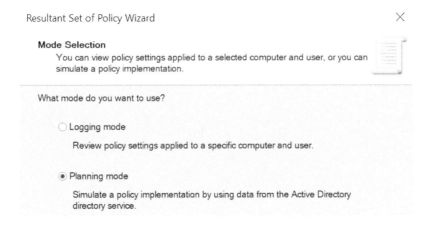

Figure 6.21 - The Resultant Set of Policy Planning mode option

After you have run the wizard, you can view the results. You can use this to review the policy settings if you want to implement new policies in your environment.

> **Important Note**
> **Planning mode** is only available when the computer is connected to an Active Directory environment.

Besides the Resultant Set of Policy tool, you also have the **GPResult** tool.

Learning about the GPResult tool

The **GPResult** command-line tool provides you with the relevant group policies that are applied to a user or a Windows 10 device. This tool creates a report that displays which GPOs are applied to a Windows 10 device and separates the user policies from the computer policies.

To see which GPOs are applied to your device, follow the next steps:

1.   Right-click **Start** and select **Windows PowerShell** (**Admin**).

2.   In the **User Account Control** dialog box, click **Yes**.

3.   Type the following command and press *Enter*:

```
gpresult /r
```

4. You should now see the **RsoP** data for your device, as shown in the following screenshot:

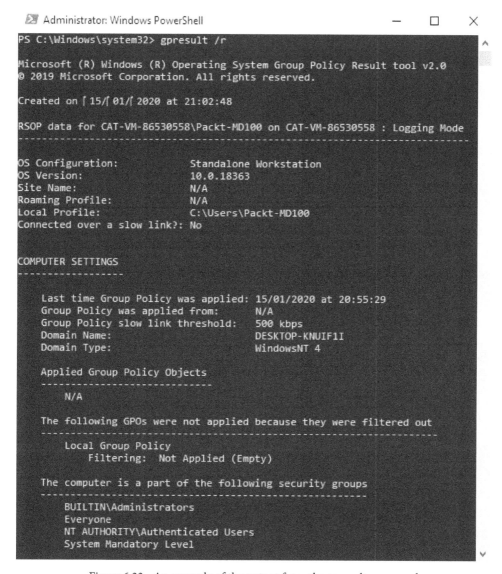

Figure 6.22 - An example of the output from the gpresult command

5. The output of the previous command will display the applied GPOs, the order of the GPOs, the details of the GPOs, the last applied time of the GPOs, the domain and functional level of the device, the domain controller is used to issue the GPO, the network speed threshold, the security groups of the user and computer are members of, and the details of the GPO filtering.

You can use command-line switches to fine-tune the report, for example, a user or a computer only. A few examples of command-line switches are as follows:

- Display the applied GPOs to a specific user:

```
gpresult /r /scope:user
```

- Display the applied GPOs to a specific computer:

```
gpresult /r /scope:computer
```

- Generate an HTML report:

```
gpresult /h c:\gporeport.html
```

In this section, we learned how you can troubleshoot group policies. The most widely used tools for troubleshooting are the **Resultant Set of Policies** (**RsoP**) tool and the **GPResult** command-line tool. Group policies are reliable on our network infrastructure and the time difference between client and server.

Summary

In this chapter, you learned the basics of the registry. The registry contains registry hives, keys, and values. You also learned about the different value types.

You also learned about configuring local policies, such as configuring the audit policy, to monitor, for example, failed login attempts. You also learned how to configure specific user rights to give users, for example, the right to change the system time. With configuring security options, you learned to allow or deny users access to specific sources, such as a CD-ROM drive.

With the implementation of account policies, you have learned how to configure a Password Policy for secure passwords and to configure an Account Lockout Policy to prevent brute-force attacks on a Windows 10 device.

In the next chapter, we will look at how we can secure data and applications within Windows 10 to make use of the features that Windows 10 offers.

Questions

1. Is the USERDIFF binary file by default present in Windows 10?

2. Can you import or export registry keys?

3. Is REG_DWORD_SZ a valid value type?

4. Can you set the **Maximum password age** setting to 123 days?

5. Can you use the **RSoP Planning Mode** on a standalone Windows 10 device?

Further reading

- **Windows registry information for advanced users**: https://support. microsoft.com/en-us/help/256986/windows-registry-information-for-advanced-users

- **Group Policy Search**: https://gpsearch.azurewebsites.net/

- **Audit Policy**: https://docs.microsoft.com/en-us/windows/security/threat-protection/security-policy-settings/audit-policy

- **User Rights Assignment**: https://docs.microsoft.com/en-us/windows/security/threat-protection/security-policy-settings/user-rights-assignment

- **Security Options**: https://docs.microsoft.com/en-us/windows/security/threat-protection/security-policy-settings/security-options

- **Gpresult**: https://docs.microsoft.com/en-us/windows-server/administration/windows-commands/gpresult

7
Securing Data and Applications

Security is essential for your devices and your end users. Data leakage seems to occur very often nowadays. Almost every day, you read that a company, a web shop, or a forum has been hacked and that their customers' details are for sale on the dark web. In this chapter, you will about learn some relevant security features that you can implement in Windows 10 to secure your system.

This chapter introduces the sixth objective, which is to know how you can configure the **User Account Control** (**UAC**) prompts, set threat management, implement disk and file encryption, and use **AppLocker** to control whether or not the end user can open applications.

The following objectives will be covered in this chapter:

- Configuring User Account Control
- Configuring Threat Protection
- Implementing encryption
- Using AppLocker

By providing you with the skills to configure User Account Control, configure **Threat Protection**, and implement encryption on disk and files in Windows 10, this chapter will help you prepare for the **MD-100** (Windows 10) exam, which is part of the **Microsoft 365 Certified: Modern Desktop Administrator Associate** certification.

Technical requirements

In this chapter, we will look at PowerShell code. This code is available on this book's GitHub page: `https://github.com/PacktPublishing/Microsoft-Exam-MD-100-Windows-10-Certification-Guide`

In the *Configuring UAC notifications* section, you will learn how you can change the UAC notifications. The steps that you are going to follow have also been recorded. You can find the relevant videos at `https://bit.ly/2LsQDqD`.

Configuring User Account Control

Most users sign in to their computers with a user account that has more privileges to run their applications and access their data files than required. Using an administrative user account for day-to-day user tasks poses significant security risks.

Windows 10 provides UAC to simplify and help secure the process of elevating your account rights. However, unless you know how UAC works and how it can affect your users, you might have problems when you attempt to carry out typical end user support tasks. This section introduces how UAC works and how you can configure UAC notifications.

Understanding User Account Control

The **User Account Control** security feature provides a way for users to raise their privilege status from a regular user account to an Administrator account, without allowing them to sign into or switch user profiles. UAC is a collection of features, not just a prompt. Such features, which include **File and Registry Redirect**, **Installer Detection**, **UAC prompt**, **ActiveX Installer Service**, and others, allow Windows users to work with user accounts that are not part of the **Administrators Group**.

Such accounts, typically called standard users, are commonly described as having the least privileges to work with. The most important fact is that the experience is usually much more secure and reliable when users sign in with regular user accounts.

With Windows 10, as opposed to older operating systems, the number of applications and activities requiring the elevation of administrator rights is lower. This helps normal users do more while receiving fewer prompts for elevation, and increases compatibility with UAC while maintaining high safety standards.

When you need administrator-level permissions to make changes to your computer, UAC will notify you, as follows:

- If you're an administrator, then click **Yes** to proceed.

- If you're not an administrator, then the person on the machine with an Administrator account must enter their password so that you can begin or resume executing the task at hand.

The following screenshot shows the **User Account Control** prompt/pop-up window:

Figure 7.1 - The User Account Control elevation prompt

If you are a standard user, providing administrative credentials gives you administrator rights to complete the task. When you complete the task, permissions revert to those that a standard user has.

This means that no one can make changes to your device without your permission, even if you use an Administrator account. This helps prevent malicious users from installing spyware and malware on your computer or making changes to it.

We will now see how UAC works.

Knowing how UAC works

Windows 10 offers two types of user accounts: **standard users** and **administrative users**. UAC simplifies users' abilities to operate as standard users and perform all necessary daily tasks. Administrative users also benefit from UAC, because administrative permissions are only available after UAC requests permission from the user for that instance.

Once you allow UAC, **Local Administrators group** members run the same access token as regular users. A process can only use the full access token of an administrator once authorized by a member of the current Administrators group.

This method forms the basis of the **Admin Approval Mode** principle. Users are only elevated to perform tasks requiring access via an administrator token. UAC asks the user to enter appropriate credentials for an Administrator account when a regular user tries to perform an administrative function. An example of a UAC prompt for end users is shown in *Figure 7.2*. This dialog box is the user prompt for the default standard behavior.

The prompt for elevation shows contextual information regarding the current executable task, which requests elevation. The meaning varies according to whether **Authenticode Technology** signs the application. There are two variations of the elevation prompt: the **consent prompt** and the **credential prompt**.

Elevation entry points do not remember that elevation has occurred, such as when you return from a shielded location or task. As a result, the user must re-elevate to enter the task again.

The Windows 10 **Operating System (OS)** reduces the number of UAC elevation prompts for a standard user who performs everyday tasks. There are times, however, when it is appropriate to return an elevation prompt. For example, you don't need elevation to view **Firewall** settings. Changing the settings does, however, require elevation as the changes have a system-wide impact.

Most of the time, you should sign into your computer with a standard user account. Without an Administrator account, you can browse the internet, send emails, and use a word processor. You do not need to move/log into an Administrator account if you want to perform an administrative function, such as installing a new program or modifying a setting that will affect other users.

Before performing the task, you will be asked by the Windows OS for permission or an administrator password. The best practice is to create standard user accounts for all of the people that use your computer. Now, let's learn about standard user accounts.

Understanding standard users

In previous versions of the Windows OS, many users were configured to use administrative permissions rather than standard user permissions. This was because previous Windows versions required users to have administrator permissions to perform basic system tasks, such as adding a printer or configuring a time zone. In Windows 10, many of these tasks no longer require administrative permissions.

When users have administrative permissions on their computers, they can install additional software. Despite organizational policies against installing unauthorized software, many users still do it, which can make their systems less stable.

When you enable UAC and a user needs to perform a task that requires administrative permissions, UAC prompts the user for administrative credentials. In an enterprise environment, the help desk can give a user temporary credentials that have local administrative permissions to complete a task. The default UAC setting allows a regular user to complete the following tasks without receiving a request from UAC:

- Installing **Windows Update** updates

- Installing **Windows Update** drivers, or drivers included with the OS

- Viewing **Windows Settings**, though a standard user is asked for elevated permissions

- Pairing **Bluetooth** equipment with the computer

- Resetting the network adapter and conducting other testing and maintenance functions on the network

Earlier, we mentioned that there are two different elevation prompts. A standard user account gets the credential prompt. The credential prompt pops up when the standard user account needs to perform an administrative task:

Figure 7.2 - The UAC credential prompt

As shown in the previous screenshot, the standard user account needs to enter an administrative user's password. In this example, this is to run the Command Prompt in Administrator mode.

Understanding Administrative users

Besides the standard user account, there are also administrative user accounts. Administrative user accounts already have the following permissions:

- Read/write/enact permissions for all resources
- All Windows permissions

Although it may seem obvious that not all users can read, modify, and delete any Windows resource, many enterprise IT departments that run older versions of Windows operating systems have no other option but to assign all of their users to the **Local Administrators Group**.

One of the benefits of UAC is that it allows users with administrative permissions to operate as standard users most of the time. When users with administrative permissions perform a task that requires administrative permissions, UAC prompts the user for permission to complete the task. When the user grants permission, the task is achieved by using full administrative rights, and then the account reverts to a lower level of permission.

The following screenshot shows us the administrator consent prompt for the Windows Command Prompt:

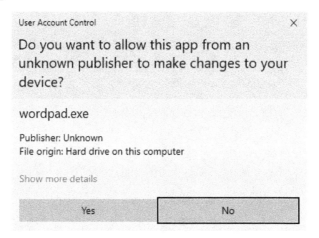

Figure 7.3 - The UAC consent prompt

When an administrative user account wants to perform an administrative task, then the consent prompt pops up. This administrative user does not need to enter a password because this user is already logged in with an Administrator account.

We will now move on and learn about the different types of elevation prompt.

Understanding the types of elevation prompt

As well as there being two different variations of elevation, there are also different types of elevation prompt. When permission or a password is necessary to complete a task, UAC notifies you with one of three different types of dialog boxes.

The different types of dialog boxes that users see and provide guidance on how to respond to them are described as follows:

- A setting or function that is part of Windows requires your permission to start executing

- Software that is not part of Windows needs your permission to run

- A program with an unknown publisher requires your consent to start

We will now move on and learn how to configure UAC notifications.

Configuring UAC notifications

In Windows 10, you can set UAC so that it notifies you when changes are made to your computer. You have four settings of the elevation prompt experience that you can customize. These are as follows:

- **Never notify me**: You never want to be notified when programs attempt to update apps or make adjustments to your computer, and when you make changes to Windows settings, you never want to be informed.

- **Notify me only when apps try to make changes to my computer (do not dim my desktop)**: You only want to be notified when programs want to make changes to your computer, without dimming the desktop, and when you make adjustments to Windows settings, you don't want to be notified.

- **Notify me only when apps try to make changes to my computer (default)**: You only want to be notified when programs want to make changes to your computer and when you make adjustments to the Windows settings, you don't want to be informed.

- **Always notify me**: You always need to be alerted when programs attempt to install software or make changes to your computer, as well as when adjustments are made to Windows settings.

If you wish to change how your UAC notifications work, follow these steps:

1. Click on **Start**.
2. Type UAC.

3. Click on **Change User Account Control settings**.

4. Use the slider to determine how Windows will prompt you.

5. Click on **OK** and in the UAC dialog box, click **Yes**:

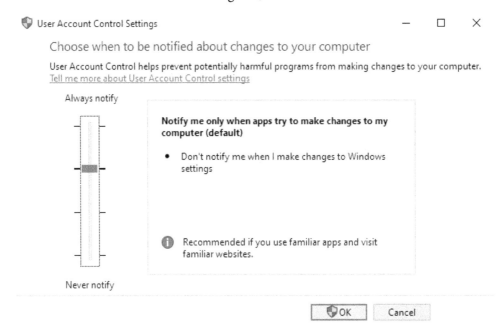

Figure 7.4 - The User Account Control Settings window

As shown in the previous screenshot, you can move the slider up and down. The default setting is **Notify me only when apps try to make changes to my computer**. *Did you notice the little shield next to the OK button?* This means that if you press **OK**, a UAC prompt will pop up to acknowledge your user rights to perform this change.

In this section, you learned what User Account Control is, how it works, and how you can configure the notification settings of UAC. In the next section, you will look at how to set threat protection and learn about different advanced protection methods.

Configuring Threat Protection

A Windows 10 computer is more vulnerable to threats that originate from the network than from any other location. This is because network attacks can target a significant number of computers, while other forms of attacks require physical access to the computer. In this section, you will understand what malware and threat protection is. Furthermore, you will learn about the advanced protection methods that you can use to reduce threat protection.

Understanding malware and threat protection

Malicious software, or malware, is software that attackers design to harm computer systems. Malware can do many things, from causing damage to the computer to allowing unauthorized parties remote access to the computer, to collecting and transmitting sensitive information to unauthorized third parties. There are several types of malware, including the following:

- **Computer viruses**
- **Computer worms**
- **Trojan horses**
- **Ransomware**
- **Spyware**

To protect you against malware infections, you need to ensure that all your software and OS updates are installed. Of course, you need to ensure that you have installed and activated anti-malware software on all your devices and that the anti-malware software is up to date with the latest virus definitions.

As well as protecting your computer, you need to ensure you teach your end users to avoid installing pirated software or media, browsing suspicious websites, and opening suspicious email attachments, even if they are from senders that you trust.

Malware can infect the devices of even the most diligent people. For example, users with good malware avoidance habits might visit a reputable website that has been compromised, and that leverages an undisclosed exploit in popular software. This could be because the software vendor has not fixed that software because they are unaware that the exploit exists. These users' devices could then become infected.

Additionally, no anti-malware solution has a perfect detection rate. It is possible to take all the necessary precautions and still have your devices become infected. Taking precautions only reduces the probability that a person's equipment will be compromised by malware, though it does not eliminate the possibility.

We'll learn about **phishing** next.

Learning about phishing scams

Phishing is a form of online identity theft. Phishing uses emails, phone calls, texts, and malicious websites designed to steal your personal data or information such as credit card numbers, passwords, account details, or other information.

Cybercriminals are skilled at tricking you into providing your personal information to them, which can lead to identity theft and loss of data. Phishing is particularly dangerous because cybercriminals mask messages and calls as legitimate, using logos and acronyms that appear to be real.

Phishing threats cannot be stopped by merely configuring a setting in Windows. Phishing scams involve exposing login credentials or other secure data when the user is tricked into exposing them to the attacker. Therefore, teaching your end users about this is necessary in order to minimize threats from phishing.

The tricks that cybercriminals use for phishing are as follows:

- **Fake websites**: If you receive a suspicious email message and it prompts you to click on a link, then you must hover over that link. If the link does not match the name or descriptive text in your email, you could have received a phishing email. If the link points to a website or company you've never heard of or visited before, this could be a phishing attempt.

- **Threats**: Emails that threaten account closure could be from a cybercriminal. If you receive an email that impulses you to take action by threatening that your account will be closed, be careful. Cybercriminals use a variety of methods to steal your information and gain access to your data through threats and misinformation.

- **Spoofing companies or people you know**: Scammers use graphics in email that appear to be connected to legitimate websites but take you to pretentious scam sites or legitimate-looking pop-up windows. Spoofing can also occur when a scammer impersonates someone you know by mimicking their email address. Always check that the address you're replying to is the correct one.

There are also a few options you can use to confirm that an email is legitimate:

- **Uncover the URL**: We can test a URL before clicking on it by placing the mouse pointer over it. Often, incorrect links are inserted into an email as a means of tricking the reader.

- **Poor grammar and spelling**: Companies rarely send messages without the text being proofread, so numerous spelling and grammar errors can signify a scam message.

- **Company contact information and brand accuracy**: Most companies have a recognizable brand identity in their emails. Look for logos, brand colors, and the message that contains their contact information.

Now that you know about the different types of phishing scams and what you can do to protect yourself against them, let's move on and understand the built-in Windows Security features we can use.

Understanding Windows Security

Devices and users need to be protected while they are online. To do this, they rely on the built-in defense features of Windows Security, which provide resilience against ever-increasing threats. The **Windows Security** feature is an app that is accessible from within the **Settings** app. The **Windows Security** app is a single portal for users to control and view their device's security, health, and online safety.

You can open the **Windows Security** app by following these steps:

1. Click on **Start**.

2. Browse to **Windows Security**.

3. The **Windows Security** app will open. This app contains an overview of the status of the Windows Security features, as well as links to other settings and support, as shown in the following screenshot:

Figure 7.5 - The Windows Security feature

This **Windows Security** page, as shown in the previous screenshot, provides a status report covering the seven areas of security. From this page, you can review the various color-coded status icons that are available, which indicate the level of safety for that area. The three color codes are as follows:

- **Green**: This is used to indicate that the device is sufficiently protected and that there aren't any recommendations to follow up.

- **Yellow**: This is used to indicate that there is a safety recommendation that should be reviewed.

- **Red**: This is used to indicate a warning, meaning that something needs immediate action.

The **Windows Security** app collects the statuses of each of the included security features and allows you to perform some configuration.

From the **Windows Security** feature inside the **Settings** app, you can open the standalone **Windows Security** app by clicking the **Open Windows Security** button, as shown in the following screenshot:

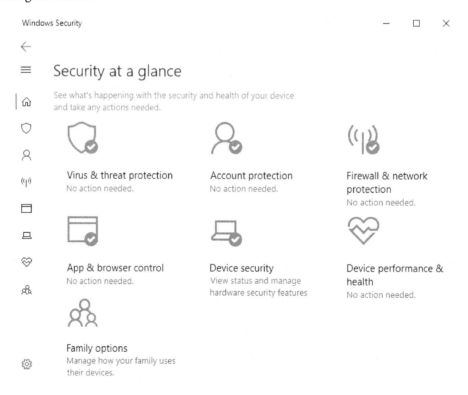

Figure 7.6 - The Windows Security standalone app

When a Windows Security item requires action from the end user, for example, to update the virus and threat protection definitions, the shield icon in the notification area of the taskbar will show a red cross to indicate that an action is required.

The previous screenshot provides you with seven security areas. These are explained as follows:

- **Virus & threat protection**: This is used to monitor threats to your device, run scans, and gather updates to help protect you against the latest threats.

- **Account protection**: This is used to access sign-in options and account settings, including features such as **Windows Hello** and **Dynamic Lock**.

- **Firewall & network protection**: This is used to manage firewall settings and monitor network and internet connections.

- **App & browser control**: This is used to review and update settings for **Windows Defender SmartScreen** and configure exploit protection settings.

- **Device security**: This is used to review built-in security options that use virtualization-based security to help protect your device from attacks that may be performed by malicious software.

- **Device performance & health**: This is used to view the status of your device's performance health.

- **Family options**: This is used for features such as **Parental control**, which allows you to keep track of your kids' online activity.

In this section, you learned the basics of the **Windows Security** app, what malware is, and its different types. In the next section, you will learn about some of the advanced protection methods available in Windows 10.

Understanding advanced protection methods

One important part of protecting Windows 10 is to take a defense-in-depth approach. Threats come in many forms and can target a variety of specific services or applications. You, as an administrator, should assume that no single solution will be able to mitigate all threats, and you should be familiar with the tools and settings available that can help you secure devices. We are going to look at such tools and settings that are helpful for securing devices available with/for Windows 10 in the following sections.

Learning about the Security Compliance Toolkit

The **Microsoft Security Compliance Toolkit** helps an organization's security administrators effectively manage the **Group Policy Objects** (**GPOs**) of their enterprise. Administrators may compare their current GPOs with Microsoft GPO baselines or other baselines using the toolkit, then edit them, save them in GPO backup file format, and apply them to test their effects via a domain controller or directly inject them into test hosts.

In the following sections, you will learn about a few security features that you can implement in your environment.

Windows Security baselines

Microsoft does have recommended configuration settings, also known as **security baselines**, that explain their security impact. These security baselines are a huge benefit to customers because they bring expert knowledge from Microsoft and their partners.

You can use a security baseline to ensure that the user and device configuration settings are compliant with the baseline. You can set these configuration settings according to a baseline via Group Policy or **Microsoft Intune**.

Windows Device Health Attestation

Windows Device Health Attestation ensures that the Windows 10 OS has not been tampered with or compromised and helps verify the overall health of the system. Certain services (such as **Exchange email**, **SharePoint**, or **Azure Active Directory** (**Azure AD**) membership) take advantage of this service and can disallow access until a Windows 10 Enterprise edition **Personal Computer** (**PC**) meets specific qualifications.

For example, when a user tries to join a new Windows 10 PC to the **Azure Active Directory**, conditional access can verify the integrity of the PC using Windows Device Health Attestation and then ensure that **BitLocker**, **Secure Boot**, or **Virtualization-Based Security** features such as **Credential Guard** are enabled. If a user elects not to allow these settings to be configured, access to the requested resource is denied.

Let's quickly understand Secure Boot in brief. **Secure Boot** is a security standard created to make sure that your PC boots up using specific software trusted by the PC manufacturers. Secure Boot support was started in **Windows 8**, and Windows 10 still supports it.

First, when starting the PC, the firmware tests the signature of each piece of booted software, including firmware drivers (**Read Only Memory** (**ROMs**) are optional), EFI programs, and the OS. If the signatures are found to be authentic and correct, the PC boots and the firmware gives control to the OS.

Secure boot prevents a dangerous and sophisticated form of malware — called a **Rootkit** — from loading on your computer when it starts. Rootkits have the same rights as the OS and can start even before the OS boots. Rootkits are also a part of a whole malware package that can bypass local logins, record passwords and keystrokes, switch private files, and capture cryptographic data.

Windows Device Health Attestation requires the use of **modern authentication**. Modern authentication is the name Microsoft uses to describe the **Azure Active Directory Authentication Library** (**ADAL**) for clients and other technologies that implement authentication using the **OAuth 2.0** and **Open ID Connect** protocols. Microsoft has built these technologies natively into Windows 10 and **Office 2016** and Microsoft-hosted services such as **Office 365**.

Windows Information Protection

Windows Information Protection (**WIP**) is a feature of Windows 10 Pro and Enterprise. This feature is intended to keep organizational data secure, regardless of the actions of end users.

When enabled, WIP watches for content that is downloaded from **SharePoint**, **Office 365**, and corporate web servers and file servers. It offers a range of controls, such as blocking content from being downloaded, warning users, or auditing their access to prevent data from being shared outside the organization.

WIP automatically protects the content that is downloaded to the device, and only approved applications can access it. An organization can also choose to securely wipe data from the device using Microsoft Intune or third-party **Mobile Device Management** (**MDM**).

WIP will provide encryption at rest using **Microsoft's Encrypting File System** (**EFS**) and will also utilize the **Microsoft-hosted Azure Rights Management Services** functionality, which is included with Office 365, to protect the data when the data egresses outside of the corporate network boundary or when it arrives on non-Windows platforms, such as **iOS** and **Android**.

Understanding Windows Defender Advanced Threat Protection

Windows Defender **Advanced Threat Protection** (**ATP**) is a platform that is designed to help enterprise networks prevent, detect, investigate, and respond to advanced threats. Unlike **Windows Defender**, which is available on each Windows 10 computer and managed by Group Policy or Intune, Windows Defender ATP is a whole new platform that helps administrators enhance security, as well as to establish centralized security control over both cloud and on-premises resources.

> **Important Note**
>
> Even though Windows Defender ATP shares the same name with Windows
> Defender in Windows 10, these are not the same products.

Windows Defender ATP can be used to monitor Windows Defender functionalities on local Windows 10 devices to maintain consistent configuration and an acceptable security level. Windows Defender ATP can also integrate with **Office 365 Threat Intelligence** and Microsoft Intune.

Windows Defender ATP uses the following combination of technologies, all of which are included in Windows 10 and the cloud service offered by Microsoft:

- **Endpoint behavioral sensors**: Embedded in Windows 10, these sensors collect and process OS behavioral signals and send the sensor data to your private, isolated Windows Defender ATP cloud instance.

- **Cloud security analytics**: Big data, machine learning, and special **Microsoft Optics** across the integrated Windows ecosystem are transformed from observations, detections, and suggested responses into advanced threats.

- **Threat intelligence**: Created by Microsoft hunters, security teams, and strengthened by partners' intelligence on threats, threat intelligence enables Windows Defender ATP to identify intruder devices, tactics, procedures, and produce warnings when data is detected in the sensor.

The aforementioned technologies, when combined, provide very efficient, proactive monitoring regarding what happens on your client machines, servers, and network. They perform automated investigations on well-known incidents and provide some actions, before an administrator is even alerted.

Understanding Windows Defender Application Control

With thousands of new malicious files being created every day, using traditional methods such as antivirus solutions provides an inadequate defense against further attacks.

When an end-user runs a process, that process has to access the data that the user has. This can cause sensitive information to be quickly deleted or transmitted out of the organization.

This could happen when an end-user knowingly or unknowingly runs malicious software. Application control can help mitigate these types of security threats by restricting the applications that your end users are allowed to run.

Learning about Windows Defender Device Guard

Windows Defender Device Guard is broken down into two functions: **Windows Defender Exploit Guard** and **Windows Defender Application Control**. Such features are a combination of business-related hardware and software security features that will lock down a system when installed together so that it can only run trusted applications that are specified in the code integrity policies of an enterprise. If the device is not trusted, it will not be able to run for a period of time.

This also means that even if an attacker manages to get control of the Windows kernel, they will be much less likely to be able to run malicious executable code with hardware that meets basic requirements.

Understanding Windows Defender Credential Guard

Windows Defender Credential Guard uses virtualization-based security to isolate secrets so that only privileged system software can access them. Credential thefts, such as **Pass-the-Hash**, can lead to unauthorized access to your systems.

This is where Windows Defender Credential Guard will prevent these attacks by protecting the **New Technology LAN Manager (NTLM) password hashes**, **Kerberos Granting Tickets**, and credentials that are stored in applications. This is done by removing these credentials from the **Local Security Authority (LSA)**.

Learning about Windows Defender Application Guard

Windows Defender Application Guard is designed for Windows 10 and the **Microsoft Edge** browser. It also helps isolate untrusted websites while your end users browse the internet. As an administrator, you need to define what the trusted sites are, which cloud resources you can trust, and, of course, you need to identify your internal networks. Everything not on your list is considered to be untrusted.

In the following screenshot, you can see how **Defender Application Guard** works on a device:

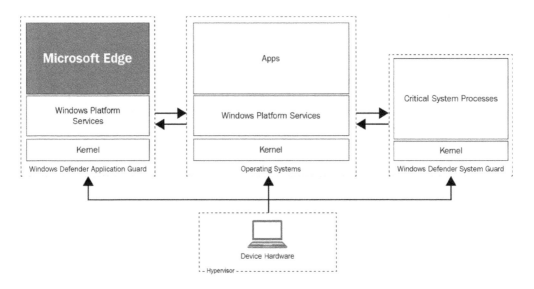

Figure 7.7 - Hardware isolation with Defender Application Guard

If an employee goes to an untrusted site through the **Microsoft Edge** browser, the browser opens the site in an isolated **Hyper-V-enabled container**, which is separate from the host OS. If the site turns out to be malicious, the host PC is protected.

Understanding Windows Defender Exploit Guard

Windows Defender Exploit Guard is a new set of host intrusion prevention capabilities for Windows 10. It allows administrators to define and manage policies for reducing surface attacks and exploits, network protection, and protecting suspicious apps from accessing folders that are typically targeted.

Now, you know about most of the different built-in features in Windows 10 that you can use to secure your OS. You know what you can do with Windows Information Protection and how you can implement the Windows Security baselines. All these Windows Defender features have been provided in this section.

Now, you need to know what the differences are between these Windows Defender features and what they do. Next, we'll learn how to implement encryption on disk or at the file level.

Implementing encryption

There are two types of encryption technologies available for Windows 10 devices: **BitLocker** and **Encrypting File System** (**EFS**). Both tools are available for use on all Windows 10 editions, except for **Windows 10 Home**. While both technologies offer robust methods of encryption, you need to understand how to implement each technique.

EFS has been available since **Windows 2000**, but very few organizations implement this type of encryption. Most organizations that require encryption choose to use **BitLocker Drive Encryption**. The difference between EFS and BitLocker is that EFS encrypts at the folder and file level, while BitLocker encrypts complete hard disks and removable drives.

First, we will understand BitLocker.

Implementing BitLocker

BitLocker allow you to encrypt an entire hard disk, which can be the Windows 10 OS drive, a data drive, or a removable drive. During the encryption process, BitLocker configures the drive that contains the OS so that you have a system partition and an OS partition. BitLocker helps to ensure that data stored on a computer remains encrypted, even if someone tampers with the machine while the OS is not running.

BitLocker offers a tightly integrated Windows 10 solution to help tackle the problem of data theft or data leakage from devices that have been lost, compromised, or improperly decommissioned. Data on these types of computers may become vulnerable to unauthorized access when a hacker either runs a software attack tool against it or transfers the hard disk of the computer to a different computer.

By enhancing Windows file and system protection, BitLocker helps to prevent unauthorized access to data. BitLocker also helps make data unavailable as you decommission or recycle computers that are secured by BitLocker.

Windows 10 now offers a newer encryption algorithm, **XTS-AES**, for BitLocker. Organizations concerned with brute-force attacks being used on their devices, given physical access is possible, they may want to consider migrating their BitLocker default encryption to **XTS-AES**. This option can be configured using Group Policy. Microsoft recommends that customers enable this level of encryption on newly provisioned devices.

BitLocker performs two functions that provide both offline data protection and system integrity verification:

- It encrypts all data that is stored on the Windows OS volume (and configured data volumes). BitLocker provides security for Microsoft applications and non-Microsoft applications, which provides benefits for the applications automatically when they are installed on the encrypted volume.

- It is configured, by default, to use a **Trusted Platform Module** (**TPM**) chip to help ensure the integrity of early startup components. It does this by ensuring that no modifications have been made to the first boot file's integrity. Once the TPM has verified that there are no changes, it releases the decryption key to the Windows OS Loader.

    When TPM detects changes, it locks any volumes that are secured by BitLocker. They remain protected, even if somebody tampers with the machine when the OS is not running.

> **Important Note**
> The Windows 10 installation process partitions the computer's hard disk to enable the use of BitLocker.

As we mentioned earlier, BitLocker uses the TPM chip to verify the integrity of the startup process by doing the following:

- It provides us with a way to check that the first boot file's integrity has been maintained and helps ensure that no adverse changes have been made to those files, such as viruses in the boot sector or rootkits.

- It improves protection in order to mitigate software-based attacks (offline). It makes sure any alternative software that could start the system does not have access to the decryption keys for the volume of the Windows OS.

- When the machine is tampered with, it locks the user out. Even if anyone has tampered with the monitored files, the system does not start. This alerts the user of tampering occurring because the system doesn't start like it usually does. BitLocker offers a simple recovery process when a system lockout occurs.

In conjunction with the TPM chip, BitLocker verifies the integrity of early startup components. This helps to prevent additional offline attacks, such as attempts to insert malicious code into these components. This functionality is necessary because the components from the earliest part of the startup process must be available in an unencrypted format so that the computer can start.

> **Important Note**
> You might need to enable the TPM functionality in your computer's **basic input/output system (BIOS)**.

If an attacker can gain access to the components of the initialization process, they can modify the code in those components and gain access to the computer, even if the data on the disk is encrypted. Once the intruder has access to confidential information such as BitLocker keys or user passwords, they can bypass BitLocker and other security measures on Windows.

BitLocker does not require a TPM chip. However, only a computer with a TPM chip can provide the additional security of pre-startup system integrity verification. To check whether a computer has a **TPM v1.2** chip, perform the following steps:

1. Open the **Control Panel**.

2. Click **System and Security**.

3. Click **BitLocker Drive Encryption**.

4. In the lower-left corner, click **TPM Administration**:

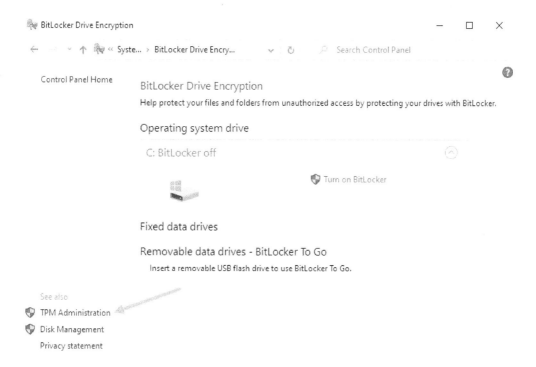

Figure 7.8 - The BitLocker Drive Encryption window

5.   The **Trusted Platform Module Management on the Local Computer** console will open:

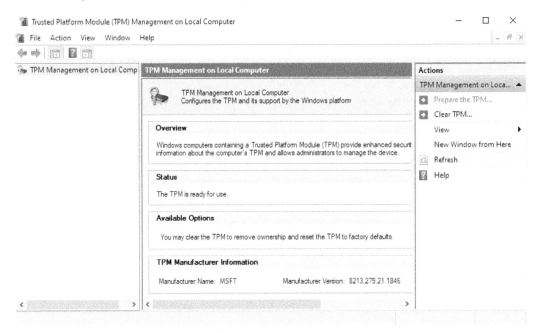

Figure 7.9 - The TPM Management on the Local Computer console

In the previous screenshot, we can see the **TPM Management** console. In this console, you will see that the machine is a TPM chip that has been installed and is ready for use. On the right-hand side of the console, you can choose some actions, such as clearing the TPM chip.

If the computer does not have the **Trusted Platform Module v1.2** chip, a message stating **Compatible TPM cannot be found** will be displayed.

> **Important Note**
> If the computer does not have a TPM v1.2 chip, you can still use BitLocker to encrypt the Windows OS volume. However, this implementation does not include a TPM and requires the user to insert a USB startup key to start the computer or resume it from hibernation. It also does not provide the pre-startup system integrity verification that BitLocker offers when working with a TPM.

Besides BitLocker, you can also use the Encrypting File System. BitLocker and EFS are built into Windows 10. Most organizations use BitLocker, but you also need to know how EFS works. You'll learn how to use it in the next section.

Implementing Encrypting File System

The built-in Encrypting File System is a powerful method that's used to restrict access to files within an NTFS environment. As we mentioned earlier, very few organizations implement file and folder encryption. In the organizations where EFS is applied, it's necessary to ensure that users and members of the IT departments acknowledge that EFS is a secure method of protecting files.

Only the origin account (other than the Administrator account) that's used for encryption has the option of decrypting the file.

Users can encrypt the files and folders they have created on an NTFS hard disk by right-clicking the file and selecting **Properties** from the context menu that appears.

In the **Advanced Attributes** dialog box, as shown in the following screenshot, select the option to **Encrypt contents to secure data**:

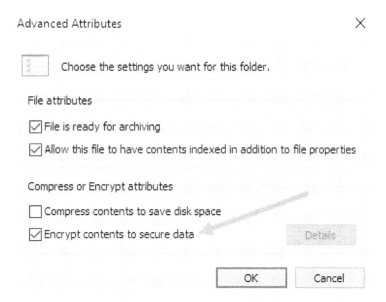

Figure 7.10 - The Advanced Attributes dialog box

Encryption should not be used without prior planning and establishing some precautions to secure the encryption keys that are used. EFS protects data from unauthorized access, and it is advantageous as a last line of defense from attacks.

EFS uses the **Windows Public Key Infrastructure** (**PKI**) and a fast encryption algorithm to protect files. The private and public keys generated during encryption ensure that only the user that encrypted the file can decrypt the file. Encrypted data can only be decrypted if the user's certificate, which is used for encryption, is available on the computer.

Some key points that you need to know about EFS are as follows:

- Encryption and decryption of files and folders happens behind the scenes and is not visible to users.

- When you close files, encryption occurs; when you open files, decryption occurs.

- EFS is only available on NTFS formatted volumes.

- EFS keys are assigned to a specific user and not to a computer.

- An EFS protected file can be moved or copied by the file owner.

- If you move the file to an EFS drive that's not supported, such as **FAT32**, then the file will be decrypted.

- Encrypted files and folders show a **padlock icon** over each file or folder.

- EFS uses the **Advanced Encryption Standard** (**AES**).

- EFS is only available on **Windows 10 Pro**, **Enterprise**, and **Education**.

In this section, you learned how to implement BitLocker and Encrypted File System. As we've mentioned several times, BitLocker is used in more organizations than EFS.

BitLocker will encrypt the whole hard disk or only the data on the hard disk. EFS is used to encrypt single files and folders. Both encryption methods use the most robust encryption that is available nowadays.

In the next section, you will learn how to use **AppLocker** to lock down applications and prevent users from running unauthorized software.

Using AppLocker

The organizations of today face many challenges in controlling which applications run on client computers. These challenges include managing the following:

- The **Universal Windows Platform** apps and desktop apps that users can access

- Which users are allowed to install new applications

- Which versions of the applications are allowed to run, and for which users

Unauthorized software can experience a higher incidence of malware infections and generate more helpdesk calls. However, it can be difficult for you to ensure that users' computers run only approved and licensed software.

You can use AppLocker to specify which software can run on a user's PC. AppLocker enables users to run the applications, installation programs, and scripts that they require to be productive while still providing the security and compliance benefits of application standardization.

> **Important Note**
>
> Only Windows 10 Enterprise and Windows 10 Education editions support AppLocker. AppLocker is unable to control processes running under the system account on any OS.

AppLocker can be useful for organizations that want to limit the number and types of applications that can run. This can be achieved by preventing unlicensed software or malware from running, and by restricting the **ActiveX** controls that are installed.

You can also reduce the total cost of ownership by making sure that workstations are homogeneous across an enterprise and that users run only the software and applications that the enterprise approves. You can also reduce the security risks and the possibility of information leaks from running unauthorized software.

Understanding AppLocker rules

You can prevent many problems in your work environment by controlling which applications a user can run. **AppLocker** enables you to do this by creating rules that specify exactly which applications a user can run. AppLocker continues to function, even when applications are updated.

Because you configure AppLocker with Group Policy, you need to understand Group Policy creation and deployment. This makes AppLocker ideal for organizations that currently use Group Policy to manage their Windows 10 computers or have per-user application installations.

To authorize AppLocker rules, you need to use the new **AppLocker Microsoft Management Console (MMC)** snap-in in the **Group Policy Management Editor** window:

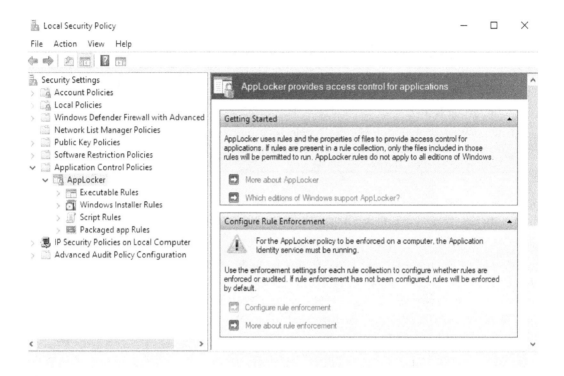

Figure 7.11 - The AppLocker MMC

AppLocker provides several rule-specific wizards. You can use one wizard to create a single rule and another wizard to generate rules automatically, based on your rule preferences and the folder that you select. The four wizards that AppLocker provides administrators with to author rules are **Executable Rules Wizard**, **Windows Installer Rules Wizard**, **Script Rules Wizard**, and **Packaged App Rules Wizard**.

At the end of each wizard, you can review the list of analyzed files. You can then modify the list to remove any file before AppLocker creates rules for the remaining files.

The events for AppLocker are stored in the Event Viewer on the local computer. You can review these events if you want to check whether your AppLocker rules have been applied as appropriate. AppLocker uses the following Event IDs, which you can use to troubleshoot AppLocker from the client:

- **Event ID 8000**: Indicates that the AppLocker policy did not apply correctly
- **Event ID 8004**: Indicates that a `.exe` or `.dll` file did not run
- **Event ID 8007**: Indicates that a script or `.msi` file did not run
- **Event ID 8022**: Indicates that the **Packaged app** is disabled
- **Event ID 8025**: Indicates that the **Packaged app** installation is disabled

AppLocker provides you with the ability to control which users can run designated desktop apps such as executables (`.exe` files), scripts, **Windows Installer files** (`.msi` and `.msp`), and **dynamic link libraries** (`.dll`). You can use AppLocker to specify which **Universal Windows apps** (`.appx`) users can install and use on their computers.

We will now move on and learn about how to configure AppLocker.

Configuring AppLocker

To enable AppLocker restrictions, for example, Universal Windows apps, you must configure the appropriate Group Policy settings by performing the following procedure:

1. Open the **Local Group Policy Editor** (`gpedit.msc`).
2. Under **Local Computer Policy**, in the left pane, navigate to `Computer Configuration\Windows Settings\Security Settings\ Application Control Policies\AppLocker`.
3. Click on **Packaged app Rules**.
4. Right-click **Packaged app Rules**.
5. Click **Create New Rule**.

6. Use the **Create Packaged app Rules** wizard to configure an application restriction policy:

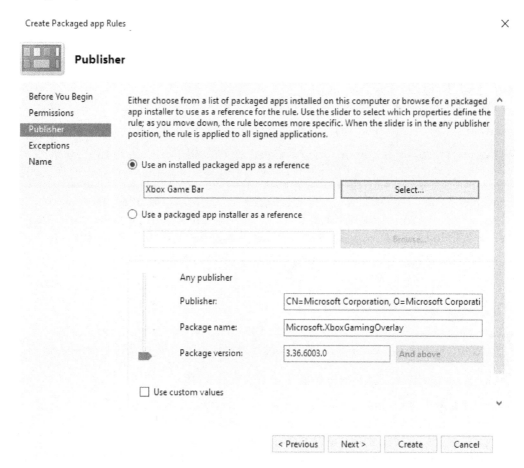

Figure 7.12 - The Create Packaged app Rules wizard

7. Click on **Create** to create the default rule.

This default rule has lower precedence, but it enables all signed packaged apps to run. To create the default rule, perform the following steps:

1. Right-click **Packaged app Rules**.

2. Click **Create Default Rules**:

Figure 7.13 - The Create Default Rules option

At this point, you have a specific package rule and a set of default rules. By default, these policies are set to enforce. You can only change the policy to audit policies by performing the following steps:

1. Right-click the **AppLocker** node.

2. Click **Properties**.

   In the **AppLocker Properties** dialog box, select the **Configured** check box adjacent to **Packaged app Rules**. In the list, depending on your requirements, select either **Enforce rules** or **Audit only** and then click **OK**:

Figure 7.14 - The AppLocker Properties dialog box

Enforcement of AppLocker rules requires that the Application Identity service runs on all computers affected by your AppLocker policy. This service identifies applications, and then processes the AppLocker policies against the identified applications. You can enable this service by opening `Services.msc` and selecting the Application Identity service. Configure the service for automatic startup, and then start the service manually. You can also start the service by configuring the setting through a GPO.

In this section, you learned what **AppLocker** is and why it is important for an organization so that they can reduce the number of applications that can be run. If an AppLocker policy does not work, you can check the **Event Viewer** for specific event IDs to troubleshoot the problem. Furthermore, you learned how to configure **AppLocker settings**.

Summary

In this chapter, you learned about the use of User Account Control to prevent unwanted programs, such as malware, from being installed on a computer. You learned about the two types of elevation prompts and also learned how to configure UAC notifications.

Furthermore, you learned what threat protection is and what types of threat protection there are. Using many of the built-in Windows Defender features makes your computer much safer. You learned what the security baselines are and how you can implement them. To protect company information, you can use Windows Information Protection.

Another form of security that you can implement is encryption. In this chapter, you learned about BitLocker and Encrypted File System. More organizations are embracing BitLocker rather than EFS, but EFS is not a bad choice.

The last thing you learned about is how AppLocker works and how you can configure AppLocker with specific application-independent rules.

In the next chapter, you will learn about the fundamentals of how you can configure connections, such as LAN and Wi-Fi.

Questions

1. Can a standard user reset the network adapter?
2. Are there four settings for UAC notifications? If yes, name them.
3. Can WIP automatically protect the content that is downloaded to the device?
4. Can EFS encrypt the whole hard disk?

5. Can BitLocker be used without a TPM chip?

6. Is AppLocker **Event ID 8023** a valid event ID?

Further reading

- **How User Account Control works**: `https://docs.microsoft.com/en-us/windows/security/identity-protection/user-account-control/how-user-account-control-works`

- **Understanding the User Account Control message**: `https://support.hp.com/us-en/document/c03313350#AbT2`

- **Microsoft Security Compliance Toolkit 1.0**: `https://www.microsoft.com/en-us/download/details.aspx?id=55319`

- **BitLocker**: `https://docs.microsoft.com/en-us/windows/security/information-protection/BitLocker/BitLocker-overview`

- **Working with AppLocker rules**: `https://docs.microsoft.com/en-us/windows/security/threat-protection/windows-defender-application-control/applocker/working-with-applocker-rules`

- **User Account Control: Admin Approval Mode for the Built-in Administrator account**: `https://docs.microsoft.com/en-us/windows/security/threat-protection/security-policy-settings/user-account-control-admin-approval-mode-for-the-built-in-administrator-account`

- **Microsoft's Authenticode Technology**: `https://www.oreilly.com/library/view/web-security-and/1565922697/ch09s02.html`

- **Windows Defender Device Guard**: `https://docs.microsoft.com/en-us/windows-hardware/design/device-experiences/oem-device-guard`

- **What's a Universal Windows Platform (UWP) app?**: `https://docs.microsoft.com/en-us/windows/uwp/get-started/universal-application-platform-guide`

Section 3: Configuring Connectivity

Connecting a Windows 10 client to a home network is easier than connecting the same device to a corporate network. In this section, you will explore the world of connectivity.

This section comprises the following chapters:

- *Chapter 8, Configuring Various Networks*
- *Chapter 9, Configuring Remote Connectivity*

8
Configuring Various Networks

Connecting a Windows client to a network has, these days, become an automatic process. When the Windows **Operating System (OS)** is installed, the default network drivers and settings are usually enough to get you connected and to locate a server or router that governs the network environment. They provide the necessary information to the client to connect to the local network.

In a typical home or public network, this is often just a matter of plugging in an Ethernet cable, or in the case of wireless connections, entering the **Service Set Identifier (SSID)** and a password, if applicable, to access resources such as the internet.

Connecting a device to an organization's network can be more complex and the default settings may not be sufficient to connect to a network or access specific resources. Regardless of the network settings or complexity, it's not an uncommon occurrence for a device to occasionally have difficulty connecting to a network.

The following topics will be covered in this chapter:

- Configuring the IPv4 settings
- Configuring the IPv6 settings
- Configuring mobile networking
- Configuring remote access
- Configuring Wi-Fi profiles
- Troubleshooting networking issues

This chapter will provide you with the skills needed to configure **Internet Protocol Version 4 (IPv4)** and **Internet Protocol Version 6 (IPv6)**, show you how to configure mobile networking and remote access, and explain how you can configure Wi-Fi profiles in Windows 10. This chapter will also help you to prepare for the **MD-100** (Windows 10) exam, which is a part of the **Microsoft 365 Certified: Modern Desktop Administrator Associate** certification.

Technical requirements

In this chapter, you will see us use PowerShell code. This code is available at `https://github.com/PacktPublishing/Microsoft-Exam-MD-100-Windows-10-Certification-Guide`.

The steps that you will follow have also been recorded. You can find these videos at `https://bit.ly/2LsQDqD`.

Configuring the IP settings

To configure networking and the connectivity between these networks, you must understand and familiarize yourself with the IPv4 or IPv6 addresses and how they work. Computers can only communicate if they can identify each other. In this section, you will learn about the IPv4 and IPv6 addresses.

Understanding the IPv4 address

You have to assign a unique IPv4 address to each computer, which is connected to the network so that the computer can identify itself to the other network-connected computers. This IPv4 address, combined with the subnet mask, will determine the location of the computer on the network. You can relate this to a street name and house number to identify the address of a house.

In the following diagram, you can see an example of the IPv4 addresses on a network:

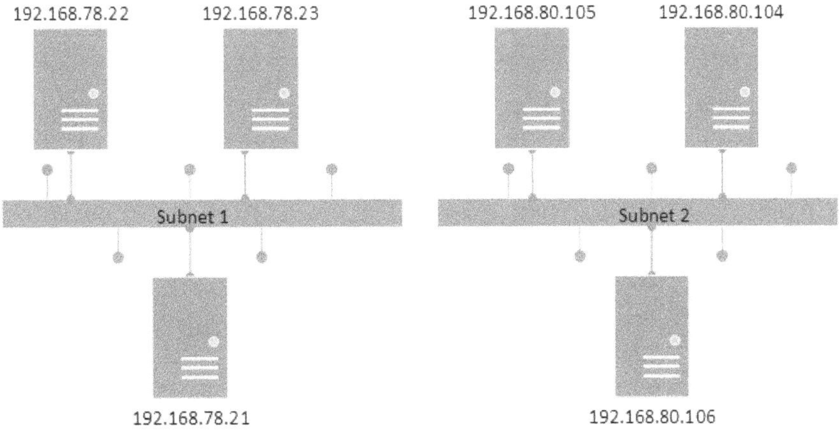

Figure 8.1 - An example of the IPv4 addresses on a network

In the previous diagram, you can see two different subnets. Computers located on their own subnet can reach each other, but if they want to reach a computer on the other subnet, they have to send a request via a gateway. You will learn about this process in the next section.

Connecting with another network host

In a typical situation, for successful communication between computers, several steps will occur. These steps are as follows:

1. A source host sends a request to connect to a destination host. The name of the destination host must be resolved to an IPv4 address.

2. Once the source host knows the destination's host IPv4 address, it uses the subnet mask to determine whether the IPv4 address is on a remote subnet or the local subnet.

3. If its destination host is on the local subnet, an **Address Resolution Protocol (ARP)** request is broadcasted on the local subnet. If its destination host is on a remote subnet, an ARP request is sent to the default gateway and then directed to the correct subnet.

4. The destination host that owns that IPv4 address will respond with its **Media Access Control (MAC)** address and a request is sent to the source's host MAC address.

5. After the exchange of MAC addresses is completed, the IPv4 communication starts and the transfer of IP data packets can occur.

IPv4 makes use of 32-bit addresses. If you switch this to a binary format, then the address has 32 characters. This format will look as follows:

```
11000000101010000100111000010100
```

IPv4 divides this address into four octets. These four octets will look as follows:

```
11000000.10101000.01001110.00010100
```

Now, take a look at this explanation of the preceding binary format with the corresponding decimal format:

- The first octet is 11000000 and, if you switch this to decimal, the result is 192.
- The second octet is 10101000 and, if you switch this to decimal, the result is 168.
- The third octet is 01001110 and, if you switch this to decimal, the result is 78.
- The fourth octet is 00010100 and, if you switch this to decimal, the result is 20.

The complete IP address is then 192.168.78.20.

Along with a subnet mask, the address identifies the computer's unique identity—which is the host ID—and the subnet that the computer resides on—which is the network ID.

This type of communication allows a computer connected to a network to communicate with other computers connected to the same network in a routed environment.

The **Internet Assigned Numbers Authority** (**IANA**) arranges the IPv4 addresses into classes. The number of hosts in a network governs the required class of addresses. **Class A** through **Class E** are the names that IANA has detailed for the IPv4 address classes.

Class A, **Class B**, and **Class C** are IP addresses that can be assigned to host computers as a unique IP address, while **Class D** can be used for multicasting. Additionally, IANA reserves **Class E** for experimental use.

Defining subnets

A subnet is a network segment. Single or multiple routers separate the subnet from the rest of the network. When your **Internet Service Provider** (**ISP**) assigns a network to a Class A, Class B, or Class C address range, you often must subdivide the range to match the network's layout. Subdividing allows you to break a large network into smaller, logical subnets.

When you subdivide a network into subnets, you must create a unique ID for each subnet, which you derive from the primary network ID.

A subnet mask helps differentiate between the network ID and the host ID of an IPv4 address, as shown in the following table:

IP address	192	168	78	20
Subnet mask	255	255	255	0
Network ID	192	168	78	0

Table 8.1 - Subnet mask differentiation

If you use subnets, you can make use of Class A, Class B, or Class C networks across multiple locations. With subnets, you can also reduce network congestion. You can achieve this by segmenting network traffic and reducing broadcasts on every network segment. With subnets, you can overcome the limitations, such as exceeding the maximum number of hosts that each segment can handle. Just like an IPv4 address, the subnet mask also has four octets to specify which part is the network ID and which part is the host ID.

In more common IPv4 networks, the subnet mask defines full octets as part of the network ID and host ID. 255 corresponds to an octet that is part of the network ID and 0 corresponds to an octet that is part of the host ID. Class A, Class B, and Class C networks use the default subnet masks. The properties of each IP address class are shown in the following table:

Class	First octet	Default subnet mask	Number of networks	Number of hosts per network
A	1 - 127	`255.0.0.0`	126	16,777,214
B	128 - 191	`255.255.0.0`	16,384	65,534
C	192 - 223	`255.255.255.0`	2,097,152	254

Table 8.2 - IP address class properties

In complex networks, such as in an organization, subnet masks might not be a simple combination of 255 and 0. As an alternative, you can split one octet, with some parts used for the network ID and some parts used for the host ID.

We use **Classless Inter-Domain Routing** (**CIDR**) methods to define subnets. This subnetting uses a different notation, which is shown in the following example:

```
172.16.78.20/255.255.248.0
```

The following classless IPv4 address is more representative:

```
172.16.78.20/21
```

`/21` represents how many bits are set to 1 in the subnet mask. This is an example of CIDR and this subnet mask now looks as in the following line in binary notation:

```
11111111.11111111.11111000.00000000
```

As you can see in the previous example, the first 21 bits are set to `1` and they indicate the subnet ID. The last 11 bits are set to `0` and they show how many bits are used to identify the host.

Now, let's understand how to use these subnets for connectivity.

Configuring connectivity to other subnets

A **default gateway** is a device on a network that serves as a forwarding host—usually, a **router**—which sends IP packets to different subnets when there is no other route specification that matches the destination IP address of an IP packet.

A router connects multiple subnets to create an **intranet**. In an intranet, any specified subnet might have more routers that connect to other local and remote subnets. To accomplish this, you must configure one of the routers as the default gateway for the local hosts so that the local hosts can communicate with the remote hosts. In most cases, you can use a **Dynamic Host Configuration Protocol** (**DHCP**) server to assign the default gateway automatically to a DHCP client. This is more straightforward than manually assigning a default gateway to each host.

Networks can contain public or private IP addresses. In the next section, you will learn the difference between the two.

Learning about public and private IP addresses

In general, hosts that are connecting directly to the internet require a public IPv4 address. However, hosts that do not link directly to the internet do not need a public IPv4 address. The public IPv4 address must be unique. IANA assigns public IPv4 addresses. Typically, your ISP allocates you one or more public IPv4 addresses from their dedicated IPv4 address pool.

The IPv4 address pool is becoming smaller, so IANA is unwilling to allocate unnecessary IPv4 addresses. Nowadays, you have technology such as **Network Address Translation** (**NAT**) that allows administrators to use a small piece of the public IPv4 addresses pool. At the same time, administrators can allow hosts on a local network to connect to hosts on the remote network and many services on the internet.

In the following table, you will see what IANA defines as the private IPv4 ranges:

Class	Mask	Range
A	10.0.0.0/8	10.0.0.0 − 10.255.255.255
B	172.16.0.0/12	172.16.0.0 − 172.31.255.255
C	192.168.0.0/16	192.168.0.0 − 192.168.255.255

Table 8.3 - Private IPv4 ranges

Routers that are connected to the internet will not forward packets initiating from, or intended for, the previously given ranges.

In networks nowadays, it is most common for organizations to have one or more public, routable IP addresses assigned to the external interfaces of their firewall appliances. For internal purposes, they use the designated private IPv4 ranges.

Assigning a host manually to an IPv4 address is a lot of work, as you already learned in an earlier section. In the next section, you will learn how you can implement automatic IPv4 addresses.

Implementing automatic IPv4 addressing

You can configure a static IPv4 configuration manually for each of your network-connected hosts. However, when you perform a manual IPv4 configuration, you must set the IPv4 address, the subnet mask, the default gateway, and the **Domain Name Server (DNS)** server. Static configuration is time-consuming and requires you to visit each host and configure the IPv4 configuration.

DHCP enables you, as an administrator, to assign IPv4 configurations automatically for a substantial number of computers without having to assign each one separately. The DHCP server receives requests for IPv4 addresses from hosts that you have configured to obtain an IPv4 address automatically. It also assigns IPv4 addresses from other scopes that you have defined for each of your subnets. The DHCP server identifies which subnet the request originated from and assigns an IPv4 configuration from the relevant scope.

DHCP helps you, as an administrator, to simplify the IPv4 address configuration process. If your DHCP server is business-critical, then you must include resilience in your DHCP server's design. This is in case of failure of a single server; we have to make sure that it doesn't prevent the whole DHCP service from functioning. The other thing you must do is to configure the DHCP scopes carefully. If you make a mistake, then this can affect the whole network and can prevent communication between the hosts.

Every network that a device connects to, such as a home or work network, might require different IPv4 configurations. Windows 10 has support for an **Automatic Private IP Addressing** (**APIPA**) and an alternate static IP address, for this scenario. In the following screenshot, you will see how this looks in the properties box of your network card:

Figure 8.2 - The Alternative Configuration tab

You can use the **Alternative Configuration** tab to control the behavior of your Windows 10 device if the DHCP server is not reachable. Windows 10 assigns itself an APIPA IPv4 address automatically, somewhere in the range of 169.254.0.0 to 169.254.255.255. With this method, you can use a DHCP server at work and an APIPA address range on your home network without the need to reconfigure the IPv4 settings. This setup can be useful for troubleshooting DHCP issues if a device can't communicate with the DHCP server.

Now, you know a lot about IPv4 address and hosts communicating with each other via subnets. Next, you will learn about IPv6. *What? Another IP address?* Yes!

Understanding the IPv6 address

Most networks currently provide IPv4 addresses, but many networks also support IPv6 addresses. You must understand the differences between IPv4, IPv6, and the IPv6 addressing scheme. Windows 10 devices use IPv6 by default, but they also support IPv6 and IPv4 in a dual-stack configuration.

The IPv6 protocol provides many benefits over IPv4. These benefits are as follows:

- **Larger address spaces**: A 32-bit address space can have 4,294,967,296 possible IPv4 addresses, whereas IPv6 uses 128-bit address spaces, which results in 340,282,366,92 0,938,463,463,374,607,431,768,211,456 possible IPv6 addresses.

- **More efficient routing**: IPv6 reduces the size of routing tables, making them more efficient and hierarchical to navigate. IPv6 allows ISPs to combine their consumer network prefixes into a single prefix and to announce this one prefix to the IPv6 internet. Besides, fragmentation in IPv6 networks is handled by the source device, rather than the router, using a protocol to determine the **Maximum Transmission Unit** (**MTU**) of the path.

- **More efficient packet processing**: The simpler packet header of IPv6 makes the processing of packets more secure. Similar to IPv4, IPv6 does not include an IP level checksum, so there is no need to recalculate the checksum at each router hop. It is possible to get rid of the checksum at the IP level because most link-layer technologies already provide checksum and error-control capabilities. Therefore, most transport layers, which handle end-to-end communication, have a checksum, allowing error detection.

- **Direct data flows**: IPv6 allows multicast, instead of broadcasting. **Multicast** provides simultaneous transmission of bandwidth-intensive packet flows (such as multimedia streams) to multiple destinations, saving network bandwidth. Disinterested hosts no longer need to process packets for transmission. However, the IPv6 header has a new field, called **flow label**, which can distinguish packets that belong to the same flow.

- **Simplified network configuration**: Auto-configuration of the address (address assignment) is built into IPv6. In the router advertisements, a router will send the local link prefix. By adding its link-layer (MAC) address and converting it into **Extended Universal Identifier** (**EUI**) 64-bit format, a host can generate its IP address.

- **Support for new services**: By removing NAT, true end-to-end communication is restored at the IP layer allowing new and useful services to be delivered.

- **Security**: For IPv6, **Internet Protocol Security** (**IPsec**) provides confidentiality, authentication, and data integrity. Corporate firewalls often block IPv4 **Internet Control Message Protocol** (**ICMP**) packets because of their ability to carry malware; however, **Internet Control Message Protocol version 6** (**ICMPv6**—which is the implementation of the ICMP for IPv6—can be enabled because IPsec can be applied to the ICMPv6 packets.

If you connect to a new network that advertises IPv6 routability, Windows 10 can check the IPv6 connectivity and use IPv6 only if the IPv6 connectivity works. Windows 10 also provides an address-sorting feature. This feature lets the Windows 10 OS decide which protocol to use when all protocol stacks are configured to support applications that support IPv4 and IPv6 addresses.

Windows 10 device utilities, such as sharing files and remote access, use IPv6 technology, such as IPsec. This includes **VPN Reconnect**, which uses version 2 of **Internet Key Exchange (IKEv2)**, a part of IPv6 authentication.

Windows 10 supports remote troubleshooting capabilities, such as **Remote Desktop** and **Windows Remote Assistance**. Remote Desktop lets administrators connect, for remote management, to multiple Windows Server sessions. To make remote desktop connections, you can use the IPv6 addresses, such as Windows Remote Assistance and Remote Desktop. These applications use Remote Desktop Protocol to allow users to access files from other computers, such as from their home computers to their office computers.

An overview of IPv6 addressing

IPv6's most noticeable distinguishing feature is its use of much larger addresses. IPv4 addresses are represented by four decimal numeral classes, such as 192.168.80.72. Each numeral class represents a binary octet. In binary format, the preceding number looks as follows:

```
11000000.10101000.01001110.00010100
```

For IPv6, the size of an address is four times that of an IPv4 address. As the following example shows, the IPv6 addresses are represented in hexadecimal form:

```
0:0:0:0:0:ffff:c0a8:5014
```

The previous hexadecimal string may seem confusing for end users, but the presumption is that users will rely on DNS names to handle hosts, ensuring that IPv6 addresses will only be typed by hand. In hexadecimal form, the IPv6 address is also easier to convert into binary form. This makes working with subnets and measuring hosts and networks simpler.

In the next section, we will learn about the types of IPv6 addresses.

Understanding the types of IPv6 addresses

The types of IPv6 addresses are similar to those of IPv4 addresses. The types of IPv6 addresses are, namely, **unicast**, **multicast**, and **anycast**.

The following sections will explain each one in detail. Let's start with unicast, first.

Unicast

A unicast IPv6 address is the same as a unicast IPv4 address. You can use this type of address to communicate between hosts one to one. Every IPv6 host has several unicast addresses. There are three types of unicast addresses:

- **Global unicast address**: These are similar to addresses for public IPv4. These addresses are routable worldwide and available on the internet portion of IPv6.

- **Link-local addresses**: Hosts use the connection local addresses when communicating on the same channel with neighboring hosts—for example, hosts communicate using link-local addresses on a single-link IPv6 network with no router. Link-local addresses always start with FE80 and they are equivalent to the IPv4 APIPA addresses.

- **Unique local unicast addresses**: Unique local addresses provide organizations with an equivalent of a private IPv4 address space, without the duplication in address space when organizations combine.

We will now move on to multicast.

Multicast

A multicast IPv6 address is the equivalent of a multicast IPv4 address. You use this type of address for one-to-many computer communication between computers that use the same multicast address.

Anycast

An anycast address is an IPv6 address allocated to multiple computers. When IPv6 addresses communicate to an anycast address, only the closest host will answer. Usually, you use this type of address to locate services or the nearest router.

You now understand the types of IPv6 addresses. In the next section, you will learn about the interface identifiers and their purposes.

Learning about the IPv6 interface identifiers

In IPv4, you typically assign a single unicast address to one host. In IPv6, however, each host can be assigned multiple unicast addresses. You need to know why IPv6 uses each of those addresses to verify communication processes on a network.

The interface identifier is the last 64 bits of an IPv6 address. This is similar to an IPv4 address host ID. Every interface on an IPv6 network must have a unique identifier for the interface. Because the interface identifier is unique to each interface, IPv6 uses interface identifiers to mark hosts individually, rather than MAC addresses.

That's it for IPv4 and IPv6. You now know the difference between these two IP addresses and how this technology works in a network. In the next section, we are going to learn how we can make use of mobile networking by using cellular networks, such as **4G** or **Long-Term Evolution (LTE)**.

Configuring mobile networking

Some devices, such as the **Microsoft Surface Pro X**, that have the Windows 10 OS installed, can support connectivity by cellular networks, such as 4G or LTE. This can be useful to end users who are unable to access Wi-Fi networks, but still need access to your corporate services and resources.

Setting up a cellular network

Before you can use cellular network connectivity, you must have a computer or laptop that supports this option. If your computer or laptop has or supports this feature, then you have to obtain a **Subscriber Identity Module (SIM)** or an **embedded SIM (eSIM)** for your Windows 10 device. After you have installed the SIM or eSIM on your Windows 10 device, you must configure Windows 10 to connect using the cellular network. Microsoft can provide this connectivity through the **Mobile Plans** app. When you start the app, the app detects your SIM or eSIM and then guides you through the setup process.

If you have a SIM or eSIM installed and you want to set up cellular network access, use the following steps:

1. Connect your device to the internet using a wired or wireless connection.

2. Select the network symbol on the taskbar, look for the name of your mobile operator, and then click on **Connect with a data plan**. This opens the Mobile Plans app, as shown in the following screenshot:

Figure 8.3 - Notification of the cellular network

3. In the **Mobile Plans** app, follow the wizard to activate a mobile plan and connect to the cellular network:

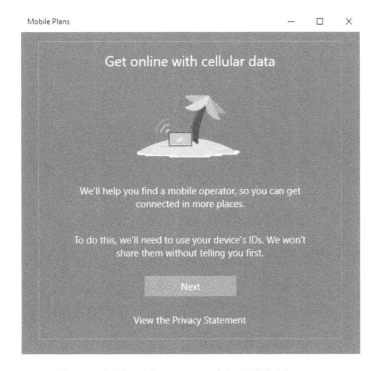

Figure 8.4 - The welcome page of the Mobile Plans app

After completing these steps, you will be connected to the internet via your cellular connection through the mobile operator. If you are working with a few colleagues in the same area and they don't have a SIM or eSIM installed on their machine, you can share your internet connection with them through the mobile hotspot feature in Windows 10.

Setting up a mobile hotspot

If you have working cellular network connectivity and you want to share this internet connection with, for example, your colleagues, you can enable the built-in **mobile hotspot** feature.

To enable and connect to the mobile hotspot, follow these steps:

1. In **Settings**, click **Network & Internet | Mobile hotspot** tab.

2. In the **Share my Internet connection from** list, choose the appropriate network connection. Depending on what kind of hardware you have, you can also choose the **Share my Internet connection over** option.

3. Click **Edit** and change **Network name** and **Network password**, as in the following screenshot:

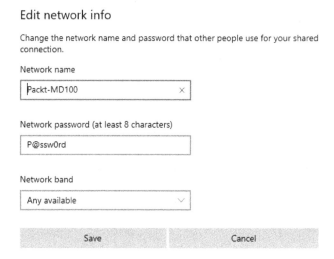

Figure 8.5 - The Edit network info window

4. Then, enable the **Share my Internet connection with other devices** button:

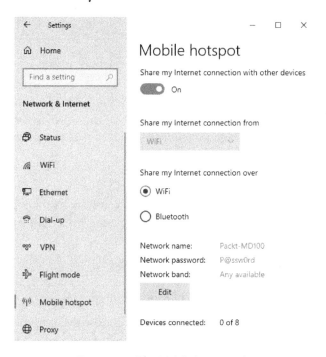

Figure 8.6 - The Mobile hotspot tab

If you followed the previous steps, then you will now see the same screen as in the previous screenshot. After this, you can disable the mobile hotspot.

You have now learned how you can connect to a cellular network and how you can enable and share your internet connection with other people and devices through the mobile hotspot feature.

In the next section, you will learn how to set up a **Virtual Private Network** (**VPN**) connection, which protocols are used by a VPN, and which types of VPN to use. You will also learn about **Always On VPN**.

Configuring remote access

Windows 10 helps users boost their efficiency regardless of where they are situated or the data they need. Windows 10 also allows the use of a VPN to allow users to access their work environments anywhere they connect.

An overview of VPNs

A VPN contains a point-to-point connection between individual network components via a public network such as the internet. Tunneling protocols allow a VPN client to link to a VPN server's listening virtual port and keep it attached. The data is encapsulated—or wrapped—and prefixed with a header to emulate a point-to-point connection. This header provides routing information that allows the data to reach its destination through a public network. The data is encrypted to ensure confidentiality to emulate a private link. Packets intercepted over the public network without encryption keys are indecipherable. There are two types of VPN connections:

- **Remote access**: Remote access VPN connections allow users at home, on customer sites, or from public wireless **Access Points** (**APs**), to access company resources that reside in the private network of their company. This is done by using the architecture offered by a public network, such as the internet.

  The VPN is a point-to-point communication between the device, the VPN client, and the server of the organization, from a user's perspective. The actual infrastructure of the shared or public network is meaningless and illogical, as it seems logical and preferable to send the data over a dedicated private connection line.

- **Site-to-site**: Site-to-site VPN connections, also known as router-to-router VPN connections, allow your organization to route connections across a public network between different offices or other organizations while maintaining secure communications.

VPN connections in Windows 10 can make use of the following protocols:

- **Point-to-Point Tunneling Protocol (PPTP)**
- **Layer Two Tunneling Protocol with IPsec (L2TP/IPsec)**
- **Secure Socket Tunneling Protocol (SSTP)**
- **Internet Key Exchange version 2 (IKEv2)**

> **Important Note**
>
> An IKEv2 VPN gives the VPN client resilience when the client either moves from one wireless hotspot to another or switches from wireless to wired.

All the previously mentioned VPN connections, regardless of their tunneling protocol, share some common characteristics, including the following:

- **Encapsulation**: Private data is encapsulated with a header with VPN technology that contains routing information, allowing the data to traverse the transit network.
- **Authentication**: Authentication ensures the two communicating parties know who they are communicating with.
- **Data encryption**: The sender encrypts the data and the recipient decrypts it to ensure data security as the data enters a mutual or public transit network. The processes of encryption and decryption rely on a common encryption key on both the sender and the recipient. Intercepted packets sent in the transit network along the VPN connection will be unintelligible to anyone who lacks the standard encryption key.

As of **Windows 10 version 1607**, you can configure several remote-access usability improvements via VPN profiles. These improvements are as follows:

- **Always On**: This feature activates automatic connections after a user signs in or there is a shift in the network.
- **App-triggered VPN**: This function activates automatic connections based on a **Universal Windows Platform (UWP)** packet family name or a file path, following the launch of the applications that you choose.

> **Important Note**
>
> Note that this functionality is available on both workgroup and domain-joined computers, unlike Windows 8.1, which is limited to workgroup computers only.

- **Traffic filters**: With this app, you can control the types of network traffic that can access your business network.

- **LockDown VPN**: This feature enforces multiple settings on VPN apps that affect their usability. For instance, you can make sure a user can't change the VPN profile or disconnect an active VPN connection. If the VPN link is not usable, you can also enforce forced tunneling and block outbound traffic.

By this point, you know what types of VPN are available and which protocol you can use and you can apply some remote access improvements. Next, we are going to create a VPN connection.

Creating a VPN connection

In this section, we are going to create a VPN connection using the following steps:

1. Click on the network icon in the notification area and then click on **Network & Internet** settings | **VPN** | **Add a VPN connection** tab.

2. In the **VPN provider** list of the **Add a VPN connection** dialog box, select **Windows (built-in)**.

3. In the **Connection name** box, add a meaningful name.

4. In the **Server name or address text** box, fill in the **Fully Qualified Domain Name (FQDN)** of the VPN server you want to connect to.

5. In the **VPN type** list, choose a VPN protocol. This protocol must match the settings and policies configured on your VPN server. If you are unsure, tap **Automatic**.

6. In the **Type of sign-in info** list, choose the correct type of sign-in option. Again, your VPN server policies must suit this environment.

7. In the **User name (optional)** box, fill in your username, and then in the **Password (optional)** box, fill in your password and then click **Save**.

If you followed the previous steps, then you will see something as in the following screenshot:

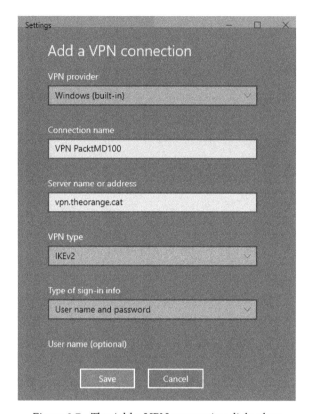

Figure 8.7 - The Add a VPN connection dialog box

To manage your VPN connection, go to **Network & Internet** | **VPN** | **VPN connection** | **Advanced** options. You can then reconfigure your VPN settings as necessary, as shown in the following screenshot:

Figure 8.8 - Extra options are visible if you click on the VPN connection

If you click the network icon in the notification area, you will see your VPN connection on the list of available networks, as you can see in the following screenshot:

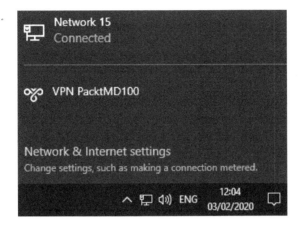

Figure 8.9 - VPN connections on the networks list

You now understand the basics of VPN connections. Nowadays, there is a demand to always have active VPN connectivity. In the next section, you learn what Always On VPN is.

Understanding Always On VPN

With conventional VPNs, the end user usually initiates and authenticates the VPN connection by opening the VPN client and authenticating it. However, there are two common disadvantages to this:

- Users need to be aware of what resources the VPN access requires and the additional steps that they need to take whenever they need to connect via VPN.

- Current VPNs are a method of *everything or nothing*. All network traffic is tunneled over the VPN when paired. This can result in large quantities of bandwidth being used on an organization's network when it's not needed.

  Remote users who frequently use publicly accessible databases and resources are the most notable example. For one or two activities, they may need VPN access, but they may unintentionally transfer all internet traffic over the organization's network, rather than directly through the ISP of the end user.

Always On VPN offers end users a more seamless experience. It allows remote access and personal owned computers for domain-joined, non-domain-joined (workgroup), or Azure AD-joined devices.

Routing policies are configured by administrators to determine when the client should direct traffic over the VPN. Policies can be based on certain criteria that are based on the user, hardware, or software. You may, for example, require device authentication for remote device management and then allow user authentication for access to internal company sites and services. Because it is governed by rules, when to connect or detach from the VPN or whether it's remote or on the internal network are things that no longer concern the user.

Many organizations that provide VPN access usually have the technology required for Always On VPN. Other than the **domain controller** and DNS servers, the Always On VPN implementation includes a **Network Policy Server/Remote Authentication Dial-In User Service** (**NPS/RADIUS**) server, a **Certification Authority** (**CA**) server, and a remote access (Routing/VPN) server. Once the system has been set up, you need to enroll clients and then securely connect the clients to your premises through several changes to the network.

Always On VPN is the successor to **Direct Access**. While it supports both options, Microsoft recommends implementing or switching to Always On VPN. Direct Access also offers seamless access but includes IPv6, so consumers are connected to the domain. Always On VPN can use either IPv4 or IPv6 and supports users that join on non-domain. Always On VPN also provides more granular restrictions on how traffic is routed and follows policies on conditional access.

Windows 10 clients are configured for Always On VPN through the **ProfileXML** setting. ProfileXML is a **Uniform Resource Identifier** (**URI**) node within the VPNv2 **Configuration Service Provider** (**CSP**).

Conceptually, CSPs work similarly to Group Policy. Similar to how you would use the Group Policy management editor to configure **Group Policy Objects** (**GPOs**), you configure CSP nodes by using **Mobile Device Management** (**MDM**) solutions, such as **Microsoft Intune**. In this case, this means configuring a specific node called ProfileXML in the VPNv2 CSP, which contains all the settings necessary. In the following screenshot, you will see an example of a VPN configuration with Always On enabled in Microsoft Intune:

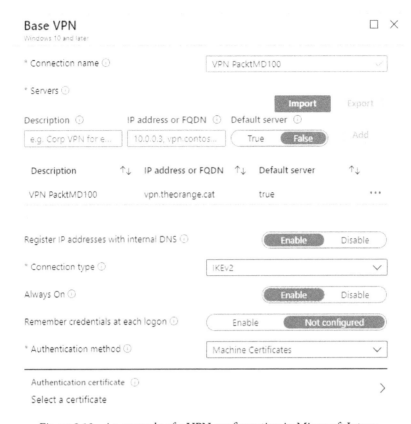

Figure 8.10 - An example of a VPN configuration in Microsoft Intune

The settings and XML files are typically created by the administrator responsible for the VPN infrastructure. Once the XML file is created, it can be deployed to clients with either a device profile in Intune or as a package in Configuration Manager. It can also be deployed using **PowerShell**.

In this section, you learned what Always On VPN is and how you can make a configuration in Microsoft Intune. In the next section, you will learn how you can configure Wi-Fi profiles in Windows 10.

Configuring Wi-Fi profiles

A growing number of devices use wireless networks as the primary method of accessing corporate intranets and the internet. Furthermore, many consumers in a corporate environment have come to expect a wireless infrastructure. Consequently, an excellent working awareness of wireless connectivity is a necessity for today's networking world. This section explores the various wireless specifications as well as the setup and support of Windows 10 wireless clients.

Understanding the technology of wireless networks

Wireless networks use radio waves to connect wireless devices to other devices in your network. Wireless networks are generally composed of wireless network devices, APs, and **802.11x wireless bridges**.

Wireless network topologies come in two types:

- **Infrastructure**: Wireless infrastructure networks consist of wireless **Local Area Networks** (**LANs**) and cellular networks, which involve the use of a device, such as an AP, to enable wireless client device communication. Wireless networks can be handled centrally.

- **Ad hoc**: Ad hoc networks can dynamically link wireless devices in a peer-to-peer configuration without using any equipment in the infrastructure.

Next, we will explore the 802.11x wireless norm.

Understanding the 802.11x norm

As of 1997, 802.11 norms have evolved. The 802.11 technology has experienced many improvements in transmission speed and security. New standards are defined by an alphabet letter, given as follows:

- **802.11a**: This is the first extension to the original specification, 802.11. It provides up to 54 **megabits per second** (**Mbps**) and operates within the range of 5 **gigahertz** (**GHz**). It is not 802.11b compatible.

- **802.11b**: This specification provides 11 Mbps and works at a range of 2.4 GHz.

- **802.11e**: This specification defines Quality of Service and multimedia support.

- **802.11g**: This norm is for the transmission at speeds of up to 54 Mbps over short distances. It is 802.11b backward-compatible and operates within the 2.4 GHz range.

- **802.11n**: This specification adds multiple-input and multiple-output, providing increased data throughput at velocities of up to 100 Mbps. This greatly enhances the performance over previous models, endorsing frequencies of 2.4 GHz and 5 GHz, respectively.

- **802.11ac**: This specification builds on the 802.11n specification to achieve 433 Mbps data rates. 802.11ac operates in the frequency range of only 5 GHz.

- **802.11ax**: This specification is the successor to 802.11ac and is marketed as **Wi-Fi 6**; it makes WLAN networks more effective. However, it is still in development.

Now, we will move on to securing our wireless networks as it is, of course, important to maintain the confidentiality and integrity of our resources.

Securing wireless networks

For companies who consider a wireless deployment, wireless protection is usually the most significant consideration. Since wireless traffic travels through open airwaves, it is vulnerable to attacker interception. Organizations also use several security tools to address these issues. Many Wi-Fi systems follow other safety standards. The outlines for the currently available security strategies for wireless networks are as follows:

- **Wired Equivalent Privacy** (**WEP**): This is the oldest form of security on the wireless network. Several systems support different versions—for example, **64-bit WEP key**, **128-bit WEP key**, and **256-bit WEP key**. The security issues surrounding WEP are well known and unless it's the only option, you can stop using WEP.

- **Wi-Fi Protected Access** (**WPA**): WPA has two variations that were developed to replace WEP—namely, **WPA-Personal** and **WPA-Enterprise**.

  WPA-Personal is more straightforward to implement for the home and small business networks than WPA Enterprise. It involves providing a password for security and using a technology called **Temporal Key Integrity Protocol** (**TKIP**). For each wireless client, the password and the SSID network create constantly changing encryption keys.

  WPA-Enterprise is used by corporate networks. It involves authentication using a RADIUS server.

- **WPA2**: This is an improved version of WPA that has become the standard for Wi-Fi authentication. WPA2 employs the **Advanced Encryption Standard** (**AES**), which uses larger key sizes for encryption.

The methods of protection that a given wireless device support depend on the vendor and the age of the device.

We have talked about the two types of network technology, the different 802.11x norms, and how you can secure your Wi-Fi network. In the next section, we will take a look at how you can configure your Wi-Fi settings and Wi-Fi profiles.

Configuring your Wi-Fi settings and profiles

Nowadays, more and more number of devices make use of Wi-Fi (wireless) networks to assess internet and corporate intranets. Thus a working knowledge of wireless connectivity is necessary for our day to day tasks.

Windows 10 makes wireless network settings very easy to connect to and configure. To manage your wireless network connections, use the following procedure:

1. Click on the wireless network icon in the notification area to see a list of the available wireless networks.

2. Click on the network that you want to connect to and click on the **Connect** button:

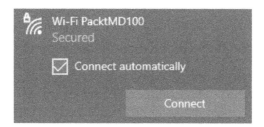

Figure 8.11 - Available Wi-Fi networks

3. Fill in the correct password of the wireless network and click on the **Next** button:

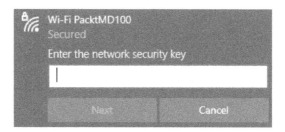

Figure 8.12 - Password dialog box

4. Make the appropriate choice for whether your device can be discoverable on the network, as shown:

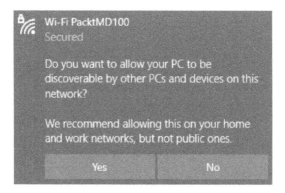

Figure 8.13 - Allow your device to be discoverable on the network

5. Once you have successfully followed the previous steps, the device will connect to the network:

Figure 8.14 - Your device is connected to the Wi-Fi network

Now that you know how to connect a Windows 10 device to a Wi-Fi network, you can, of course, manage these networks via the WiFi page on the **Network & Internet** settings page. To do so, follow these steps:

1. Go to **Settings | Network & Internet | WiFi** option.

2. On the **WiFi** page, click on the **Manage known networks** setting.

3. On the **Manage known networks** page, click on the network that you want to manage.

4. Click on **Properties** to manage the connection or click on **Forget** to remove the connection:

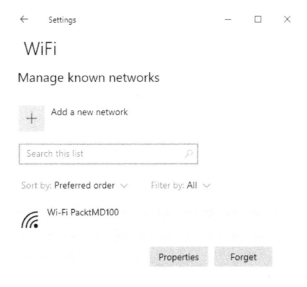

Figure 8.15 - The Manage known networks page

You can also configure specialized wireless assets from **Network and Sharing Center**. To do so, on the **Network and Sharing Center** page, select your wireless network adapter name. You can view the properties of your wireless connection within the **WiFi Status** dialog box. Click on **Wireless Properties** to view the additional information, including the connection security settings.

> **Important Note**
>
> To configure the wireless profiles, you can use Windows Server GPOs. This prevents users from having to set their wireless connections manually.

You have learned how to connect to a Wi-Fi network on Windows 10. It's pretty straightforward and definitely not rocket science. However, you may run into some networking issues. So, in the next section, you will learn about some tools for troubleshooting network connectivity.

Troubleshooting networking issues

You will have to troubleshoot networking issues in Windows 10 every now and then.

Windows 10 comes with several tools that you can use to diagnose network issues. The tools you can use are as follows:

- **Event Viewer**: Event logs are files that document significant events, such as when a process experiences an error on a computer. In the system log, IP conflicts are reflected and may prevent services from starting. When these events occur, Windows must record the incident in a log.

  To read the file, you can use **Event Viewer**. When you troubleshoot issues on Windows 10, you can view the events in the event logs to determine the cause of the problem. You can use Event Viewer to view the **Application**, **Security**, **Setup**, and **System** logs, which you can find under the **Windows Logs** node.

  When selecting a log and then selecting an event, the details of the specified event are given in a preview pane under the event list. Check for errors or alerts relating to the network services in the **System** log to help diagnose network problems, as in the following screenshot:

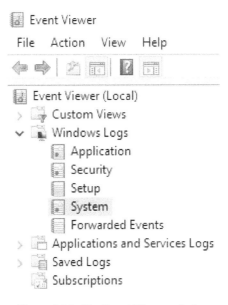

Figure 8.16 - The Event Viewer window

- **Windows Network Diagnostics**: The **Diagnose Connection Problems** option helps to diagnose and repair a problem if you have a Windows 10 networking issue. Windows Network Diagnostics presents a possible description of the problem and a viable solution. The solution could require the user to intervene manually. You can open the **Windows Network Diagnostics** page via the **Network & Internet** page in the **Settings** app:

Figure 8.17 - The Windows Network Diagnostics page

- ipconfig: The ipconfig command shows the current configuration of a **Transmission Control Protocol/Internet Protocol (TCP/IP)** network. You can also use ipconfig to allow the DHCP and DNS settings to update. You may need to flush the DNS cache, as shown in the following screenshot:

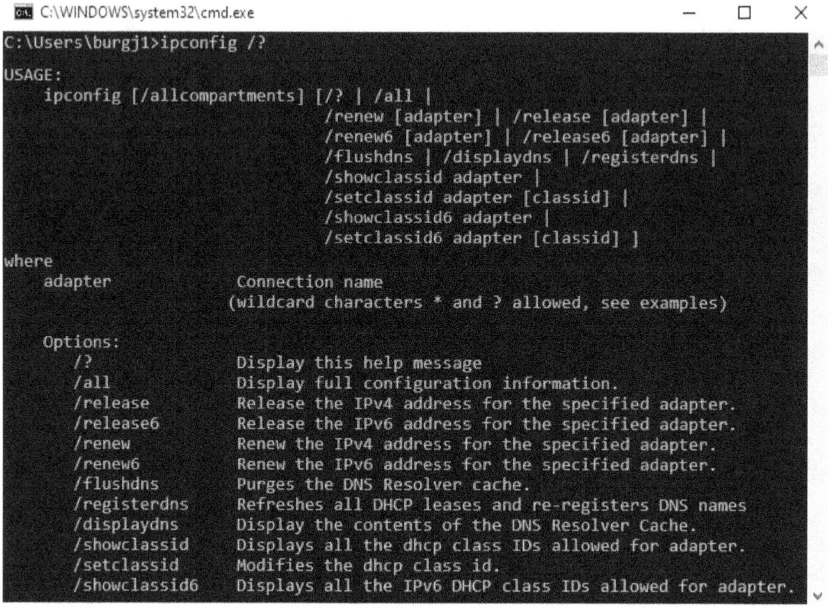

Figure 8.18 - The available command-line switches for the ipconfig command

- ping: To check the connection to another TCP/IP device at the IP level, you can use the ping command. This command sends and receives echo question messages from the ICMP and shows the receipt of the corresponding echo response messages.

> **Important Note**
> Firewalls may block ICMP requests. As a result, you may receive false negatives when using ping as a troubleshooting tool.

ping is the first TCP/IP command that you use for troubleshooting communication, as shown in the following screenshot:

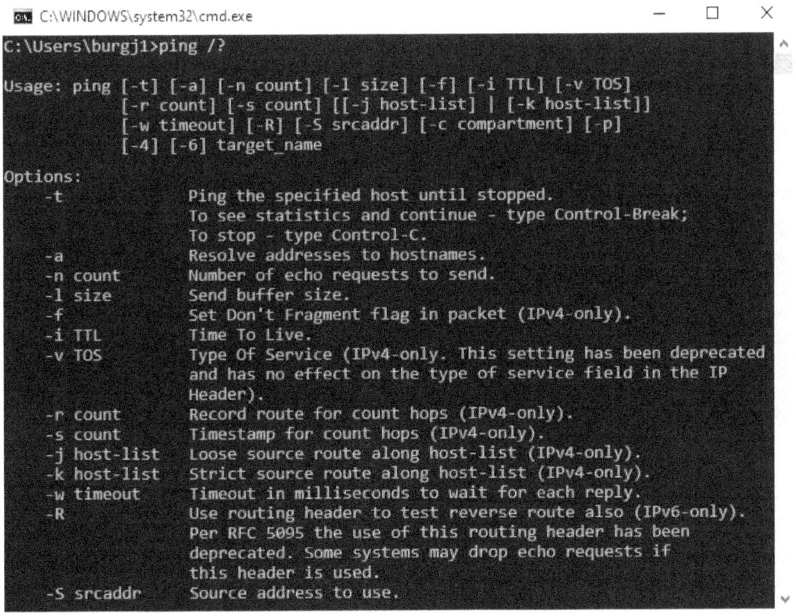

Figure 8.19 - The available command-line switches for the ping command

- `tracert`: The `tracert` command determines the route taken by sending ICMP echo requests to a destination computer. The displayed path is a list of the interfaces between a source and a destination router. This method also calculates which router failed and what the speed or latency is. If the router is busy, these results might not be reliable because the router assigns a low priority to the packets, as shown in the following screenshot:

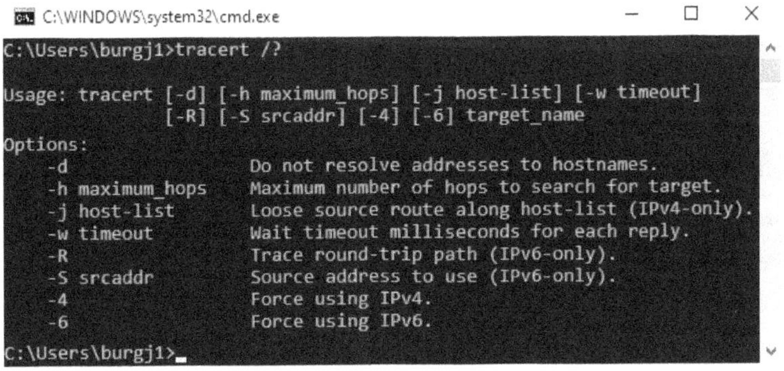

Figure 8.20 - The available command-line switches for the tracert command

- nslookup: The nslookup command displays information that the DNS network can be evaluated against, as shown in the following screenshot. Apart from the presence of the necessary records, you can use the tool to confirm the connection to the DNS server:

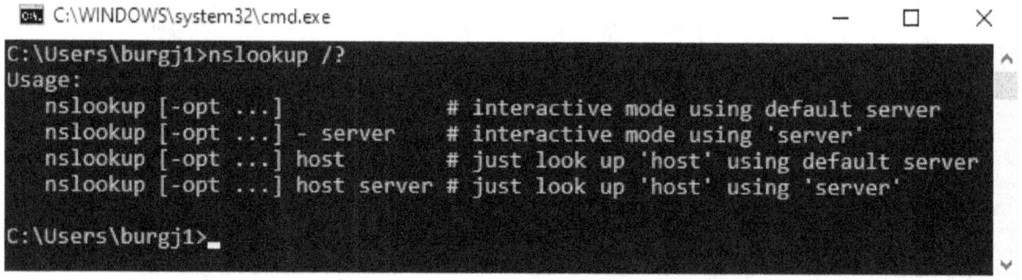

```
C:\Users\burgj1>nslookup /?
Usage:
    nslookup [-opt ...]              # interactive mode using default server
    nslookup [-opt ...] - server     # interactive mode using 'server'
    nslookup [-opt ...] host         # just look up 'host' using default server
    nslookup [-opt ...] host server  # just look up 'host' using 'server'

C:\Users\burgj1>_
```

Figure 8.21 - The available command-line switches for the nslookup command

- pathping: The pathping command traces a path through the network in a similar manner to the tracert method. However, pathping offers more detailed statistics through a network about the individual steps or hops taken. The command, as shown in the following screenshot, provides more detail because it sends 100 packets for each router, allowing it to set trends:

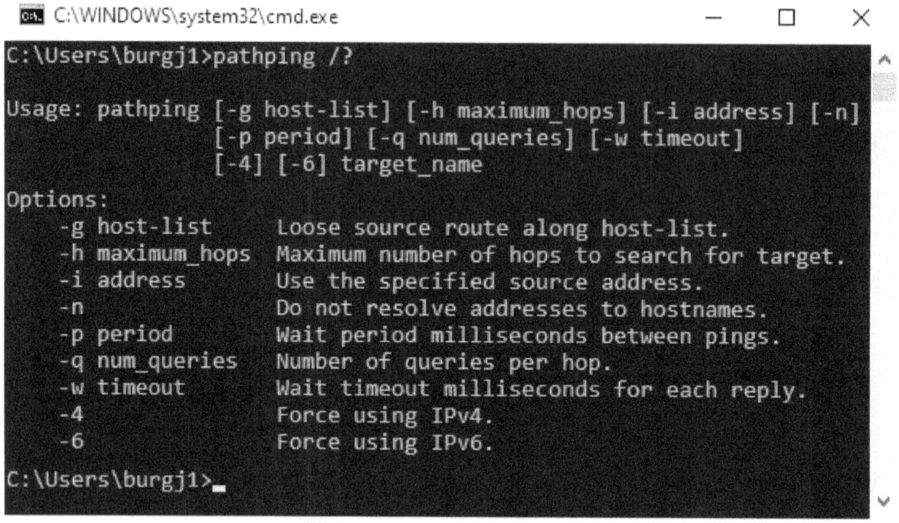

```
C:\Users\burgj1>pathping /?

Usage: pathping [-g host-list] [-h maximum_hops] [-i address] [-n]
                [-p period] [-q num_queries] [-w timeout]
                [-4] [-6] target_name
Options:
    -g host-list      Loose source route along host-list.
    -h maximum_hops   Maximum number of hops to search for target.
    -i address        Use the specified source address.
    -n                Do not resolve addresses to hostnames.
    -p period         Wait period milliseconds between pings.
    -q num_queries    Number of queries per hop.
    -w timeout        Wait timeout milliseconds for each reply.
    -4                Force using IPv4.
    -6                Force using IPv6.
C:\Users\burgj1>_
```

Figure 8.22 - The available command-line switches for the pathping command

- **PowerShell**: Configuring network connection settings can be achieved using **Windows PowerShell**. You can also use Windows PowerShell cmdlets to troubleshoot network configurations:

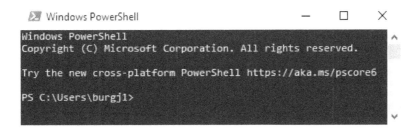

Figure 8.23 - The Windows PowerShell window

In this section, you learned about the possible tools to track networking issues in Windows 10. As you can see, there are many options to do this, but each command has its own command-line switches. It is advised that you carry out some practice tests because some command-line switchers will be on the exam.

Summary

In this chapter, you learned what IPv4 and IPv6 addresses are and how they work to communicate between two or more hosts. Another essential part of an IP address is the subnets, which indicate whether the computer is on the same network or another network. You also learned what public, private, and APIPA IP addresses are.

We talked about how you can connect your Windows 10 device to a cellular network and how you can share this internet connectivity with the built-in hotspot feature. Furthermore, you learned about the VPN possibilities in Windows 10 and how a VPN communicates with different protocols that you can use. You also learned how you can create a VPN connection and other VPN options, such as implementing Always On VPN so that users are always automatically connected to company resources on your corporate network.

Aside from the previously mentioned connectivities, you learned about the Wi-Fi 802.11x norms and you are now able to secure your wireless network. Furthermore, you now know how you can connect to a Wi-Fi network. Also, after reading this chapter, you are aware of the possible network issues you may encounter, how to troubleshoot those issues, and which tools you can use for this.

In the next chapter, you will learn about remote management via PowerShell to a Windows 10 device. By reading this chapter, you will understand how you can connect to a Windows 10 device with the use of the Remote Desktop Protocol.

Questions

1. Can you use a Class E network?

2. How many hosts can you connect to in a Class B network?

3. Which mechanism can you use to configure alternate IP settings?

4. Can Microsoft provide you with a cellular plan?

5. Is IKEv1 a valid VPN protocol?

6. Is WEP encryption the most secure Wi-Fi encryption that you can use?

Further reading

- **Understanding TCP/IP addressing and subnetting basics**: https://support.microsoft.com/en-us/help/164015/understanding-tcp-ip-addressing-and-subnetting-basics

- **Six benefits of IPv6**: https://www.networkcomputing.com/networking/six-benefits-ipv6

- **IPv4 address converter**: https://www.vultr.com/resources/ipv4-converter/

- **IPv6 explained for beginners**: http://www.steves-Internet-guide.com/ipv6-guide/

- **IEEE 802.11**: https://nl.wikipedia.org/wiki/IEEE_802.11

9
Configuring Remote Connectivity

When you use a lot of computers to manage devices in several locations, you must know how to enable and configure remote connectivity. It is also essential that you are able to handle those computers by using the remote management tools provided by **Windows 10**.

Windows 10 provides you with several tools that you can use to manage your organization's computers remotely. We will cover the **Remote Assistance**, **Remote Desktop**, and **PowerShell Remoting** tools in this chapter, as well as many other management console snap-ins. Knowing which resources to use to serve a given situation can help you handle the needs of your users faster.

We will cover the following topics in this chapter:

- Configuring remote management
- Configuring Remote Desktop access
- Enabling PowerShell Remoting

By providing you with the skills to use remote management with the built-in tools on Windows 10, after reading this chapter, you will be able to handle remote connectivity with ease.

Technical requirements

In this chapter, you will see us use PowerShell code. This code is available on the GitHub page at `https://github.com/PacktPublishing/Microsoft-Exam-MD-100-Windows-10-Certification-Guide/tree/master/Chapter09`.

Throughout this chapter, you will need to follow steps to configure many settings. The steps that you will follow have been recorded for your convenience. You can find the videos at `https://bit.ly/2LsQDqD`.

Configuring remote management

Remote management is a very effective and useful way for Windows administrators to access their (or others') computers and all of their contents remotely. It offers access functionality for a variety of computers and is optimized for remote **Personal Computer** (**PC**) control.

You can use a variety of tools to manage Windows 10 devices remotely. The five built-in tools for remote management are as follows:

- **Quick Assist**: This is the successor of the Remote Assistance tool. It provides interaction with a remote user, which you them to view or take control of a user's computer remotely. To initiate a session, you have to exchange a six-digit security code.

- **Remote Assistance**: This is a built-in tool that provides interaction with a remote user. By using this tool, you can view or take control of a user's computer remotely and perform remote management on its system.

- **Remote Desktop**: This is a built-in tool that you can use to access a computer remotely over the **Remote Desktop Protocol** (**RDP**). It does not provide user interaction and requires the user of the computer to sign out before you can access the computer remotely.

- **PowerShell**: PowerShell is a powerful command-line management tool used to script environments. You can use it to perform management functions on Windows 10. You can also use PowerShell to manage remote computers. This is known as **PowerShell Remoting**.

- **Microsoft Management Console** (**MMC**): This is an extensive interface for management applications. To perform management tasks with MMC, a specific tool—a **snap-in**—is loaded to the console. You can use MMC snap-ins to manage Windows 10 devices remotely.

Depending on the remote management tool you have decided on, you will almost certainly need to configure the target computer and, possibly, the local management computer to use the selected remote management tool.

In the next section, we will see how you can configure the firewall to allow remote management before we can use one of these tools.

Configuring the firewall to allow remote management

Before you start using remote management, you have to enable it through Windows Defender Firewall. You can do this by taking the following steps:

1. In **Control Panel**, click **System and Security | Windows Defender Firewall** option.

2. Then, in **Windows Defender Firewall**, click on the **Allow an app or feature through Windows Defender Firewall** option.

3. After that, in the **Allowed applications** window, click on the **Change Settings** option.

4. Then, in the **Allowed apps and features** list, scroll down and select the appropriate management feature. For example, we selected **Remote Assistance**, which enables the chosen management feature, as shown:

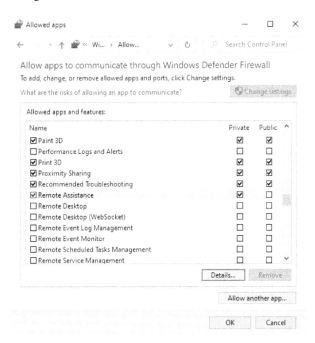

Figure 9.1 - The Allowed apps dialog box

In the preceding screenshot, you can also see the **Private** and **Public** checkboxes. In this example, if you also want to allow Remote Assistance over the internet, then you have to check the **Public** checkbox as well as the **Private** checkbox.

5. Lastly, click **OK**.

The available remote management features that you can turn on in the firewall are as follows:

- **Remote Assistance**
- **Remote Desktop**
- **Remote Event Log Management**
- **Remote Event Monitor**
- **Remote Scheduled Tasks Management**
- **Remote Shutdown**
- **Remote Volume Management**
- **Virtual Machine Monitoring**
- **Windows Defender Firewall Remote Management**
- **Windows Management Instrumentation**
- **Windows Remote Management**

It takes a lot of work to configure these settings manually on each computer and enable the appropriate remote management features. Instead of doing so manually, you can set these options with **Group Policy Objects** (**GPO**s) in an **Active Directory** domain.

You now know which services you have to allow on the Windows Defender Firewall to perform remote management. First, we will enable the Remote Desktop tool.

Enabling Remote Desktop

Remote Desktop is a useful Windows feature that allows you to access another computer from a PC on your network or from the internet. This function requires both computers to be connected to the internet and turned on. If these conditions are met, you can remotely use your PC to fix problems on any other computer. This feature also gives you full access to all the files stored on the other computer, as well as the live desktop.

You can use Remote Desktop on your Windows 10 PC or on your **Android** or **iOS** devices to connect to a PC that is far away.

Before you can use Remote Desktop, you will need to set up the remote PC to allow remote connections by taking the following steps:

1. On the remote PC, open **Settings** and select **System | Remote Desktop** option.

2. Click on the switch to change it from **Off** to **On**.

3. In the pop-up dialog box, click on **Confirm**:

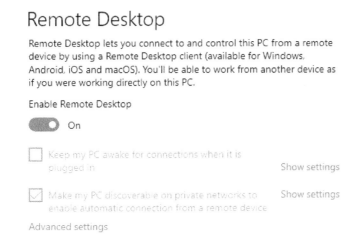

Figure 9.2 - The Remote Desktop services enabled on the remote computer

As you can see in the previous screenshot, the Remote Desktop services are enabled on the remote computer. From this moment onward, you can initiate a Remote Desktop connection to the remote computer.

So far, we have seen how to enable Remote Desktop. The next section shows us how we can configure Remote Assistance to map remote management.

Configuring Remote Assistance

A network administrator can access a device on a network with remote management tools and technologies to take control of and perform tasks on it, without needing to be physically present in front of the computer.

Reducing the number of trips required to service problem computers saves both time and money. Users can also use and operate on their machines/systems. Remote Assistance is a bundled Windows 10 service that helps a technician take control of a computer to troubleshoot and carry out maintenance tasks without having to travel directly to that machine.

This helps the technician solve any problems without having to leave their home or office. To allow this, the end user must be present and the user can terminate the session at any time. A system such as this is usually only used to troubleshoot remote computers and is not used to telecommute or access files or directories.

Remote Assistance connections are, by default, enabled for Windows 10 computers. If this is not the case on your computer, you can change this in the **System Properties** dialog box, as shown:

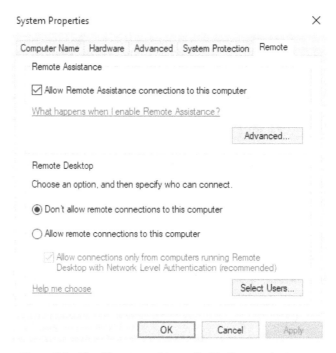

Figure 9.3 - Checkbox to enable or disable Remote Assistance

In the previous screenshot, you can configure the settings for **Remote Assistance** and **Remote Desktop** to allow or block another person from taking over your computer remotely.

There are a few ways of getting to the dialog box shown in the previous screenshot. One of the methods is as follows:

1. Right-click on the **Start** icon.

2. Then, select **System | System info** on the right-hand side of the window.

3. Click on **Remote Settings** in the left pane.

4. Check the box for **Allow Remote Assistance connections to this computer** and then click the **OK** button.

In this section, you learned how to take control of a remote computer by configuring Remote Assistance or by enabling **Remote Desktop**. Next up, we will show you how you can use MMC to perform management tasks on a remote computer.

Using MMC

You can use the RDP protocol to connect to a remote computer with both Remote Desktop and Remote Assistance. You can perform any management tasks after you have established a connection in the same way as if you had physical access to that remote computer. This, however, is not the case when using either the Windows Management Console or PowerShell Remoting.

For MMC, by changing the **Windows Defender Firewall** configuration, you need to give permission to the proper remote management functionality that you wish to take advantage of. You can then load the correct management console snap-in and select the desired remote computer.

The MMC snap-in is used to handle remote computers in a straightforward manner. Some management snap-ins allow you to specify additional computers from the console to connect to. You can right-click on the uppermost node in the navigation pane and then click on the **Connect to another computer...** option, as shown:

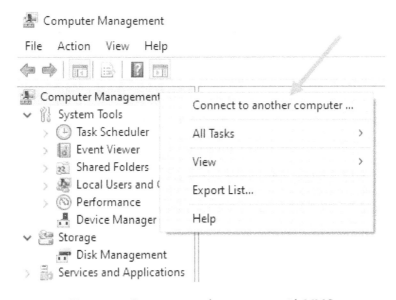

Figure 9.4 - Connect to another computer with MMC

If the management snap-in that you want to use does not allow you to connect to a remote computer by running `mmc.exe` and attaching the correct snap-in to the empty console, then you can create a new management console by choosing **Another computer**, as shown:

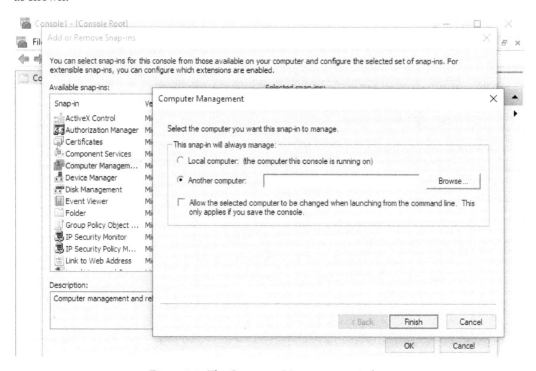

Figure 9.5 - The Computer Management window

It is essential that you realize that you will be recognized by the remote computer. This means you must authenticate your connection using a username and password on a target computer that has the appropriate management rights. This is easy to do because you can use the domain admin credentials in an **Active Directory Domain Services** (**AD DS**) domain environment. In a non-domain-joined environment, such as a **workgroup** computer, it is more difficult to connect remotely to a computer. Generally speaking, you must be able to provide the credentials of a local administrator of the target computer.

After you have activated the correct remote management features in **Windows Defender Firewall** and changed your MMC to use the appropriate credentials to connect to a remote computer, remote management is no different than local management.

So, we have now configured and enabled the required tools—namely, Remote Desktop, Remote Assistance, and MMC—for remote management tasks. In the next section, you will learn how you can use these tools to connect to a computer and perform remote management tasks.

Configuring Remote Desktop access

When Remote Desktop or Remote Assistance is allowed on a device, you can connect to the machine using Remote Desktop or Remote Assistance. When you are connected to the remote computer, you can use that computer as if you have signed in locally and perform all the management tasks that your user account has the right to do. This makes Remote Desktop a particularly useful tool.

Using Remote Desktop

To use Remote Desktop, you first need to create a remote desktop connection by taking the following steps:

1. Type `Remote Desktop Connection` in the search box on the taskbar.

2. Click on **Remote Desktop Connection**.

3. Then, fill in the full name or IP address of the remote computer, as in the following screenshot:

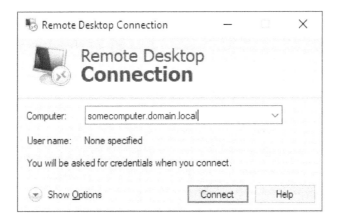

Figure 9.6 - Remote Desktop Connection window

4. After that, click on **Connect**.

    For now, we will just discuss how we can connect to a remote computer, not all of the different connection properties. You can configure additional connection properties by using the options in the tabs, as shown:

Figure 9.7 - Various connection properties of an RDP connection

As you can see in the previous screenshot, there are four tabs that you can use to configure your RDP connection properties. It is advised that you look through these connection properties. If you need to connect to a computer multiple times, then you can save the configuration to a `.rdp` file.

Instead of starting a **Remote Desktop** session through the **Graphical User Interface** (**GUI**), you can also start a **Remote Desktop** session via the command line with some parameters. You will learn more about this in the next section.

Customizing the Remote Desktop settings from the command line

The **Remote Desktop Service** app can be accessed by running `mstsc.exe` from the command line or from the **Windows Run** dialog box. This command allows administrators to start the application with several parameters configured.

There are different command-line syntaxes that you can use for `mstsc.exe`, which are as follows:

```
mstsc.exe [<Connection File>] [/v:<Server>[:<Port>]] [/admin]
[/f] [/w:<Width> /h:<Height>] [/public] [/span]
mstsc.exe /edit <Connection File>
mstsc.exe /migrate
```

We will now explain some of the parameters from the preceding example:

- `<connection file>`: Specifies the name of the `.rdp` file
- `/v:<server>:<port>`: Specifies the remote computer and, optionally, a different port number
- `/admin`: Connects you to the administering session of the server
- `/f`: Starts the Remote Desktop session in full screen mode
- `/w:<width> /h:<height>`: Specifies the width and height of the Remote Desktop window
- `/public`: Runs Remote Desktop in public mode, which means passwords and bitmaps are not cached
- `/span`: Spans the Remote Desktop session across multiple monitors
- `/edit <connection file>`: Opens the specified `.rdp` file for editing
- `/migrate`: Migrates legacy connection to the new `.rdp` files

An example of executing a Remote Desktop session to the `PACKTDC1` server, spanning the session across multiple monitors, is shown in the following screenshot:

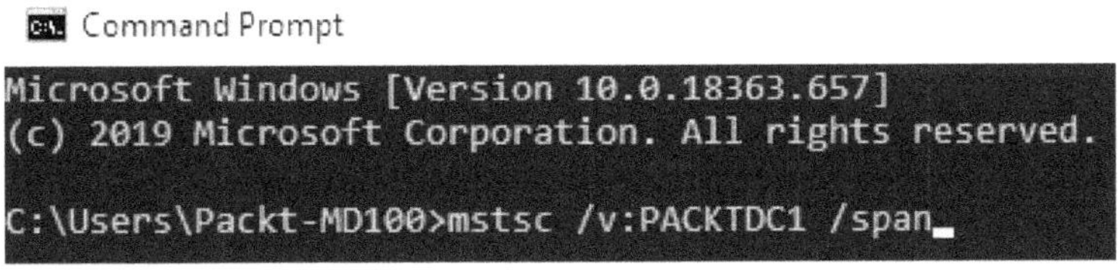

Figure 9.8 - An example command line for executing mstsc.exe

You can also start configuring RDP files through the GUI or the command line. You can also configure Remote Desktop with GPOs in an AD DS domain environment. To configure these settings, take the following steps:

1. Open **Group Policy Management**.

2. Then, locate the appropriate GPO.

3. Open the GPO for editing and navigate to `Computer Configuration\Policies\Administrative Templates\Windows Components\Remote Desktop Services`, as shown:

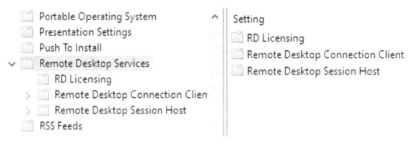

Figure 9.9 - The Remote Desktop Services GPO setting

As you can see in the previous screenshot, there are three more subfolders with settings that you can configure for **Remote Desktop Services**.

In this section, you have learned how to connect to another computer with the Remote Desktop app or via the command line. In an AD DS domain environment, you can use a GPO to configure these settings. You now know how to work with Remote Desktop, so we can proceed on to understanding the next tool—Remote Assistance.

Using Remote Assistance

To use Remote Assistance, the user must be at the computer that they are having problems with (for example, a software issue). The user must initiate a Remote Assistance session and the remote user must approve the connection before it can be made.

You can request remote assistance by taking the following steps:

1. Type `Remote Assistance` or `Invite someone` in the taskbar's search box.

2. Then, choose the **Invite someone to connect to your PC and help you, or offer to help someone else** option.

3. This will open up the **Windows Remote Assistance** wizard. Then select the **Invite someone you trust to help you** option, as shown:

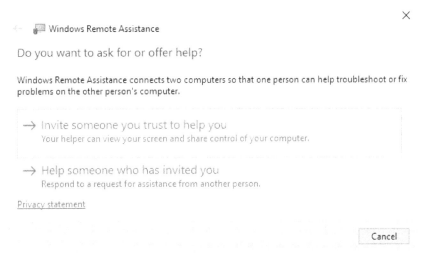

Figure 9.10 - The Do you want to ask for or offer help? window

4. After you have clicked **Invite someone you trust to help you,** you have three options to send this request to your helper. The following screenshot shows you these three options, which are **Save this invitation as a file, Use email to send an invitation,** and **Use Easy Connect** (only available if enabled):

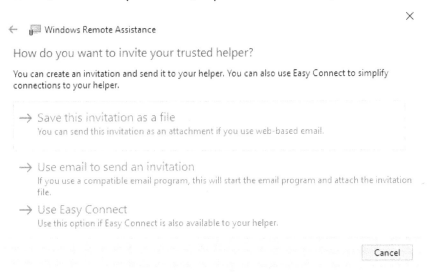

Figure 9.11 - The How do you want to invite your trusted helper? window

5. After your helper receives the invitation file and opens it, a secure connection is set up and the helper can help you with your problem.

You now know how to use Remote Desktop and Remote Assistance, but Microsoft also released a new tool called **Quick Assist**. In the next section, you will learn how you can use this tool.

Using Quick Assist

Microsoft Quick Assist is the successor to Remote Assistance and was introduced to **Windows 10 version 1607**.

Quick Assist lets two people share a computer over a remote connection so that one person can help solve problems on the other person's computer, just as with Remote Assistance. The version of Windows 10 that you have installed may determine whether Quick Assist or Remote Assistance is available to you.

To start with Quick Assist, follow these steps:

1. Type `Quick Assist` in the taskbar's search box and then choose **Quick Assist**.

2. The **Quick Assist** app will open, as in the following screenshot:

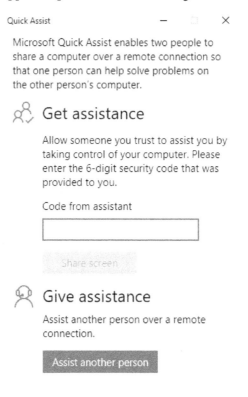

Figure 9.12 - The Quick Assist start screen

The previous screenshot shows how, depending on your situation, you can choose from the following options:

- If you want to get assistance from someone, fill in the six-digit code that you received and click on **Share screen**.

- If you wish to assist someone, click on **Assist another person** and give the other person the six-digit generated code.

In this section, you learned how you can use the Remote Desktop, Remote Assistance, and Quick Assist tools to help another person resolve their problems.

To manage domain-joined or workgroup computers, you can also use Windows PowerShell Remoting. In the next section, you will learn what PowerShell Remoting is and how you can use it.

Enabling PowerShell Remoting

PowerShell can be used to control remote computers with **Windows PowerShell Remoting**. First, you need to learn how to allow and configure it.

PowerShell is commonly available across the Windows platform, including on both Windows 10 and Windows Server. Therefore, it makes sense to use PowerShell to execute management tasks on both local and remote machines because you can pass those skills on to other management situations.

Most cmdlets in PowerShell can be used with the `-ComputerName` parameter, making it a bit easier to use the command remotely than defining the name of the computer that you wish to run the command against. Run the following cmdlet as an example of how to determine the IP configuration of a remote computer:

```
Get-NetIPConfiguration -ComputerName PACKTCL1
```

However, not all cmdlets accept the `-ComputerName` parameter, and you must enable and configure PowerShell Remoting (explained further in the *Enabling PowerShell Remoting* section) for these parameters.

The PowerShell Remoting function is used to allow you to connect to one or more remote computers and execute one or more cmdlets or scripts on those remote computers, returning the results to your local computer.

The remote features of Windows PowerShell are supported by the **Web Services Management** (**WS-Management**) protocol and the **Windows Remote Management** (**WinRM**) service, which implements WS-Management on Windows. Computers running Windows 7 (and later versions) have **WinRM 2.0** (or higher).

> **Important Note**
>
> To use the PowerShell Remoting features, you must start Windows PowerShell as an administrator by right-clicking on the Windows PowerShell shortcut and selecting **Run As Administrator**. You can start this program as an administrator when you start to run or execute PowerShell from another application, such as the **Command Prompt** (cmd.exe).

By following these steps, you can check the availability of WinRM and configure PowerShell Remoting:

1. Start **PowerShell** as an administrator by right-clicking on the PowerShell shortcut.

2. Then, select **Run As Administrator**.

3. The WinRM service is configured to manual startup. You must change the type of startup to **Automatic** and start the service on every computer that you want to work on. You can verify that the WinRM service is running on the **PowerShell** prompt by using the following command:

```
Get-Service winrm
```

The output of the previous command can be seen in the following screenshot:

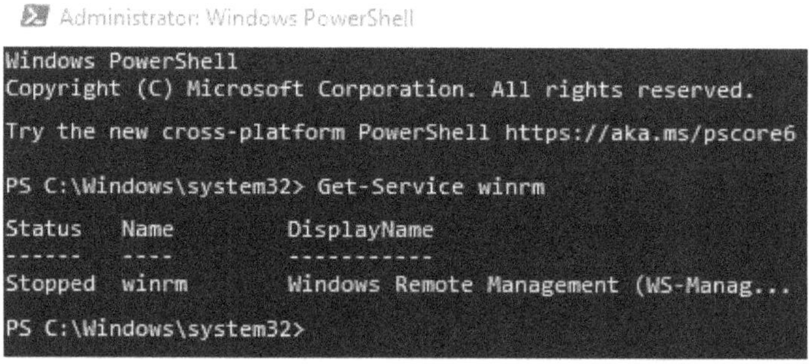

Figure 9.13 - Output values of the winrm cmdlet

As you can see in the previous screenshot, the output of the **Status** property value is **Stopped**. To manage this computer, the **Status** property value should be **Running**.

4. To configure Windows PowerShell for remote access, type in the following command:

```
Enable-PSRemoting -Force
```

When you execute the previous command in a **Windows PowerShell** window, the output will look as in the following screenshot:

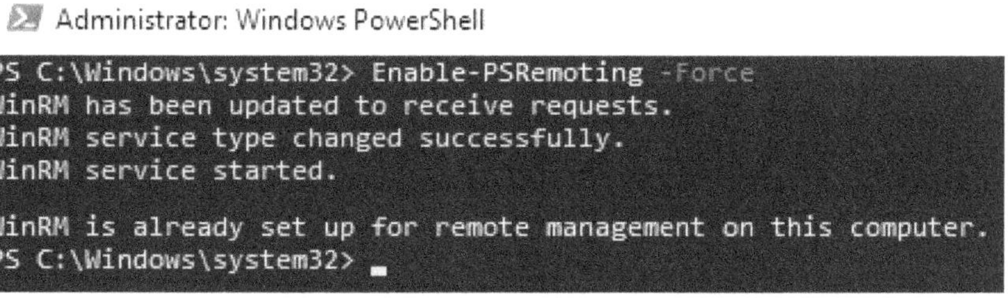

Figure 9.14 - Output of the Enable-PSRemoting -Force cmdlet

5. After you have executed the previous cmdlet and the output is similar to what can be seen in the preceding screenshot, if you re-run the Get-Service WinRM cmdlet, you will see that the **Status** property value has changed to **Running**, as shown:

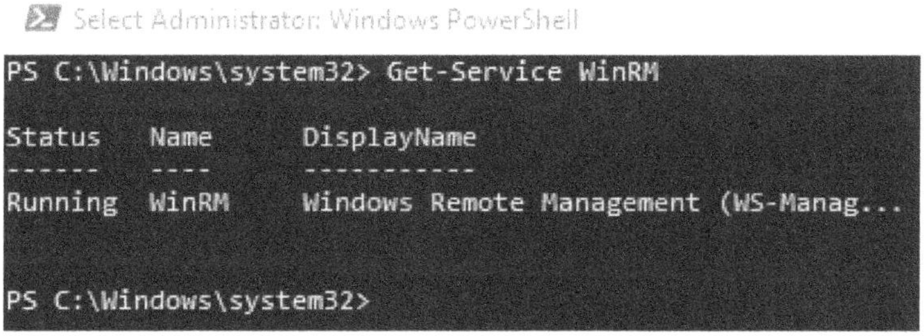

Figure 9.15 - The WinRM service is now running

In many cases, you'll be able to work in other domains with remote computers. However, if the remote computer is not on a trusted domain, your credentials may not be authenticated by the remote computer. To allow authentication, you need to add the remote computer to the **WinRM Local Computer Trusted Hosts** list.

To do this, run the following code:

```
winrm set winrm/config/client '@{TrustedHosts="RemoteComputer"}
```

At this point, `RemoteComputer` should be the name of the remote computer, as follows:

```
winrm set winrm/config/client '@{TrustedHosts="PACKTCL2"}'
```

You must either use **Hypertext Transfer Protocol Secure** (**HTTPS**) as the transport or add the remote machine to the `TrustedHosts` configuration settings when operating on computers in workgroups or homegroups. If you can't connect to a remote host, then you should verify whether the service is running on the remote host and make sure it accepts requests by executing the following command on the remote host:

```
winrm quickconfig
```

This command analyzes and configures the WinRM service on that particular remote host.

In this section, you learned how to enable PowerShell Remoting and checked whether the services were running. You can now carry out management tasks via PowerShell Remoting on remote computers. You also now know that enabling PowerShell Remoting on a domain environment is much simpler than setting up PowerShell Remoting on a workgroup environment.

Summary

In this chapter, you learned a lot of new things about performing remote management tasks on remote computers, such as how you can configure Windows Defender Firewall to allow remote management. You also learned about the built-in tools to perform remote management on remote computers—Remote Desktop, Remote Assistance, MMC, and Windows PowerShell Remoting.

You also learned which tools you can use to give support to or ask for support from other people. You can now use Remote Desktop, Remote Assistance, and Quick Assist for this type of support. MMC and PowerShell Remoting are used for remote management tasks on remote computers, such as workstations or servers, but you can also use Remote Desktop for remote server management.

In the next chapter, you will learn about the different ways to troubleshoot errors in Windows 10, such as file recovery and recovering a complete Windows 10 installation or application. We will also look at troubleshooting during the startup or boot process of Windows 10.

Questions

1. Is Quick Assist a remote management feature that you can turn on in the firewall?

2. Is the RDP protocol used by the Microsoft Management Console to connect to remote hosts?

3. Can you start the Remote Desktop Connection app via the command line and specify specific connection properties?

Further reading

- **Solve PC problems over a remote connection with Quick Assist**: `https:// support.microsoft.com/en-us/help/4027243/windows-10-solve-pc-problems-with-quick-assist`

- **How to configure the Remote Desktop options**: `https://www.dummies.com/ computers/computer-networking/configure-remote-desktop-options/`

- **Mstsc**: `https://docs.microsoft.com/en-us/windows-server/ administration/windows-commands/mstsc`

- **How to run PowerShell commands on remote computers**: `https://www. howtogeek.com/117192/how-to-run-powershell-commands-on-remote-computers/`

Section 4: Maintaining Windows

In this section, you will get an understanding of how to troubleshoot the operating system and apps, as well as how to deal with other errors. We will also look at the different update strategies.

This section comprises the following chapters:

- *Chapter 10, Understanding Troubleshooting and Recovery*
- *Chapter 11, Managing Updates*
- *Chapter 12, Managing Log Files*

10
Understanding Troubleshooting and Recovery

Your organization most likely has a file recovery strategy in place to recover user data stored on network file servers or storage devices that are accessible through the network. It's important to remember, however, that users often save their work to local computers. Therefore, you must provide a local file recovery method, so that you can recover these data files if users accidentally delete them or they get corrupted.

The following topics will be covered in this chapter:

- Performing file recovery
- Recovering Windows 10
- Troubleshooting the startup/boot process
- Troubleshooting applications

This chapter will provide you with the skills to troubleshoot applications, troubleshoot the startup/boot process, and perform file recovery and recover Windows 10. This chapter will help you to prepare for the **MD-100** (Windows 10) exam, which is part of the **Microsoft 365 Certified: Modern Desktop Administrator Associate** certification.

Technical requirements

In this chapter, you will see PowerShell code. The code is available on the following GitHub page: `https://github.com/PacktPublishing/Microsoft-Exam-MD-100-Windows-10-Certification-Guide/tree/master/Chapter10`

Throughout this chapter, you need to follow some steps to configure settings. These steps are also recorded. You can find the videos here: `https://bit.ly/2LsQDqD`

Performing file recovery

A computer contains various types of data that it stores at different locations. Types of computer data include configuration files for the **Operating System** (**OS**), user-related settings for the device, and user data. The latter might consist of documents, photographs, spreadsheets, and other file types. Computers are highly reliable, and most operating systems are stable and recoverable, but there are issues that can sometimes result in data loss.

To avoid data loss, we strongly recommend that user data is maintained on file servers or cloud-based solutions, where it is readily accessible and securely backed up. Windows tools, such as **Folder Redirection** or **OneDrive**, include transparent and secure offline access to reliable storage for users.

A system malfunction could be as easy as resetting the **Personal Computer** (**PC**) or providing a new PC in familiar situations and workloads, allowing the user to continue working on login. Enabling these solutions will result in considerable time savings when troubleshooting and dealing with data-loss-related costs and when resources are needed to support the recovery of desktop data.

But it is not always possible to store all data remotely. So, you need to be able to recover local data in case of hardware failure or other situations such as the following:

- A user unintentionally removes or deletes a file or a whole folder.

- Malware or a virus infects a computer, and user files are modified or encrypted.

- A user makes several modifications to a file but later decides that the changes were unnecessary and wants to access the original file.

- There is a natural disaster such as a fire, flood, or hurricane, and it destroys the machine.

- Data from a user does not frequently synchronize with the file server and is then stolen. The user wants new versions of the data to be accessed.

A computer can store data files and settings in multiple locations, and you need to make sure you secure them all. Windows 10 includes some tools that can help to protect your data and back up local files, including the following:

- **Folder Redirection** and **Offline Files**: Folder Redirection redirects local files from the user profile to the file server in a domain system. Offline Files include a local copy of the redirected files and make them available even if there is no network access to the file server.

- **Work Folders**: You can use Work Folders for whatever domain membership you might have. Work Folders synchronize data files between users and computers on the file servers.

- **File History**: Upon allowing File History, it will automatically create a backup of changed user files on the local drive, removable drive, or network location. File History backs up directories in user-profiles and databases, and additional folders may be added. By default, File History copies the changed files every hour in secure folders, and Windows 10 stores them forever, as long as there is ample storage space.

- **Backup and Restore (Windows 7)**: While the tool's name includes Windows 7, it is a part of Windows 10. It's supposed to restore files in Windows 10 from a Windows 7 backup.

- **Synchronization of user data with Microsoft OneDrive or OneDrive for Business**: If your user account is connected to a Microsoft account or your business uses OneDrive for Business, you can synchronize data files with the cloud and between the devices you are using.

- **Creation of a system image**: A system image is not meant to be a solution for Backup and Restore, but it provides an exact copy of all of the data that was on a computer when you built it. There's no way to create a system image production schedule. You can transfer images of the device to hard disks, DVD sets, or network locations. A system image contains a virtual hard disk (`.vhdx` file) for every volume of the device you are creating the image for. Within **File Explorer**, you can mount the virtual disk and independently access and restore each file. If you want the entire system image to be restored, you can use the **Windows Recovery Environment (Windows RE) System Image Recovery** option.

- `Wbamin.exe`: This command-line tool can be used to create backups and restore the backup content.

- **File Explorer** (`robocopy.exe`): You can use either File Explorer or the `robocopy.exe` tool to copy files to other media or a network location manually.

- **Microsoft Azure Backup**: Azure Backup is not included in Windows 10. But if you have a subscription to Microsoft Azure, you can create a Backup Vault, download and install the **Azure Backup Agent**, and then back up Windows 10 to Microsoft Azure.

In this chapter, we will not deal extensively with the different tools of backup or File History. The advice is to look at that independently and what the possibilities are. In the next section, you will learn about the File History feature and how it works.

Understanding File History

When using the File History feature, Windows 10 automatically saves copies of your files to a removable local drive or a network shared folder. Upon allowing File History, it regularly saves a copy of your updated files to a designated location. Windows 10 saves updated files every hour and holds new versions of files forever. You can, however, configure the interval at which the saves occur and how long Windows 10 will keep files saved.

> **Important Note**
> The location of the File History storage you choose can be on a local drive, a removable drive, or a location on the network.

File History saves by default the files from the following directories, which can be found at `C:\Users\<username>`:

- `Saved Games`
- `Links`

- Downloads

- Favorites

- Contacts

- OneDrive

- Desktop

- 3D Objects

- Searches

File History also saves files from the following libraries:

- Pictures

- Documents

- Videos

- Music

The preceding directories can be seen in the following screenshot:

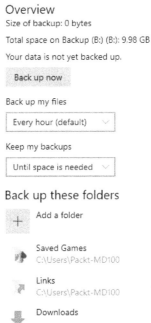

Figure 10.1 - The Backup options page

By using File History, you can secure files in two ways:

- In the **Settings** app, use the **Backup** option in the **Update & Security** section. To access that option, click **Settings | Update & Security | Backup | More options** in the **Back up using File History** window, which can be seen in the following screenshot:

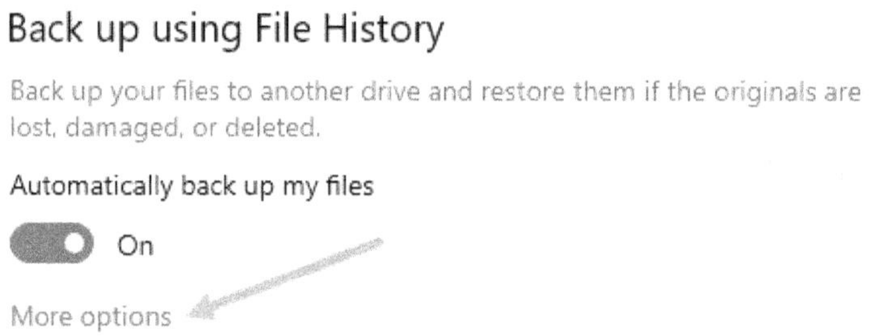

Figure 10.2 - More options link in the Back up using File History window

> **Important Note**
> You cannot add additional folders to the File History item in **Control Panel**.

- File History also protects folders that you add to one of the protected libraries. Configuring File Explorer to show libraries and modifying the library properties to include additional folders can help to secure these folders. If you create a new library, it will automatically be protected by File History.

Using the File History feature in the **Control Panel**, you can change the File History settings. You can also change these settings from the **Settings** app by clicking **Update & Security | Backup | More options** link in the **Backup** tab using **File History**. By using the item File History in the **Control Panel**, you can start a backup manually. Additionally, you can configure how often backups should be performed and how long backups should be retained. You can also define the drive that will hold backups of the File History and exclude from File History folders and libraries.

You can use **File Explorer** to return to previous versions of files that are covered by File History. You can use it by right-clicking the file or folder to restore files and then clicking on the **Previous Versions** tab.

You can also navigate to the folder that contains a changed or deleted file, press **History** to open **File History** on the **Home** ribbon, and then view the recoverable files. Alternatively, you can directly use the **Restore your files with File History** option, allowing you to compare changed files and recover deleted or updated files.

File History backs up protected folders into a folder hierarchy and names the top folder as the username of the logged-in account. File History will back up the data to the **Data** folder's subfolders, as shown in the following screenshot:

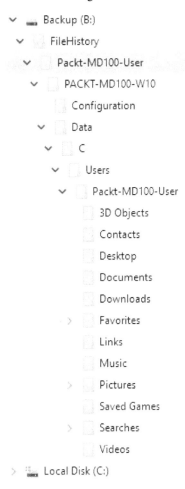

Figure 10.3 - The folder structure of the backup

From the previous screenshot, you can see that File History names the first level subfolder after the computer from which the data stored is backed up and names the **Configuration** and **Data** subfolders of the second level.

> **Important Note**
> Previous versions of **OneDrive** files and folders are accessible via the online OneDrive portal. For companies with **OneDrive for Business** and **SharePoint**, consult with **SharePoint Manager** for versioning settings.

Now you know about File History and how you can turn this feature on. In the next section, you are going to understand the functionality of the **Previous Versions** tab.

Learning about the Previous Versions tab

The **File Explorer** tab for **Previous Versions** is a feature included in Windows 10. This feature allows users to view, restore, or reverse previous versions of files, directories, or volumes. File History or restore point data fills in the **Previous Versions** tab. Therefore, to be able to use the Previous Versions function, you must configure either File History or restore the points.

The Previous Versions tab for all files is empty until either you run File History for the first time or, while using the **Backup and Restore (Windows 7)** feature, you make the original backup. File History data populates the Previous Versions tab only for files that are covered by File History. For instance, in Folder1, you can change File1.txt, but if File History does not protect Folder1, then the Previous Versions tab remains empty.

The Windows 7 (Backup and Restore) feature works similarly. This allows you to use preceding versions for any file on a **New Technology File System** (**NTFS**) volume that contains the backup. For example, if you are using the Backup and Restore (Windows 7) tool to back up Folder1, only the data from restore points for Folder1 and all of its contents will fill in the **Previous Versions** tab. The following screenshot shows you the **Previous Versions** tab for File1.txt:

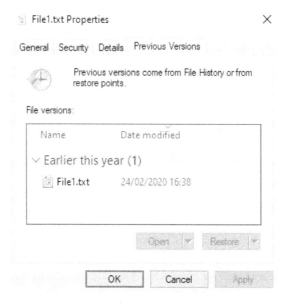

Figure 10.4 - The Previous Versions tab

If you configure File History and use the Backup and Restore (Windows 7) tool, the **Previous Versions** tab will be filled in by data from both sources. After that, each time File History runs, a new version of the file becomes available for any file protected by File History.

> **Important Note**
>
> The **Previous Versions** tab shows **Previous versions come from File History or restore points.** This message does not, however, apply to restore points created by **System Restore**. This message refers to the points that are generated by the **Backup and Restore (Windows 7)** tool.

When a backup is created by the Backup and Restore (Windows 7) tool, it also automatically adds a new version of the file. If the backup is generated by File History or Backup and Restore (Windows 7), you can only restore files and folders to the versions included in the backup.

> **Important Note**
>
> The function of Previous Versions is available in Windows 10, irrespective of which file system you are using. Nevertheless, the Windows 7 (Backup and Restore) tool can only back up data from NTFS volumes. So, File History will only protect specific files, if you want to use the Previous Versions option for files on the **File Allocation Table** (**FAT**) file system.

In this section, you learned how the Previous Versions feature can be used and learned about its benefits. But you have to be aware of specific requirements and benefits that are suitable to your environment. In the next section, we are going to compare the file recovery options.

Comparing file recovery options

Each Windows 10 file recovery option has specific requirements and benefits, and all options offer protection and recovery of NTFS volume files and folders. Nevertheless, their design does have important differences. When you consider, for example, which file recovery option to use, ask yourself the following questions:

- *How often does an option create backups of the protected content?*

- *What kind of content and file systems does an option protect?*

- *Can an option protect and recover a computer's system state?*

- *Can I use a different computer to recover content than that on which I created it?*

Windows 10 offers two options for file recovery: **File History** and **Backup and Restore (Windows 7)**. You don't have to install any apps to use these tools, but you need to configure them first. If you need to restore files that you are protecting using either of these methods, you can use the Previous Versions function. Windows 10 doesn't provide **Azure Backup**, as Azure Backup is a paid service of Azure. So, before using Azure Backup to restore files, you have to make sure of the following:

1. Purchase a **Microsoft Azure** subscription.

2. Create a backup vault.

3. Install the **Microsoft Azure Backup** agent.

4. Register the computer with the backup vault.

> **Important Note**
> Azure Backup does not integrate with the Windows 10 Previous Versions feature. You can use the Microsoft Azure Backup program to manage Azure Backups.

All three options, namely, File History, Backup and Restore (Windows 7), and Azure Backup, can secure and restore files and folders saved on an NTFS disk, which is Windows 10's most common file system. If files are stored on other file systems, such as FAT, FAT32, **Extensible File Allocation Table** (**exFAT**), or **Resilient File System** (**ReFS**), you can only use File History to protect and retrieve them. The Windows Backup and Restore (Windows 7) tool and Azure Backup do not support those file systems. If you need the ability to recover a full Windows 10 device, and not just files and directories, the Windows Backup and Restore (Windows 7) tool is necessary. This tool alone can create a system state image that uses **bare-metal recovery**.

When configuring File History, this creates by default a backup of the protected content every hour. You can customize the File History to make backups more often, with 10 minutes being the shortest time, and 24 hours being the longest time that you can set up. The Windows Backup and Restore feature (Windows 7) offers a weekly software backup, every Sunday at 19:00 hours, set by default.

When using the Backup and Restore (Windows 7) functionality, you can adjust the backup frequency to an hourly basis, and you can schedule backups that occur more regularly when using **Task Scheduler**. Conversely, Azure Backup is unable to create backups more often than three times a day.

Both the Backup and Restore (Windows 7) tool and Azure Backup are capable of recovering files and folders on the same computer that created the backup and on different computers. However, File History can recover files and folders only on the computer that created the backup. If you have permissions, you can access backup folders in File History and manually restore files from any computer because the backup that File History performs is based on files.

In this section, you compared the different file recovery options, that are available in Windows 10. In the next section, you will learn to troubleshoot issues with file recovery.

Troubleshooting file recovery

If you wish to use file recovery, backup copies of files and folders that you want to recover must exist. The copies must be accessible, and you must have the appropriate file and folder recovery tool. **File History**, the Windows 7 Backup and Restore tool, and Azure Backup will not create backup copies until you configure them. For example, a previous version of the file will not be available in the **File Properties** dialog box on the Previous Versions tab until File History or the Windows Backup and Restore (Windows 7) tool creates a backup copy of that file.

If you are using Azure Backup, you can store backup copies of locally located files and folders in a shared folder or Microsoft Azure. If you want to do file recovery, backup copies must be made available. For example, if you create backup copies on a removable disk, you need to attach that disk to your Windows 10 computer, that is, if you want to do file recovery.

If you store backup copies in a shared folder, you need network connectivity to the file server and permissions to access the shared folder to recover files. If your backup is stored in Microsoft Azure, the following must be in place:

- Internet connectivity
- The Microsoft Azure Backup program
- Vault credentials
- A passphrase to enable the file recovery that is to be done

The current vault credentials can always be downloaded from the Microsoft Azure portal.

On the computer that you make a backup on, a passphrase is created, and you use it to encrypt your backup. You should store your passphrase safely since, without a valid passphrase, you won't be able to recover data. You need to provide vault credentials and a passphrase if you want to recover files on a computer other than the one you've created the backup on. If you misplace or lose the passphrase that you used to encrypt the backup, you can't access backup content.

> **Important Note**
>
> If you are unable to access a remotely saved file backup, you should use standard network troubleshooting. If a file backup is stored locally and the backup location is not accessible, you should perform local storage troubleshooting. For example, if the local disk is connected and displays in **Device Manager** and **Disk Management**, you should look in **Event Viewer** for any disk-related entries.

File History stores backups within a hierarchy of folders. When using Previous Versions or File History, you can restore the backup only to the computer on which the backup was created. If you want to restore files and folders from a backup, you need to manually copy and rename the files and folders on different computers than the one you created it on.

In this section, you learned how you could perform file recovery through different methods, such as File History and Backup and Restore. You learned how to configure File History and the Previous Versions tab to recover files and folders. Furthermore, you know that the Windows 10 file recovery option has specific requirements and benefits, and all options offer protection and recovery of NTFS volume files and folders. The decision to implement the right choice of file recovery is strongly dependent on the needs of your organization.

In the next section, you are going to learn how you can recover Windows 10.

Recovering Windows 10

Windows 10 is a reliable OS. Occasionally, however, you will encounter problems with devices from your users that require you to perform some recovery of the OS. The nature of the problem will decide the particular course of action, and as a result, Microsoft has provided several recovery options in Windows 10.

Some of these are relatively benign and allow you to investigate and resolve the underlying problem with little effect on the OS. Others are more intrusive and can result in the OS being rolled back to an earlier point in time or even to its initial state. These recovery tools are listed as follows:

- **Recovery Drive**
- **System Restore**
- **Windows Recovery Environment (WinRE)**
- **Reset this PC**
- **Fresh start**

Let's see what each of these tools do in Windows 10.

Configuring a Recovery Drive

Many Windows 10 PCs will have a recovery partition containing a full system image. If your computer isn't starting correctly, you can start the recovery partition.

Disk drive space is often smaller on many small form factor devices and tablets than what is available on a laptop or desktop. This may limit the availability to include a recovery partition for an **Original Equipment Manufacturer** (**OEM**) on devices shipped with Windows 10. If there is no partition to recover, you can still create a recovery drive based on a **bootable USB drive**. You can boot into the Recovery Environment using this drive. You will then need to access a system image created by you or provided by the OEM.

To **Create a recovery drive**, follow these steps:

1. Click on **Start**.

2. Search for `Recovery Disk` and open the app; this will open the Recovery Drive window, as shown in the following screenshot:

Figure 10.5 - Recovery Drive wizard

3. Make sure that **Back up system files to the recovery drive** is selected.

4. Then, click **Next**.

5. In **Select the USB flash drive**, choose your USB flash drive and click **Next**, as shown in the following screenshot:

Figure 10.6 - The Select the USB flash drive dialog box

6. Click the **Create** button to **Create the recovery drive**:

Figure 10.7 - Create the recovery drive dialog box

7. The wizard is now **Creating the recovery drive**:

Figure 10.8 - Wizard is now creating the recovery drive

If your computer has a recovery partition, you will see a link to uninstall the recovery partition from your PC when the recovery drive has been provisioned on the removable media. This relates to the recovery partition of Windows 10 devices and not the newly created Recovery Drive. If you want your device to free up space, you must select this option. It is essential to store the recovery drive in a safe place because if you lose the recovery drive and delete the recovery partition, you will not be able to recover your device.

> **Important Note**
>
> Some devices will support the use of **Secure Digital High-Capacity** (**SDHC**) memory cards. The **Recovery Drive** Wizard will be able to use an SDHC card as an alternative to a USB flash drive.

After they are created, you should carefully label your Recovery Drive files. Note that a **64-bit** (**x64**) Recovery Drive can be used only to reinstall a 64-bit architecture device. The Windows 10 Recovery Drive can't be used to repair older Windows versions.

Now you know how you can configure a Recovery Drive. Up next, we will take a look at how you can set System Restore.

Learning about System Restore

In an earlier version of Windows, such as **Windows XP** or **Windows 7**, you might have used System Restore to restore a computer that has become unstable. System Restore has been retained in Windows 10 and offers a familiar and reliable system recovery method by restoring the OS to a restore point created during the stability period.

Windows 10 does not automatically enable System Restore features. System Restore takes snapshots of your computer system, then saves them as points of restore. These restore points represent a point in time when it was running successfully for the configuration of the computer. The use of System Restore does not affect user data.

After you have enabled System Restore points, Windows 10 will automatically create them when the following actions take place:

- You install a new application or driver.
- You uninstall certain programs.
- You install updates.

Windows 10 also creates System Restore points:

- Manually, whenever you choose to create them

- Automatically, once daily

- Automatically, if you decide to use System Restore to restore to a previous point in time

System Restore creates a new restore point in this last instance, before restoring the system to an earlier state. This gives you an option for recovery if the restore operation fails or leads to problems. Nevertheless, if you are in safe mode and you restore to a former state, Windows RE will not generate a restore point for the current state.

Follow these steps to turn on **System Restore** and manually create a restore point:

1. Type in the **Search** bar `Create a restore point` and open the app. The resultant window is shown in the following screenshot:

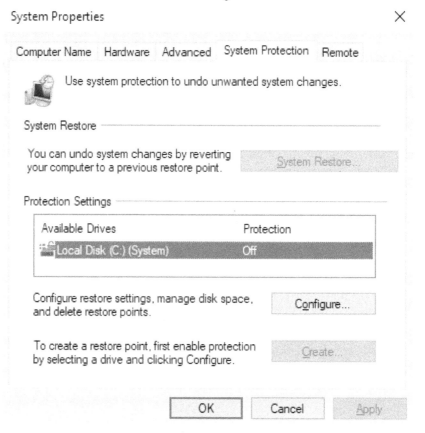

Figure 10.9 - The System Properties tab

> **Tip**
>
> You can also open **System Properties** with the keyboard shortcut *Windows+Pause/Break* and then click in the left pane on **System Protection**.

2. Then, click on the **Configure...** button:

Figure 10.10 - The System Protection for Local Disk (C:) dialog box

3. Select the **Turn on system protection** option.

4. You can additionally move the slider under **Disk Space Usage** to allow room on the restore points to be saved.

You can also customize **System Restore** using **PowerShell**. Some of the commands you need to review are as follows:

*   `Enable-ComputerRestore`: This command allows System Restore feature on the specified drive.

*   `Disable-ComputerRestore`: It disables the System Restore feature on the specified drive.

- `Get-ComputerRestorePoint`: It gets the restore points on the local computer.

- `Checkpoint-Computer`: It creates a System Restore point on the local computer.

If the amount of space reserved for restore points is full, the oldest restore points will be removed automatically by System Restore. If more restore points are needed to be used, a more significant proportion of the hard disk must be allocated to the feature.

If the program has created restore points, you are safe, and the system should be recoverable.

To recover your system, you can launch the **System Restore** wizard from either of the following:

- **System Protection**: If your system allows you to sign in to Windows, you can start the **System Restore...** option in the **System Properties** dialog box and follow the wizard to restore to a restore point that was created earlier:

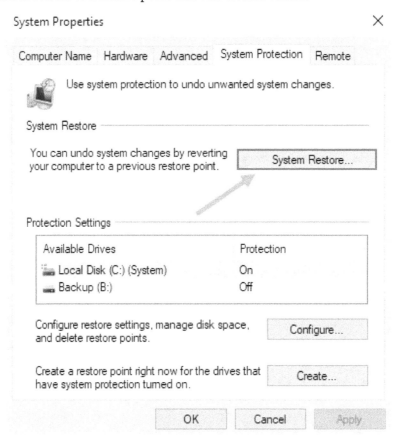

Figure 10.11 - The System Restore option

- **Windows Recovery Environment (Windows RE)**: If the system doesn't allow you to sign in, you can boot from the **Advanced** options to the Windows RE and start the **System Restore** wizard.

In this section, you learned how you could enable and create restore points in Windows 10. To restore a restore point, you could use the Windows RE. We will handle this feature in the next section.

Understanding the Windows Recovery Environment

If your Windows machine fails to start correctly, a variety of methods can be used to help to solve the problem. Such resources are discussed in this section.

Windows RE is a **Windows Preinstalling Environment** (**Windows PE**) based recovery tool. Windows RE uses two main features. These main features are: diagnosing and repairing automated startup issues and providing a unified platform for further advanced recovery tools.

If you want to access the Windows RE environment and your Windows 10 has started (booted) normally, you can access Windows RE by following any one of these steps:

- Click **Start** | the **Power** option, then hold the *Shift* key while clicking **Restart**.
- Click **Start** | **Settings** | **Update & security** | **Recovery** option under **Advanced Startup**, then click **Restart now**.
- At the login screen, click **Shutdown**, then hold the *Shift* key while selecting **Restart**.
- Boot to recovery media.
- From Command Prompt, run the following command:

```
shutdown /r /o
```

If you are unable to boot Windows successfully, you can access Windows RE by doing one of the following:

- Attach the media in Windows 10, then power on the computer. Execute the **Windows 10 Media Setup** program, if requested. After configuring the **Language and Keyboard** settings, pick the **Repair your computer** option, which scans the computer for Windows installations, and then press the **Troubleshoot** button.
- Some systems will support pressing a *function* key during boot (such as *F11*).

> **Important Note**
>
> The previous method of using *F8* or *Shift+F8* is no longer reliable.

Windows 10 includes an on-disk version of Windows RE. If a computer running Windows 10 detects a startup failure, it can automatically fail to run Windows RE on-disk.

Windows OS Loader sets a status flag during initialization, which indicates when starting the process. `Winload.exe` clears this flag before showing the sign-in screen for Windows. When the boot fails, the flag will not be visible to the loader. Consequently, Windows OS Loader detects the flag when the device starts next time; it believes a startup failure has occurred and then launches Windows RE instead of Windows 10.

The benefit of automatic failover to **Windows RE Startup Repair** is that when a startup problem occurs, you may not need to test the troubled device.

> **Important Note**
>
> Notice that for Windows OS Loader, the system has to start successfully to remove the status flag. If the control of the machine is disrupted during the activate-up phase, Windows OS Loader will not remove the flag and will instead automatically start **Start-up Repair**.

Remember that the presence of both **Windows Boot Manager** and Windows OS Loader is necessary for this automatic failover. If any of these components are missing or damaged, automatic failover can not function, and you must perform a manual evaluation and repair of the startup environment of the device.

Now you know how the Windows Recovery Environment works, let's go to the **Reset this PC** feature.

Learning about the Reset this PC option

There are several explanations of why a consumer may want their machine reset. For example, if a user has significant configuration issues or bugs or the system does not run correctly, they might choose to reset their Windows 10 machine. The user can intend to repurpose the computer and give it to a member of the family.

You can reset the device using the **Reset this PC** feature. The Reset this PC tool reinstalls Windows 10, but it can retain computer settings and files depending on your choices. Optionally, the Reset this PC tool can remove most of the applications and leave the computer only with the default Windows 10 installation.

> **Important Note**
> You do not need Windows 10 media to use the Reset this PC feature.

From the **Settings** app or the Windows RE, you can access the Reset this PC feature. In either case, you can select the option to protect your files or delete everything from the device in the Reset this PC tool. When you decide to remove everything, you can specify that you only remove your data or that you clean the drive thoroughly.

It takes considerably more time to clean your drive entirely. It's more secure, though, because you can't easily retrieve the deleted files. The Reset this PC device still maintains the size and names of disk partitions irrespective of your range, and it always eliminates applications and drivers that are not part of the initial Windows 10 installation process.

The Reset this PC tool can only be run as a local user from the Settings app. When you run it from the Settings app, you don't need to provide credentials, and you select the option to protect your files. The Reset this PC tool will warn you of the applications it is going to delete, and you will need to reinstall them manually.

If you are running Reset this PC from the Windows RE accessible on a local drive, you will need to pick the local user and provide the credentials to the user. You won't be told of the apps it will uninstall, in any case. In either case, after completing the process, the Reset this PC tool will add a list of the removed apps to the local user's screen.

Although Windows 10 is reinstalled by the Reset this PC function, it retains computer settings such as computer name, domain membership, and local users. The Reset this PC feature removes device drivers and programs that were not a part of the default update for Windows 10 but retains all user settings and files.

When you run the Reset this PC tool and choose to remove all, and if your device has more than one drive, you will be asked to decide whether you want to delete all files from all drives or remove all data from the drive where Windows 10 is installed. You will also need to decide whether the Reset this PC operation should only wipe your files or clean the drive thoroughly.

The Reset this PC procedure will erase all disk space multiple times before installing Windows 10 if you choose to clean your drive entirely. If you don't want to recover your files, such as before selling your Windows 10 device or giving it to a family member for personal use, you can choose this option. The Reset this PC procedure removes all software, settings, and data that are not included in the default Windows 10 installation if you decide to uninstall all.

Up next, you will find some considerations for using the Reset this PC tool.

Consider the following when you are deciding whether to use the Reset this PC tool with the **Keep my files** option:

- The choice of **Keep my files** isn't as detrimental as just deleting my files and cleaning the drive options entirely. Although the Reset this PC tool preserves your data and settings, it removes all programs that were not included in the initial Windows 10 update.

- If you start the **Reset this PC** tool with the **Keep my files** option from the Windows RE, which is accessible from the local drive, you need a local user with administrative permissions. If you use **Keep my files** from the Windows 10 media within the Reset the PC tool, anyone with physical access to the device can use the Reset feature of this PC tool.

- You have to reinstall all applications and reapply any updates that have been made since the Windows 10 device was first installed.

- You don't need a backup or Windows 10 media to use the **Keep my Files** option from the Reset this PC tool.

When choosing to use the Reset this PC tool with the **Just remove my files** or **Fully clean the drive** options, you need to consider the following:

- The Reset this PC tool eliminates all software and desktop applications from your **Windows Store**. Only the programs that are included in the default Windows 10 update will be available on the device.

- To use Reset this PC with the **Just remove my files** or **Fully clean the drive** options, you do not need any special permissions.

- Your configuration settings for files, settings, and computer are set to their original, post-installation state.

- You must reinstall all programs and reapply any updates that have been made since the Windows 10 device was first installed.

- You don't need a backup or Windows 10 media to perform Reset this PC with the **Just remove my files** or **Fully clean the drive** options.

To start the recovery process, follow these steps:

1. Launch the **Settings** app.
2. Click **Update & Security | Recovery** option.
3. On the **Reset this PC** page, click **Get Started**.

4. In the dialog box, you will be presented with two options, namely, **Keep my files** and **Remove everything**, as shown in the following screenshot:

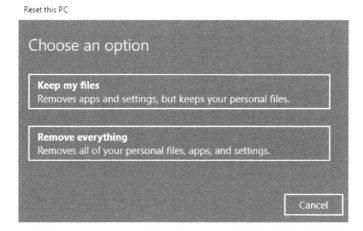

Figure 10.12 - Reset this PC dialog box

5. Choose one of the options that suits you, and click **Reset** to restart the PC and allow the reset process to begin.

You'll have a list of removed apps on your desktop after the reset process is complete, and you've signed in.

Besides all of the options mentioned previously, you also have the **Fresh Start** feature.

Understanding the Fresh Start feature

Windows 10 also offers a different way of resetting the system called **Fresh Start**. Fresh Start performs three actions, as follows:

*   Reinstalls Windows 10 while retaining your data
*   Removes all installed apps and bloatware
*   Installs the latest security updates

When the system restarts after the **Fresh Start** has been completed, you can sign in with the same username and password, and it will retain all of your data. You need to reinstall any additional applications that you had installed before. If you need access to the list of removed applications, during the process, a file will be created that can be found on the desktop after you sign in to the computer. Within the **Fresh Start** page in the **Windows Security** app, you will see a history of when you have used the **Fresh Start** feature and a link to the removed apps list.

> **Important Note**
> Any apps that came preinstalled on your system by the OEM will have also been removed.

You can access the **Fresh Start** feature using the following steps:

1. Launch **Windows Security**.

2. Select **Device performance and Health**.

3. Scroll down to **Fresh Start** and click on **Additional information,** as shown in the following screenshot:

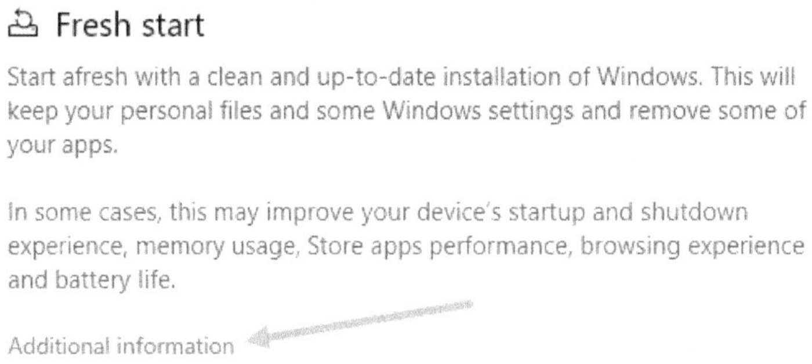

🖴 Fresh start

Start afresh with a clean and up-to-date installation of Windows. This will keep your personal files and some Windows settings and remove some of your apps.

In some cases, this may improve your device's startup and shutdown experience, memory usage, Store apps performance, browsing experience and battery life.

Additional information

Figure 10.13 - Fresh start window

4. Then, click on **Get Started**.

5. Read the warning and click **Next** to proceed.

6. **Fresh Start** will then display a list of apps that will be removed, then click **Next**.

7. On the **Let's Get Started** page, click **Start**. Then, the PC will start the reset process, which can take up to 20 minutes.

At this point, you have the knowledge to recover Windows 10 with the previously mentioned recovering options. You have two more options, such as using a system image backup and using a system repair disk. These two mentioned options are not necessary for the exam, so we will not be handling those two options.

The next section will be about troubleshooting the Windows 10 startup and boot process.

Troubleshooting the startup/boot process

Windows 10 has a competent and reliable architecture for the startup. You rarely need to get involved in solving startup problems. When one arises, however, it can be difficult to solve unless you understand the underlying mechanism.

Windows includes boot loader components designed for quick and secure loading of Windows. These three components are given as follows:

- **Windows Boot Manager** (`Bootmgr.exe`): **Windows Boot Manager (BOOTMGR)** first loads as the computer starts and then reads the **Boot Configuration Data** (**BCD**). BCD is a startup configuration information database that is stored in a registry-like format on the hard disk.

- **Windows OS Loader** (`Winload.exe`): `Winload.exe` is the boot loader for the OS invoked by Windows Boot Manager. `Winload.exe` loads the device drivers for the OS kernel, namely, **Windows NT operating system kernel** (`ntoskrnl.exe`) and `BOOT_START`, which, together with BOOTMGR, make it functionally identical to NTLDR. `Winload.exe` initializes memory, loads drivers to continue, and transfers control to the kernel afterward.

- **Windows Resume Loader** (`Winresume.exe`): BOOTMGR transfers the information to `Winresume.exe` only if the BCD contains information about a current hibernation file. Then, BOOTMGR exits and starts/initiates `Winresume.exe`. After it starts to execute, it reads the image file for hibernation and uses that file to restore the OS to its running state for pre-hibernation.

> **Important Note**
>
> Windows 10 enables fast startup by default. When the Windows 10 computer is shut down, Windows stores part of the state of the OS into the `hiberfil.sys` file. When you start your Windows 10 machine next time, this condition will be reloaded during initialization. Often, this process is called **Hybrid Startup**. This behavior can be controlled via the **Control Panel | Power Options | Change what the power button does | Turn on fast startup (recommended)** option.

You just learned that three components are necessary to startup Windows 10 from cold boot or hibernation. In the next section, you will learn the seven steps of the startup process of Windows.

Understanding the startup process

Once you turn on a computer, the initialization process will load the **basic input/output system** (**BIOS**) module or **Unified Extensible Firmware Interface** (**UEFI**) on more recent or modern computers. When loading the UEFI or BIOS, the machine accesses the boot disk's **Master Boot Record** (**MBR**), followed by the drive startup's boot sector.

The cold startup process of Windows 10 has seven steps, as follows:

1. First, the UEFI or BIOS does a **Power-On Self-Test** (**POST**). From a startup perspective, before loading the OS, the BIOS allows the device to access peripherals such as hard disks, keyboards, and computer monitors.

2. Then, in the UEFI or BIOS, the computer uses the information to locate a mounted hard disk that should contain an MBR. After that, BOOTMGR is called and loaded by the computer, which then locates an active drive partition on the discovered hard disk's *sector 0*.

3. Then, BOOTMGR reads the BCD file from the active partition, collects information about the different operating systems mounted on the computer, and then shows a boot menu, if applicable.

4. For a resume operation, BOOTMGR either transfers control to `Winload.exe` or calls `Winresume.exe`.

5. Otherwise, `Winload.exe` initializes memory and loads drivers that are set to start at startup. Such drivers (configured in the registry with a start value of 0 and called **BOOT_START** drivers) are essential components of hardware such as disk controllers and peripheral bus drivers. `Winload.exe` then transfers the access to the kernel of the OS, that is, `ntoskrnl.exe`.

6. Then, the kernel initializes and loads the drivers at a higher level (except for **BOOT_START** and services). In this step, as the **Session Manager** (`Smss.exe`) initializes the Windows subsystem, you'll see the screen turn to graphical mode.

7. Then, the Windows OS loads the `Winlogon.exe` service, which displays the **Sign-in** page. **Windows Explorer** loads once the user has logged in to the system.

In this section, you learned about the seven steps of the startup process of a Windows OS. Nowadays, you have seen that many manufacturers are implementing UEFI boot instead of BIOS boot to give more enhanced security to your computer. In the next section, you will learn about **Secure Boot**.

Learning about Windows Secure Boot

Secure Boot is a Windows 10 feature on UEFI-based devices that can help to enhance your device's protection by helping to prevent unauthorized software from running on your computer during the startup. Secure Boot checks every piece of software that has a valid digital signature. The verification applies to the OS itself.

With Secure Boot on a device, each piece of software is checked by the device against the databases of known good signatures kept within the firmware. Using this method, the firmware will only run software that it deems free of tampering.

The Secure Boot phase under Windows 10 requires UEFI-based firmware. The Secure Boot process uses UEFI to avoid the launch of unknown or potentially unwanted OS boot loaders (such as firmware **rootkits**) between the system's firmware start and the start of the Windows 10 OS.

Important Note

Some desktop computer manufacturers might allow you to deactivate Windows 10 Secure Boot via UEFI. However, on UEFI-based tablet devices running Windows 10, this may not be possible.

With Windows 10, Secure Boot is mandatory, and it greatly increases the quality of the startup process.

In this section, you learned about Secure Boot on UEFI-based devices and about Secure Boot's ability to secure your Windows 10 environment. In the next section, you will understand about the BCD store and what it does.

Understanding the Windows 10 BCD store

The **Windows 10 BCD store** is an extensible database of objects and elements that can include hibernation image details and individual configuration options to start Windows 10 or an alternative OS. For new firmware models, the BCD store offers an improved mechanism for describing the boot configuration details.

The boot sector loads BOOTMGR during startup, which in effect accesses the BCD store, and then uses that information to view the user's startup menu (if there are several boot options) and to load the OS. Such parameters were previously found in the `Boot.ini` file (in BIOS-based operating systems) or the **Non-Volatile Random Access Memory (NVRAM)** entries in the **Extensible Firmware Interface (EFI)** operating systems.

Windows 10, however, removes the BCD store `boot.ini` file and NVRAM entries. The BCD store is more flexible than `boot.ini` and can be extended to computer platforms that do not use BIOS to start the device. You can also apply the BCD store to firmware versions, such as EFI-based computers.

Windows 10 stores the BCD as a hive for the registry. The BCD registry file is in the active `\Boot` directory partition for BIOS-based systems. The BCD registry file for EFI–based systems is on the partition of the EFI device.

Now you understand more about the Windows 10 BCD store, and you learned how the BCD store works when you boot up your Windows 10 computer. The following section is about troubleshooting application installer issues and how you can resolve these kinds of problems.

Troubleshooting applications

This section is about troubleshooting applications. That's something different than troubleshooting the Windows 10 OS. Most large organizations manage application installations from a central location.

Desktop support staff, however, are involved in deploying applications during initial development and when troubleshooting failed installations. Therefore, you need to learn how to determine why the installation of a desktop app fails and how to solve those problems that might prevent the installation.

Troubleshooting Windows Installer issues

Windows 10 runs updates using **Windows Installer**. Both versions of **Windows 7** and older versions of the Windows OS include **Windows Installer 5.0**.

If the program you want to install is packaged as a `.msi` file and is accessible from the destination computer, you can either double-click the `.msi` file or run `msiexec.exe` from elevated Command Prompt to install a desktop app. To install an application from a shared folder, for example, execute the following command from an elevated prompt:

```
Msiexec.exe /i \\PACKTDC1\apps\application1.msi
```

You may receive one of the following error messages during the installation of an application:

- **The Windows Installer Service could not be accessed.**
- **Windows Installer Service could not be started.**
- **Could not start the Windows Installer service on the Local Computer.**

One of the causes of problems with Windows Installer is applications that don't complete their installation or uninstallation successfully. In some cases, restarting the computer can force the operation to continue. You may need to reinstall or repair the program before you can uninstall it. However, in a worst-case scenario, you may need to uninstall an application, including its registry entries manually. You can use any of the following methods to troubleshoot Windows Installer issues:

- Verify that **Windows Installer** is functioning by running the following command at Command Prompt:

```
msiexec.exe
```

- Verify that the Windows Installer service is configured to start manually and that it starts without errors.

- Re-register Windows Installer, but first `unregister` by using the following command:

```
msiexec /unregister
```

After executing the preceding command, make sure to run the following command as well:

```
msiexec /register
```

- Reboot the computer to reset any running installations.

- Remove any software that may clash with the software you are attempting to install.

In rare cases, another application that is running may be preventing the installation or removal of the device. Try to identify a problem application so that you can disable services and applications that start automatically.

To resolve application deployment issues, you need to understand why the deployment failed. In the next section, you will learn some standard resolving methods for deployment issues.

Resolving application deployment issues

Being able to solve deployment problems with desktop applications depends on your understanding of why the deployment failed. When you understand why a desktop application doesn't deploy properly, you can then decide the appropriate methods for resolving the problem.

The following is a list of approaches used to overcome deployment problems with desktop applications:

- **Run as administrator**: For installations with desktop applications that do not correctly elevate installation permissions, you can manually elevate permissions by right-clicking the installation file and then clicking **Run as Administrator**.

- **Install the necessary dependencies**: If you are unable to install a desktop application due to missing dependencies, then you have to install the correct dependencies. If the missing dependency affects multiple computers, the best way to fix the missing dependency on all computers needs to be decided. You may need to update the base image, which you can then deploy along with the dependency.

- **Application Compatibility Toolkit** (**ACT**): ACT is a suite of software that you use to ease the installation and execution of earlier Windows OS applications on newer versions. **Application Compatibility Manager** is one of the methods at ACT.

  You can use this method to create an inventory of installed applications and then determine whether those applications are experiencing problems while running on Windows 10. During conversion to a new OS, you will usually be using ACT. As a part of the **Windows Assessment and Deployment Kit**, you can install ACT.

- **Correct AppLocker configuration**: If **AppLocker** blocks the installation of valid desktop applications, then you need to change the AppLocker rules setting.

In the case of automated deployment, when deployed manually, the application will install and perform correctly but will fail when using an automated deployment process. While the application itself should not be ruled out, when a manual installation works and the automatic installation doesn't, the installation is often stopped because of a lack of permissions. You have to verify that whichever deployment tool you use has the correct permissions to install the program.

A desktop application operational issue is any case where a desktop application does not work correctly from the user's perspective. Some of the problems you or your users can experience include the following:

- **Missing application features**: You can select which features to install in many applications. The default installation options for an application might not include all of the features a user requires.

- **Missing Windows OS features**: Some applications require proper functioning of the Windows OS features. This includes various **Microsoft .NET Framework** versions.

- **Incorrect configuration**: The default settings post-installation of an application might not be sufficient. You can configure the program settings to suit your needs, such as the default locations for saving files and folders. Some desktop apps might also need the firewall to have open ports. Users may not have access to start all apps, or some file permissions may be inadequate for users to run the app.

- **Poor performance**: Applications could be running slower than users could expect. This can happen when users perform a specific task, when devices don't meet minimum hardware requirements or they are used regularly.

- **Application errors**: Every fault the program shows on the screen is an issue in the operation of a desktop application.

- **Incorrect database connection settings**: Some desktop applications use a database server as a store for data. If you don't correctly configure the link to the database, the application cannot function properly.

- **Application blocking by AppLocker**: To enable or block applications on Windows 10 computers, you can configure AppLocker. If AppLocker blocks an authorized desktop app, you will have to try to solve the problem.

Issues concerning desktop application operations can affect the performance of a user's work. Therefore, you need to define and solve these problems as quickly and as accurately as possible.

You will bring it through a rigorous testing process before you deploy a desktop app, which involves every day user activities. Desktop support staff often do this research, but you may want users to be included in this testing process too. The desktop app may not function as you would expect during testing, which results in the need for more troubleshooting.

Users are the most popular source for information on issues with device operations after you install a desktop app. Use on-screen error messages and event logs while examining problems with desktop application operations. In some instances, these messages and logs provide sufficient information to solve the problem. In other cases, you may need to do more work. Additional research might include searching the vendor's website, searching the internet, or contacting vendor support.

In this section, you learned various methods with which you can troubleshoot some Windows Installer issues. If a desktop application is successfully installed, there can be some problems with the applications as well. In the next section, you will learn how you can resolve operations in desktop applications.

Learning to resolve application operations issues

Your success in solving a problem with a desktop application process depends on your consistency in the problem description. The following methods include some ways to resolve the problems with desktop app operations:

- **Install a requested feature**: If there is a missing application function that a user needs, then you can disable it. Finally, you have to decide whether other users also need the functionality, and if so, determine how best to accommodate them. You may need to update the installation process of the program or update an image of the OS containing the application.

- **Reconfigure the application**: When you incorrectly configure a desktop app, you can reconfigure it to meet the requirements that have been specified. If multiple users need to reconfigure, the best way to upgrade multiple computers is to be decided. You can choose to update your group policy, update the application deployment process, or update an image of the OS containing the application.

- **Repair or reinstall the application**: If a desktop app faces errors or is unable to start, the issue might be resolved by fixing the program. During the process of repairing an application, the configuration files are set to the correct version and rewrite the computer-specific registry entries. It does not impact user-specific entries within the registry. If an application patch does not fix the problem, try reinstalling the program.

- **Apply application updates**: These software updates update the application issues found by the vendor of the software. Installing timely application updates can prevent problems with desktop application operations from occurring in your environment and may solve any performance problems.

- **Upgrade the application to a newer version**: Some issues relating to application operations enable you to update to a more recent application version. For example, you may need to update an app to a 64-bit version to improve the performance and access more memory. Newer versions may also offer new features.

- **Identify performance issues and bottlenecks**: The performance issues that are usually reported by the users are vague. By using tools such as Performance Monitor or Resource Monitor, you need to identify the source of the problem. Improving performance may rely on hardware upgrades, or users might need to run fewer applications on the device simultaneously. You might also need to change the performance expectations of the users.

- **Reconfigure AppLocker rules**: If AppLocker rules prevent a legitimate desktop app from running, these rules must be reconfigured to allow the desktop app to run, using the application path, the publisher, or the hash value.

So, now you know how to resolve issues with desktop applications. But in Windows 10, you can also install applications via the **Windows Store**. The applications that you are installing from the Windows Store are **Universal Windows Platform** (**UWP**) apps. These types of applications work differently than traditional applications.

Resolving Universal Windows Apps issues

The Windows Store will alert you when there are problems with an application and will immediately try to solve the problem in most situations. You may encounter situations where an app won't start, and the Windows Store won't be able to solve the problem. This section will address some of the most common issues you can experience while running Universal Windows Apps.

You can run the **Apps troubleshooter** if you have issues with an application or if the Windows Store app isn't loading. This tool will detect and repair Universal Windows applications and Windows Store software issues. It's only available in English, but the tool can be used on computers that are using any other language. The following screenshot shows you the **Windows Store Apps** window:

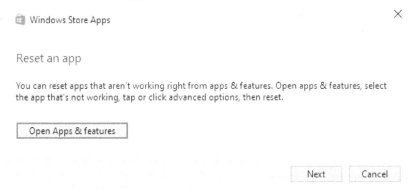

Figure 10.14 - The Apps troubleshooter application

If the problem can't be solved by the troubleshooter, then it is recommended that you try any of the following suggestions:

- **Built-in Administrator can't run Universal Windows Apps**: You cannot run Universal Windows Apps when signed in as the built-in administrator because of the default configuration. To run Universal Windows apps, you must allow **User Account Control: Admin Approval Mode for Built-in Administrator account**.

- **Allow Universal Windows applications to run at User Account Control** (UAC): Universal Windows applications can only start when UAC is allowed. If you have UAC disabled, it must be re-enabled to run Universal Windows Apps.

- **Windows Firewall could block the app**: Windows Firewall blocks those Universal Windows Apps to protect your device. Microsoft suggests configuring the **Windows Firewall rules** for the proper functioning of an application.

- **Group Policy could block the application**: AppLocker may be preventing certain Universal Windows Apps from installing and running. Microsoft recommends reconfiguring AppLocker rules to allow the installation and execution of an application.

- **Verify that your applications are valid**: When you run into problems with starting Universal Windows Apps, you should first test whether the Windows Store apps have any updates. You should make sure that the application updates are allowed automatically to avoid this problem.

- **Clear the cache for the Windows Store**: If the Windows Store app does not start, or the Windows Store app can't connect to the store, this problem could be fixed by clearing the **Windows Store cache**. You can reset the Windows Store cache by typing the following command in Command Prompt and then pressing *Enter*:

```
WSReset.exe
```

- **Synchronize the licenses to apply**: If the license for the application you want to start isn't compatible with the computer that you want to start the application on, then synchronizing the licenses could solve the problem.

If the previously mentioned suggestions with starting your Universal Windows App have not solved your problem, then I suggest reinstalling the program. To reinstall the program, you need to uninstall it first and then open the Windows Store app to reinstall it.

In this section, you have learned some methods to troubleshoot Universal Windows Apps with, for example, the Apps Troubleshooter tool, which you can download from the **Microsoft Download Center**.

Summary

This chapter was all about recovery and troubleshooting from files to Windows 10 to applications. You learned how to enable and configure File History and make use of the Previous Versions tab to go back to a previous version of a document or other types of files. Furthermore, you can decide which type of file recovery you can use in your organization and how you can troubleshoot issues with file recovery.

Another crucial thing you have learned is how you can recover Windows 10 through different mechanisms, such as Fresh Start and using a recovery drive.

Sometimes it can happen that Windows 10 won't boot at all, due to a corrupt boot loader or a similar issue. So you learned the process of booting Windows 10 and how you can troubleshoot this as well.

The last part of this chapter was about troubleshooting applications, such as UWP apps and desktop applications, through deployment and operational issues.

In the next chapter, you are going to learn to manage updates in Windows 10. It is common knowledge that it is essential to keep your Windows 10 and applications up to date. You will discover several key strategies to keep Windows 10 up to date.

Questions

1. Is Microsoft Azure Backup a built-in tool in Windows 10?

2. Does File History, by default, back up Windows libraries?

3. Can the recovery drive have a size of 4 GB?

4. When you go back to an earlier created restore point, will your personal data be affected then?

5. Can you enter the Windows Recovery Environment with the *F8* key?

6. Can you use the ACT tool to test your legacy software on Windows 10?

7. Is the `IISReset.exe` command the correct one to clear the Windows Store cache?

Further reading

- **How to use all of Windows 10's backup and recovery tools**: `https://www.howtogeek.com/220986/how-to-use-all-of-windows-10%E2%80%99s-backup-and-recovery-tools/`

- **Backup and Restore in Windows 10**: `https://support.microsoft.com/en-us/help/4027408/windows-10-backup-and-restore`

- **Backup Windows 10 to Microsoft Azure Backup**: `https://www.thomasmaurer.ch/2018/10/backup-windows-10-microsoft-azure-backup/`

- **Create a recovery drive**: `https://support.microsoft.com/en-us/help/4026852/windows-create-a-recovery-drive`

- **Managing restore points with PowerShell**: `https://mcpmag.com/articles/2012/02/21/powershell-windows-restore.aspx`

- **Windows Recovery Environment (Windows RE)**: `https://docs.microsoft.com/en-us/windows-hardware/manufacture/desktop/windows-recovery-environment--windows-re--technical-reference`

- **How to reset your Windows 10 PC**: `https://www.laptopmag.com/articles/reset-windows-10-pc`

- **How to factory reset Windows 10 using the Fresh Start option**: `https://www.windowscentral.com/how-reset-windows-10-pc-factory-settings#reset_freshstart_windows10`

- **Released Versions of Windows Installer**: `https://docs.microsoft.com/en-us/windows/win32/msi/released-versions-of-windows-installer?redirectedfrom=MSDN`

- **Fix problems with apps from Microsoft Store**: `https://support.microsoft.com/en-us/help/4027498/microsoft-store-fix-problems-with-apps`

11
Managing Updates

It is a considerable challenge keeping computer systems secure from external threats, such as malware and hackers. For earlier versions of Windows, with the **Windows Update** app, you could determine whether the **Operating System (OS)** was updated automatically with new functionality, security updates, and improvements. Many users opted to disable the **Install updates automatically** option, which made their systems vulnerable to attack.

Windows 10 changed the game in terms of updates and reliability, as new updates are now rolled out frequently. These updates are automatically downloaded and installed by Windows Update.

The following topics will be covered in this chapter:

- Selecting the appropriate servicing channel
- Configuring the Windows Update options
- Checking for updates
- Validating and testing updates
- Troubleshooting updates

By providing you with the skills to learn several key strategies to keep Windows 10 up to date, this chapter will help you configure Windows Update by selecting the appropriate servicing channels. You will also gain insight into how you can test, validate, and troubleshoot updates. By learning these skills, you are preparing for the **MD-100** (Windows 10) exam, which is part of the **Microsoft 365 Certified**: **Modern Desktop Administrator Associate** certification.

Technical requirements

In this chapter, you will see that we use PowerShell code. This code is available on the GitHub page: `https://github.com/PacktPublishing/Microsoft-Exam-MD-100-Windows-10-Certification-Guide/tree/master/Chapter11`

Throughout this chapter, you will need to follow some steps to configure settings. All of the steps covered in this chapter that you will need to follow have also been recorded. You can find those videos at `https://bit.ly/2LsQDqD`.

Selecting the appropriate servicing channel

New versions of Windows are usually released every couple of years. The introduction of these new versions to an organization then becomes a project, either by using a **wipe-and-load** process to install the latest version of the OS on, existing machines or by transitioning, as part of the hardware replacement cycle, to the newer version of the OS.

Either way, it takes a tremendous amount of time and energy to complete specific tasks. A new configuration has been introduced to **Windows 10**. This new model, called **Windows as a service**, allows organizations to reconsider how they implement and update Windows. Updating Windows is no longer a project that occurs every couple of years, but is in fact, now a continuous cycle.

In this section, you will get to know Windows as a service, how you can select the appropriate servicing channel for your organization, and how you can distribute the updates with deployment rings.

Getting to know Windows as a service

Instead of only adding new functionality to new releases that come out every couple of years, Windows as a service strives to include new capabilities twice a year. Before 2020, the build versions were **YY03** or **YY09**. From 2020, the build versions will be **YYH1** and **YYH2**. New features are introduced or modified two to three times a year while maintaining a high degree of consistency between the hardware and application.

The key to having substantially shorter development cycles while retaining high quality standards is a creative community-centered approach to testing, which was introduced by Microsoft for Windows 10. The group, known as **Windows Insider**, consists of millions of users worldwide.

As Windows Insiders opt in to the community, they test several builds over a product cycle and provide Microsoft with feedback through an iterative approach called **flighting**. Builds distributed as flights offer essential data to the Windows development team on how successful builds actually work when used.

Flighting with Insiders now also helps Microsoft check builds on much more sophisticated hardware, devices, and networking environments than they could in the past. It also helps them to detect problems much faster. As a result, Microsoft believes that distributing flights based on the community allows a faster pace of innovation and a higher quality of public release than ever before.

While Microsoft releases flight builds for Windows Insider, it continues to publish two forms of Windows 10 updates to the wider public:

- **Feature updates**: These are software updates that enable the latest new apps, experiences, and functionality already running on Windows 10 devices. Since software updates include a full copy of Windows, they are also what consumers can use to install Windows 10 on existing devices that currently run on **Windows 7** or **Windows 8.1** and on new devices that don't have an OS.

- **Quality updates**: These quality updates concentrate on deploying security patches, as well as other critical updates. Microsoft plans to deliver an average of two to three new feature upgrades each year and to publish software updates when required for any feature upgrades that are still in support. Microsoft will continue to issue updates on **Patch Tuesday** for operations. Microsoft also publishes additional service updates for Windows 10 outside the Update Tuesday phase, when needed, to address customer needs.

Windows 10 Home users have no say about how these updates are handled by their machines. Users in enterprises and educational organizations that use the **Windows 10 Pro**, **Windows 10 Enterprise**, or **Windows 10 Education** versions are, however, able to control their upgrade experience using the following options:

- **Servicing channels**: To fit with the new method of providing Windows 10 feature updates and quality updates, Microsoft introduced this concept to allow customers to define how often their devices are updated. These channels are the **Windows Insider Program**, the **Semi-Annual Channel**, and the **Long-Term Servicing Channel (LTSC)**.

- **Deployment rings**: By using **Group Policy Objects** (**GPO**) or **Microsoft Intune**, you can define deployment rings. These deployment rings use a specified channel of service and additional Windows settings to decide when updates are applied. You can monitor the updates to that group by configuring groups of computers with matching settings.

In the next section, we will look at the different servicing channels that you can choose from. By using these servicing channels, companies can decide how frequently their computers are updated.

Selecting the servicing channels

Microsoft introduced the concept of servicing channels to allow customers to define how often their devices are updated. Servicing channels were also introduced to align with the new method of delivering Windows 10 feature updates and quality updates.

Microsoft has launched the following new Windows 10 service options:

- **Windows Insider Program**: Gaining exposure to feature updates early, before they are available to the Semi-Annual Channel, can be exciting and useful for potential end user interactions for many IT pros. It also means being able to check for any problems with the next Semi-Annual Channel rollout. Feature flighting with Windows 10 enables Windows Insiders to access and deploy preproduction code to their test machines, gaining early insight into the next project.

- **Semi-Annual Channel**: Feature updates are included in the semi-annual servicing channel as soon as Microsoft publishes them. This service model is suitable for pilot trials and the testing of Windows 10 feature upgrades, as well as for consumers, including developers who need to immediately work with the new features. After the latest update has gone through pilot delivery and testing, you pick what time it goes to the main rollout.

- **Long-Term Servicing Channel** (**LTSC**): Due to their functions, specialized devices, such as **Personal Computers** (**PCs**) that monitor medical equipment, point-of-sale devices, and **Automated Teller Machines** (**ATMs**), frequently need a more extended service period.

   It is critical that these apps are kept as stable and safe as possible so that the user interface updates are up to date. The LTSC servicing model prohibits Windows 10 Enterprise LTSC devices from providing regular feature updates and only offers consistency updates to ensure that the protection of the system remains current. The LTSC is only available on the **Long-Term Servicing Branch** (**LTSB**) version of Windows 10 Enterprise.

> **Important Note**
>
> Windows 10 Enterprise LTSC is a dedicated version of LTSC. LTSC is not intended for installation on any or all of an organization's PCs. This platform can only be used by special-purpose computers. A computer with **Microsoft Office** installed on it is, as a general rule, a general-purpose tool, usually used by an information worker, and is, therefore, best suited for the Semi-Annual Channel service.

We will now move on to understanding deployment rings.

Using deployment rings

You can create deployment rings by selecting a suitable service channel and then configuring the feature update and deferral values for the quality update. You may decide whether you need a machine test community that gets updates early on.

You may also choose to build a computer group that will receive updates quickly after release. You may want to allow the bulk of your remaining computers to receive updates after checking for them. You can achieve this by using deployment rings.

You can use the GPO settings to configure deployment rings for domain-joined devices running **Active Directory Domain Services (AD DS)** and use the **Microsoft 365 Endpoint Manager Admin Center** to configure deployment rings for non-domain-joined computers.

You can use the Microsoft 365 Endpoint Manager admin center to set deployment rings, as in the following screenshot. Details of this phase are beyond the scope of this book since they are not covered on the MD-100 Windows 10 exam:

Figure 11.1 - Deployment rings in the Microsoft Endpoint Manager portal

At this point, you can decide which servicing channel is most appropriate for your organization.

You now know the difference between quality updates and feature updates. You have also learned what deployment rings are and which tools you can use in your environment. In the next section, we are going to learn how to configure the Windows Update options.

Configuring the Windows Update options

You will be able to customize the **Windows Update** settings after you have planned your deployment rings. You can do this either on a per-computer basis, using the **Settings** app, or by using GPOs to configure computers that are AD DS domain-joined.

To configure the **Windows Update** settings on an individual computer, follow these steps:

1. Open **Settings | Update & Security** option. The following screenshot shows the window that will show up:

Figure 11.2 - The Windows Update settings

As you can see in the preceding screenshot, there are several options that you can configure, including the following:

*   **Pause updates for 7 days**: As of **Windows 10 1903**, this setting will pause Windows updates for 7 days, but before Windows 10 1903, this setting was set to a value of 35 days. So, when you click on the **Pause updates for 7 days** option, the following screen is displayed:

Figure 11.3 - Updates are paused for the next 7 days

*   **Change active hours**: These settings allow the user to decide the period that they expect their system to be in use.

- **View update history**: This setting provides link access to uninstall updates and access the recovery options.

- **Advanced options**: Under the **Advanced options** section, you can configure **Update options**, **Update notifications**, **Choose when updates are installed**, and other settings.

After you have configured and selected your appropriate servicing channel, you can optimize the download and delivery of the Windows updates on your network by enabling the **Delivery Optimization** feature in Windows 10. With this feature, you can decrease the internet traffic to the Windows Update servers. In the next section, you will learn about this delivery optimization feature.

Understanding Delivery Optimization

Windows Update's **Delivery Optimization** feature allows updates to be implemented quicker than in previous Windows versions. After an update has been activated on one PC in your local network, all computers in the network get the same updates without having to download them directly from Microsoft.

If **Delivery Optimization** is enabled, your device can also submit parts of apps or updates that have been downloaded to other PCs locally or on the internet. Follow these steps to enable **Delivery Optimization**:

1. Open **Settings | Update & Security** option.

2. Select **Delivery Optimization**. The resultant window is as follows:

Figure 11.4 - The Delivery Optimization settings

This method resembles typical peer-to-peer file sharing applications. Only partial file fragments of the update files are downloaded from any source, which accelerates the delivery and improves process protection. When you require distribution optimization, you can choose how your PC can receive notifications and apps from other PCs using the following options:

- **PCs on my local network**: Windows may attempt to download the updates or apps from other PCs on your local network.

- **PCs on my local network and PCs on the internet**: Windows will attempt to download from other PCs on your local network and will even search for internet PCs that are configured to share parts of updates and apps.

You can configure **Delivery Optimization** through **Microsoft Intune** or a GPO for domain-joined computers, but that is beyond the scope of this book.

In this section, you learned how to configure Windows Update settings, and you now know what the different settings are, such as **Change active hours** and **Advanced options**. Furthermore, you learned how Delivery Optimization is used to speed up the downloading of Windows updates.

In the next section, you will learn how you can check for updates on Windows 10.

Checking for updates

Typically, manually checking for updates isn't required on Windows. You can do this quickly by following these steps:

1. Open **Settings | Update & Security** option.

2. Click on the **Check for updates** button on the **Windows Update** page, as shown:

Figure 11.5 - The Check for updates button

Windows connects to **Windows Update** and gets a list of any updates that are pending, as you can see in the following screenshot, where an update is downloading:

Windows Update

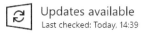

Updates available
Last checked: Today, 14:39

2020-03 Cumulative Update for Windows 10 Version 1909 for x64-based Systems (KB4541335)
Status: Downloading - 49%

Figure 11.6 - Downloading an update from Windows Update

If updates are available, they start downloading and installing automatically, even if you have configured settings in a GPO to only notify you of downloading and installing.

You have now learned how to check for updates manually. If any updates are pending, then these updates will be downloaded and installed.

In the next section, we are going to learn how you can test and validate updates.

Validating and testing updates

You need to know how updating Windows will affect users' devices. Therefore, you need time to verify and check the changes before they are made available to your organization.

We have already discussed how to use a servicing channel to build the notion of deployment rings, along with deferment values. Using deployment rings helps you to get and check potential updates before continued deployment.

You can also consider using additional services to distribute updates to Windows, rather than relying solely on Windows Update servers. You can choose between the following deployment tools to spread the Windows updates in your organization:

- **Windows Server Update Services** (**WSUS**): This is a server role for **Windows Server 2019**. WSUS downloads updates from servers running Windows Update. You can then customize how it propagates these changes to your client computers. This gives you time to check the changes and verify them.

- **Windows Update for Business**: Essentially, you should think of this as similar to WSUS. Nevertheless, Microsoft retains it in the cloud and it is available for computers running Windows 10 Pro or Windows 10 Enterprise.

- **Microsoft Endpoint Configuration Manager** (**MECM**): If you already use MECM to handle deployment, you can use it to control updates as well. MECM offers you superior power and versatility for managing notifications. MECM was previously called **System Center Configuration Center**.

- **Microsoft Endpoint Manager**: Microsoft Endpoint Manager, formerly called **Microsoft Intune**, is a cloud-based device and an app-management platform. It is especially useful for the management of non-domain connected devices. With Microsoft Endpoint Manager (Intune), updates can be approved, deployed, and removed.

When testing updates, you must make sure that the latest updates work for all computers, their peripherals, and applications. This is particularly important when considering how feature updates are implemented.

You have now learned how to test and validate Windows updates with the use of deployment rings. You also learned which distribution mechanisms you can deploy Windows updates to your client computers with.

In the next section, you will learn how to troubleshoot updates through different methods.

Troubleshooting updates

If a system does not receive updates, then you have to review the **Settings** app and group policy settings. We have to review them to ensure updates are not deferred or paused.

So, to troubleshoot, in this case, you have to check that the two Windows Update services are running—namely, the **Windows Update** service and **Background Intelligent Transfer Service**.

You can find these services in the **Services** snap-in. Use the following steps to find that snap-in:

1. Click on the **Start** icon.
2. Type in Services.msc.
3. Then, click on **Services**.
4. The **Services** snap-in will open, as shown:

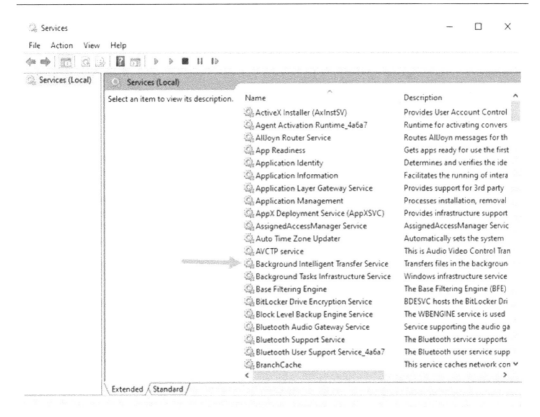

Figure 11.7 - The Services snap-in

In the previous screenshot, you can see all the services that are available on Windows 10. To use the troubleshooter, you need two specific services from the list, which are pointed out in the previous screenshot. These are the **Windows Update** service and **Background Intelligent Transfer Service (BITS)**.

The first is the **Windows Update** service, which checks the locally installed updates and what is available on the update servers. Also, the **Windows Update** service manages to download, install, and monitor the status of the updates. The following screenshot shows you the **Windows Update** service:

Windows Update   Enables the detection, download, and installatio...   Running   Manual (Trig...   Local System

Figure 11.8 - The Windows Update service

The second service is **Background Intelligent Transfer Service**. BITS is a supplementary service that manages the most effective transfer of the update files. For Windows Update to work correctly, both services should be running. The following screenshot shows you the second service:

Background Intelligent Transfer Service   Transfers files in the background using idle netw...   Running   Automatic (...   Local System

Figure 11.9 - Background Intelligent Transfer Service

If these two services are up and running, you can use the Windows Update troubleshooter. To find the troubleshooter, follow these steps:

1. Open **Settings | Update and Security** option.

2. Select the **Troubleshoot** tab and you will see the **Run the troubleshooter** button, as shown:

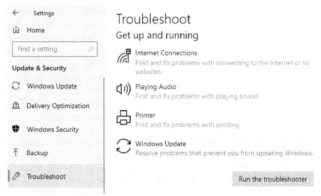

Figure 11.10 - The Windows Update Troubleshoot tab

If you click **Run the troubleshooter**, Windows will attempt to check the necessary services and will try to connect to the Windows Update server. If Windows identifies a problem, suggestions will be made about how best to address those problems.

The troubleshooter is just one option that you can try. However, if the problem still exists, then you can try one of the following options:

*   Uninstall an update via **Control Panel**.

*   Uninstall an update via **Settings**.

*   Uninstall an update via **Command Prompt**.

You will learn how you can roll back Windows updates via these methods in the next section. Rolling back updates is necessary if an update is causing issues on your test workstation.

Rolling back updates

With the routine of daily updates being used as the method to keep devices stable and up to date, there can be times where an update creates issues, so you need to consider removing the update that is causing the issue. You may have experience with driver rollback; the same principle is used to roll back Windows updates.

Often, only a single Windows update needs to be removed. This function can be carried out in many ways, including via **Control Panel**, the **Settings** app, or **Command Prompt**. You will learn how to remove an update in the following sections.

We will first see how to use Control Panel in the next section.

Uninstalling an update via the Control Panel

If you choose to use Control Panel, you can see a list of installed updates and further updates that can be installed by following these steps:

1. Click on the **Start** icon and type in `Control Panel`.

2. Then, go to **Control Panel | Programs | Programs and Features** option.

3. After that, click on **View installed updates**. The resultant window is shown in the following screenshot:

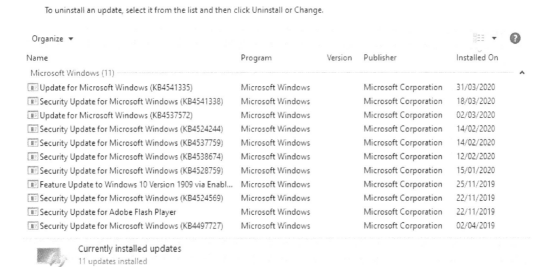

Figure 11.11 - The installed updates screen

4. Then, select an update that you want to uninstall from the list.

5. After that, in the **Uninstall an update** dialog box, click **Yes** to confirm.

6. Click **Accept** in the UAC dialog box if prompted.

7. Finally, you will be prompted to restart your computer:

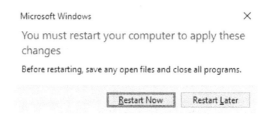

Figure 11.12 - The dialog box prompting you to restart your computer

Once you have restarted your computer, the uninstalled update will have been removed from Windows 10.

Next, we will see how to use the **Settings** app to uninstall updates.

Uninstalling an update in Settings

The **Settings** app opens the same list of installed updates in the **Control Panel**. If you want to use the **Settings** app, follow these steps:

1. Go to **Settings | Update & Security | Windows Update** option.

2. Then, click on the **View update history** option. The resultant window is shown in the following screenshot:

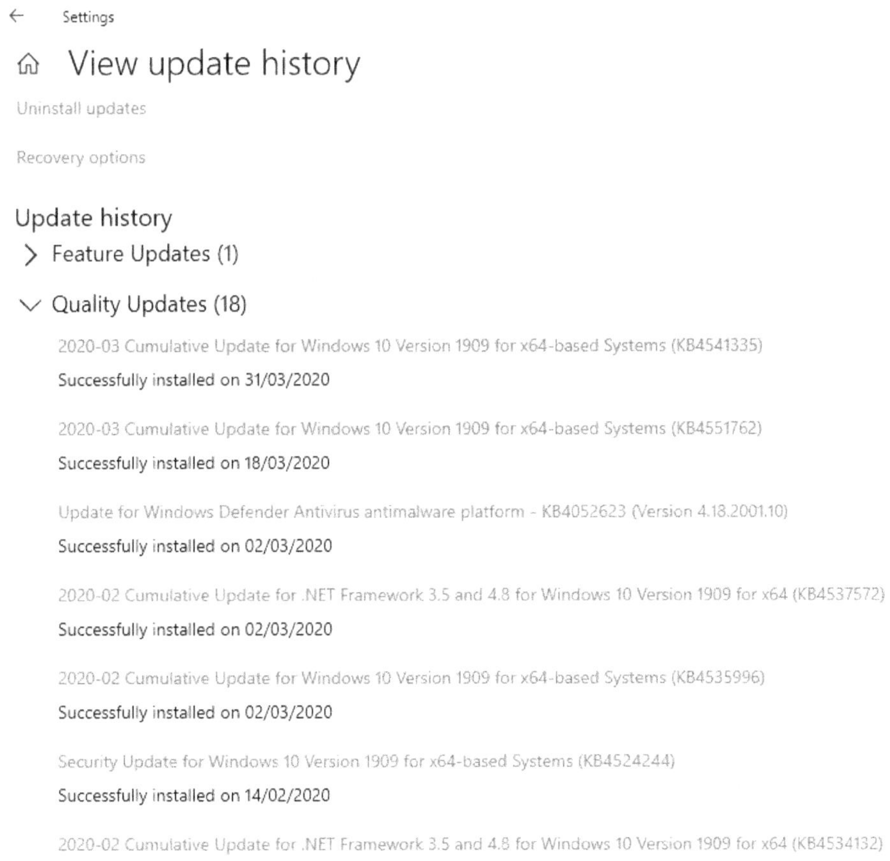

Figure 11.13 - The View update history page

3. After that, click on **Uninstall updates** at the top of the screen.

4. From here, follow *step 5* and onward from the *Uninstalling an update via the Control Panel* section to uninstall an update.

We will now look at using Command Prompt to remove an update in the next section.

Uninstalling an update via Command Prompt

Often, you will need to remove the same update from multiple devices. You can use the Command Prompt or PowerShell to script the command. After you have created the script, you can distribute it to various devices using **Group Policy** or PowerShell. Of course, you need to do this after you have checked the command-line tool on your test system.

To create a list of installed update packages on a Windows 10 system, you can use the **Windows Management Instrumentation Command-line** (**WMIC**) utility, as shown:

```
Try the new cross-platform PowerShell https://aka.ms/pscore6

PS C:\Users\Packt-MD100-User> wmic qfe list brief /format:table
Description     FixComments  HotFixID     InstallDate  InstalledBy          InstalledOn  Name  ServicePackInEffect  Status
Update                       KB4537572                 NT AUTHORITY\SYSTEM  3/2/2020
Security Update              KB4497727                                      4/1/2019
Security Update              KB4516115                 NT AUTHORITY\SYSTEM  11/22/2019
Update                       KB4517245                 NT AUTHORITY\SYSTEM  11/25/2019
Security Update              KB4524244                 NT AUTHORITY\SYSTEM  2/14/2020
Security Update              KB4524569                 NT AUTHORITY\SYSTEM  11/22/2019
Security Update              KB4528759                 NT AUTHORITY\SYSTEM  1/15/2020
Security Update              KB4537759                 NT AUTHORITY\SYSTEM  2/14/2020
Security Update              KB4538674                 NT AUTHORITY\SYSTEM  2/12/2020
Security Update              KB4541338                 NT AUTHORITY\SYSTEM  3/18/2020
Update                       KB4541335                 NT AUTHORITY\SYSTEM  3/31/2020

PS C:\Users\Packt-MD100-User>
```

Figure 11.14 - Overview of the installed updates in PowerShell

To generate a list of the installed update packages on your device, open **Command Prompt**, or **PowerShell** and type in the following command:

```
wmic qfe list brief /format:table
```

By specifying the package number (from **Microsoft Knowledge Base**) of the update to be uninstalled, you can use the **Windows Update Standalone Installer** (**WUSA**) command-line tool (wusa.exe) to remove the update.

For the previous method, the syntax is as follows:

```
wusa.exe /uninstall /kb:<KBnumber>
```

Replace <KBnumber> with the actual KB number in the command if you wish to uninstall the update. The WMIC and WUSA command functions can be used in either PowerShell or Command Prompt.

In this section, you learned about the many methods you can use to identify and solve update issues with different techniques. You now know which services are essential for Windows Update to work correctly. Furthermore, you learned how you can uninstall and roll back updates in different ways.

Summary

You learned, throughout this chapter, that it's essential to keep your Windows 10 devices up to date. You learned what the term Windows as a service is and that there are three servicing channels that you can use in your organization. By using deployment rings in your organization, you can have control over the deployment of your updates. You can configure deployment rings with GPOs or with Microsoft Endpoint Manager.

You can now configure Windows Update on a machine via a GPO or Microsoft Endpoint Manager. You can also change the active hours, pause any updates, or view the update history. You now know about the various ways of finding and solving upgrade problems using different techniques, as well as which resources are important for Windows Update to update properly. Also, you now know how to uninstall and roll back updates in different ways.

You learned that you can configure delivery optimization to speed up the downloading of updates to client computers. Furthermore, you learned which distribution mechanism to use so that you can deploy Windows updates to your client computers.

You are almost at the end of this book. The next chapter is all about log files; Windows 10 has many built-in log files and you will explore these different log files and how you can read them.

Questions

1. Can anyone opt into the Windows Insider Program?

2. Is the Semi-Annual Channel (Targeted) a valid servicing channel?

3. If you manually check for updates, can you install the updates at a later time?

4. Is it necessary to test and validate updates before you deploy them to the rest of your organization?

5. Are Background Tasks Infrastructure Service and Windows Update services critical for Windows updates?

Further reading

- **Overview of Windows as a service**: https://docs.microsoft.com/en-us/windows/deployment/update/waas-overview

- **Build deployment rings for Windows 10 updates**: https://docs.microsoft.com/en-us/windows/deployment/update/waas-deployment-rings-windows-10-updates

- **Delivery Optimization for Windows 10 updates**: https://docs.microsoft.com/en-us/windows/deployment/update/waas-delivery-optimization

- **Windows Server Update Services (WSUS)**: https://docs.microsoft.com/en-us/windows-server/administration/windows-server-update-services/get-started/windows-server-update-services-wsus

- **Deploy updates using Windows Update for business**: https://docs.microsoft.com/en-us/windows/deployment/update/waas-manage-updates-wufb

- **Learn about Configuration Manager**: https://docs.microsoft.com/en-us/configmgr/core/understand/introduction

- **Microsoft Intune is a Mobile Device Management (MDM) and Mobile Application Management (MAM) provider for your devices**: https://docs.microsoft.com/en-us/mem/intune/fundamentals/what-is-intune

- **Description of the Windows Update Standalone Installer in Windows**: https://support.microsoft.com/en-us/help/934307/description-of-the-windows-update-standalone-installer-in-windows

12
Managing Log Files

Once Windows 10 computers are installed, they need to be monitored and managed. Windows 10 provides various tools for controlling your computer, including **Event Viewer** and a range of performance management features, such as **Resource Monitor** and **Performance Monitor**.

As well as knowing how to control your computers, you must also be familiar with how to handle vital **Operating System(OS)** elements, such as printing, indexing, and the various Windows services.

The following topics will be covered in this chapter:

- Configuring and analyzing event logs
- Managing performance
- Managing the Windows 10 environment

This chapter provides you with the skills you need to analyze event log errors on the current version of Windows 10. This will help you maintain the performance and environment of Windows 10. This chapter will also help you to prepare for the **MD-100** (Windows 10) exam, which is part of the **Microsoft 365 Certified: Modern Desktop Administrator Associate** certification.

Technical requirements

In this chapter, you will see us use PowerShell code. This code is available at `https://github.com/PacktPublishing/Microsoft-Exam-MD-100-Windows-10-Certification-Guide/tree/master/Chapter12`.

In this chapter, you will need to follow the steps to configure some settings. The steps that you will follow have also been recorded. You can find these videos at `https://bit.ly/2LsQDqD`.

Configuring and analyzing event logs

Event logs are a key built-in security resource in all Windows Operating Systems and can be accessed from Windows Event Viewer. They provide information about occurring system events. Event logs are created by the Event Log service as a background operation and can contain information, alerts, and error messages about Windows components, installed applications, and system behavior.

We will learn how to configure and analyze event logs in this section. In addition to log groups for individually installed applications and different Windows component categories, Event Viewer offers classified lists of important Windows log events, including applications, security, setup, and system events. Individual accidents provide comprehensive details about the type of incident that occurred, the cause of the incident, and specific technical information to assist with troubleshooting the accident.

Event Viewer also helps you merge logs from several machines into a single computer while using subscriptions. Event Viewer can, eventually, be programmed to perform an action when particular events occur. This may involve sending you an email message, launching an app, running a script, taking individual maintenance acts to alert you of an event, or trying to fix a possible problem.

Windows 10's Event Viewer has the following features:

- **The option of viewing several logs**: You can search through several logs for different incidents, making it easier to investigate issues and troubleshoot problems that may occur in numerous logs.

- **The inclusion of customized views**: You can use filtering to limit searches to only the things you are interested in and you can then save these views.

- **The ability to set up tasks that are scheduled to run in response to events**: Reactions to incidents can be automated. Event Viewer combines with **Task Scheduler** to execute these reactions.

- **The capacity to build and maintain subscriptions to activities**: You can capture and store events from remote computers.

> **Important Note**
> You need to create an inbound rule on **Windows Firewall** to allow **Windows Event Log Management** to capture events from remote computers.

By now, you will know what Event Viewer is. In the next section, we will move on to understanding event logs.

Understanding event logs

In the previous section, you learned what the Event Viewer is, and what it is used for. To get better insight of the Event Viewer and the event logs, we will go a little deeper in the Event Viewer. So first, we are going to open Event Viewer, take the following steps:

1. Click **Start** icon.

2. Type in event viewer.

3. Click on **Event Viewer**.

4. The **Event Viewer** app will open, as shown:

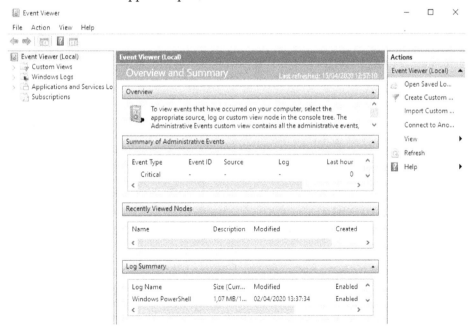

Figure 12.1 - Event Viewer app

As you can see in the preceding screenshot, upon opening the window, the console retrieves and displays the events that have occurred on your computer. You can configure **Event Viewer** from remote computers to work with the event log; so, you can allow remote management in your firewall.

There are two different types of log files:

- **Windows Logs**: These logs include **Application**, **Security**, **Setup**, **System**, and **Forwarded Events**. The following screenshot shows you these logs:

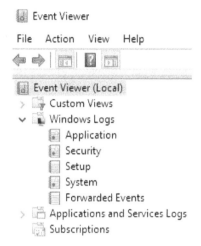

Figure 12.2 - An expanded tree of the Windows Logs node

- **Applications and Services Logs**: These logs include other logs from applications and services to record application-specific or service-specific events. You can also see these logs in the previous screenshot.

Since logs are created as part of the OS, they can provide forensic information to help you understand issues that are difficult to diagnose using real-time system analysis.

More details about the **Windows Logs** files are as follows:

- **Application**: This log contains events logged by installed applications.

- **Security**: This log contains auditable events, such as logon, logoff, privilege use, and shutdown.

- **Setup**: This log records events logged by Windows during setup and installation.

- **System**: This log contains the events logged by Windows 10. This is the primary system log.

- **Forwarded Events**: These are used when event forwarding is operational. This log records forwarded events from other computers.

Select each of the Windows logs in **Event Viewer** and look at the types of events created. On the right side, the **Actions** pane contains tools and wizards to help you deal with logs, including saving logs, clearing/deleting log entries, opening a previously saved log, and adding a task to an event.

The maximum file size of a Windows 10 event log is 20 **Megabytes** (**MB**) by design. When the program exceeds the maximum scale, it replaces old events with new events.

Open **Event Viewer** and take some time to get familiar with it by reviewing some of the logs, as in the following screenshot:

System Number of events: 617				
Level	Date and Time	Source	Event ID	Task Category
ⓘ Information	08/05/2020 08:29:57	WindowsUpdateClient	44	Windows Update Agent
ⓘ Information	08/05/2020 08:26:28	Application Popup	26	None
ⓘ Information	08/05/2020 08:24:33	Service Control Manager	7040	None
⚠ Error	08/05/2020 08:22:06	WindowsUpdateClient	20	Windows Update Agent
ⓘ Information	08/05/2020 08:21:48	WindowsUpdateClient	43	Windows Update Agent
⚠ Warning	08/05/2020 08:21:43	DistributedCOM	10016	None
⚠ Warning	08/05/2020 08:21:43	DistributedCOM	10016	None
⚠ Warning	08/05/2020 08:21:43	DistributedCOM	10016	None
ⓘ Information	08/05/2020 08:21:42	IsolatedUserMode	5	None
ⓘ Information	08/05/2020 08:21:39	Service Control Manager	7045	None
⚠ Warning	08/05/2020 08:20:54	DistributedCOM	10016	None
⚠ Error	08/05/2020 08:20:43	Service Control Manager	7009	None
⚠ Warning	08/05/2020 08:20:38	DistributedCOM	10016	None
⚠ Warning	08/05/2020 08:20:29	DistributedCOM	10016	None
⚠ Warning	08/05/2020 08:20:28	DistributedCOM	10016	None

Figure 12.3 - Some examples of event log types

In the previous screenshot, you can see that there are multiple types of occurrences, which have the following meanings:

- **Information**: These logs provide information on changes to a part or system operation that are typically a positive outcome.

- **Warning**: These incidents are not detailed, but they may be more significant and should be investigated.

- **Error**: These events warn you that there has been a problem.

- **Critical**: These incidents are the most severe and may result in failure or loss of function. These events are highly important and suggest whether there is or has been a problem.

- **Audit Success/Failure**: If auditing is enabled, those log entries will appear in the security log.

Instead of using the default layout of Event Viewer, you can create custom views for the specific logs you want to investigate. In the next section, you will learn how you can create these custom views.

Creating Custom Views

Event logs contain large quantities of data, which can make it challenging to limit your task of understanding those events that concern you. To accommodate this, the view in Windows 10 can be configured to allow you to query and sort only the events you wish to examine. You can also save, export, import, and share Custom Views.

Event Viewer allows you to search through several logs for individual incidents and show all the occurrences that may be relevant to an incident that you are investigating. You'll need to build a custom view to define a filter that spans several logs.

In **Event Viewer**, go to **Create Custom View** under the **Actions** window. These Custom Views can be filtered according to various parameters, as shown:

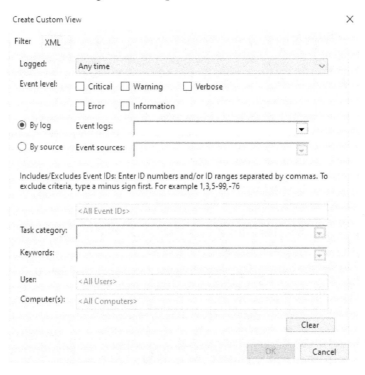

Figure 12.4 - The Create Custom View dialog box

In the previous screenshot, you can see the various fields used. They are described as follows:

- **Logged**: This states the time that the event was logged.
- **Event level**: This is used to display the type of level, such as **Error** or **Warning**.
- **By log**: This is used to select the logs to include events for.
- **By source**: This is used to select specific event IDs to include or exclude.
- **User**: This shows the user context of the event.
- **Computer(s)**: This shows the computer that the incident occurred on.

Use the following steps to build a custom view in **Event Viewer** that only shows the **Critical** events in the **System** log:

1. Go to **Event Viewer** | **Actions** | **Create Custom View** option.
2. From the **Filter** tab, select the **Critical** checkbox under **Event level**.
3. Use the **By log** drop-down option to expand **Windows Logs**.
4. Select the **System** checkbox from the dropdown and then click **OK**:

Figure 12.5 - The filter created by following the previous steps

5. After that, in the **Save Filter to Custom View** window, choose a name, such as System-Critical, for the log and click **OK**:

Figure 12.6 - Giving the custom view a name and a description

The Custom View immediately refreshes and displays the log entries that match the set criteria. Your Custom View filter is located in the left pane under the **Custom Views** node. The output of the previous steps is shown in the following screenshot:

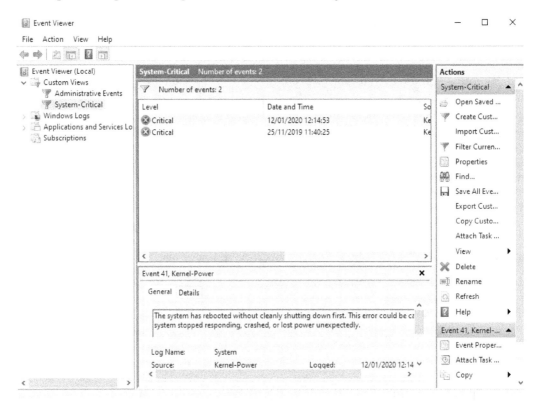

Figure 12.7 - The Custom View result that we created

In the previous screenshot, you can see all the events listed. Double-click the **Event log** entry. This will display its **Property** dialog box. The **Event Properties** dialog box, along with a **Copy** button, can be seen under the **Actions** menu. It provides you with additional details so that you can transfer the event data to the clipboard and either work with the data or request assistance. Descriptions of incidents are now easier to understand than in previous Windows versions. Even the experience of reading event log entries can help develop your understanding to find out what the problem is.

You know how you can create a custom view for a Windows 10 computer. With Event **Subscriptions**, you can collect event logs from other computers, instead of manually connecting to them. You will learn more about this in the next section.

Configuring Event Subscriptions

Event Viewer helps you view events on a single screen. However, troubleshooting a problem may require you to look at a series of events that are stored on multiple computers in multiple logs. Event Viewer allows you to gather copies of events from various remote computers for this purpose and then store them locally. Create an event subscription to determine which events to receive. After a subscription is active and the events are recorded, these forwarded events can be interpreted and manipulated as you would with any other locally stored events.

You need to configure the forwarding and collecting computers to use the event-collecting function. The functionality for event collection is based on the **Windows Remote Management** (**WinRM**) and **Windows Event Collector** (**Wecsvc**) services. All of these services operate on computers that are active in the process of forwarding and collecting.

We can perform the following steps to allow subscriptions:

1. Type the following command in an elevated Command Prompt to enable **Windows Remote Management** on a source computer and then press *Enter*:

```
winrm quickconfig
```

The `winrm quickconfig` command starts the WinRM service and configures a port listener to send and receive messages. The output of this command is shown in the following screenshot:

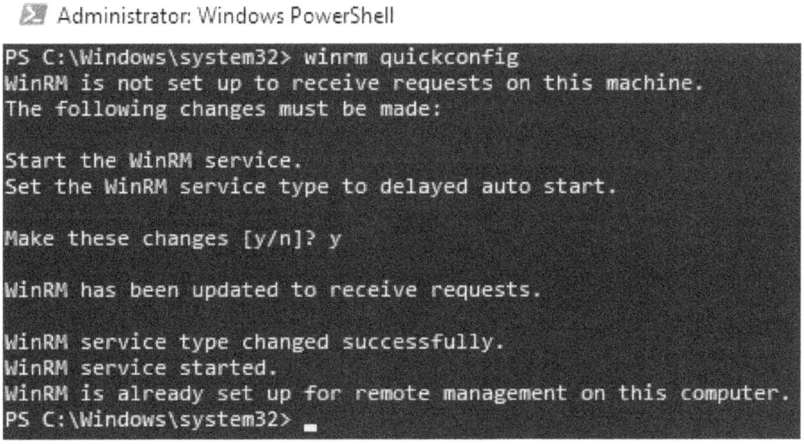

Figure 12.8 - The output of the winrm quickconfig command

2. On the collector machine, which is the machine that receives the messages, type the following command in an elevated Command Prompt to activate the **Windows Event Collector** service, then press *Enter*:

```
wecutil qc
```

The `wecutil qc` command helps you build and manage subscriptions to events sent from remote computers. The output of this command is shown in the following screenshot:

```
Administrator: Windows PowerShell
PS C:\Windows\system32> wecutil qc
The service startup mode will be changed to Delay-Start. Would you like to proceed ( Y- yes or N- no)?y
Windows Event Collector service was configured successfully.
PS C:\Windows\system32> _
```

Figure 12.9 - Output of the wecutil qc command

3. Add the collector's computer account to the local group of event log readers on each of the source computers.

You have now learned to configure Event Subscriptions to gather remote event logs from other computers. In the next section, you will learn how to create a subscription to see the logs from other computers.

Creating a Subscription

After you have configured Event Subscriptions on a source computer and the remote computers, you can create a subscription to receive event logs from remote computers. There are two kinds of subscriptions—**collector-initiated** and **source computer-initiated**.

In a collector-initiated subscription, the subscription must provide a list of all the origins of the events. The source computer-initiated subscriptions allow you to identify an event collector's subscription without specifying the event source computers.

To create a collector-initiated subscription, follow these steps:

1. Go to **Event Viewer | Subscription** menu.

2. If the option to start Windows Event Collection service appears, click **Yes**.

3. Then, in the **Action** pane, click **Create Subscription...**:

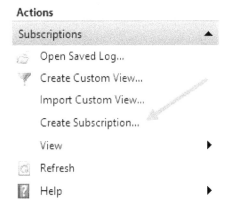

Figure 12.10 - The Create Subscription option

4. After that, type in a name and description for the subscription, as shown:

Figure 12.11 - The Subscription name field

5. Then, under **Subscription type and source computers**, click **Collector initiated**, then the **Select Computers...** option:

Figure 12.12 - Subscription type and source computers section

6. After that, in the **Computers** dialog box, click **Add Domain Computers...**, then select the computer to be polled for subscriptions and click **OK**:

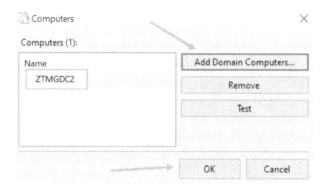

Figure 12.13 - Computers dialog box

7. Under **Events to collect**, click **Select Events…**, then define the event criteria to be used to match and collect events and click **OK**:

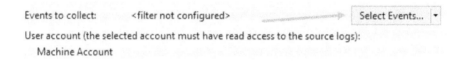

Figure 12.14 - Events to collect option

8. Click **OK** to save the changes made to the options and make the Subscription active.

The previous steps will create a subscription that is listed in the **Main** pane of the **Subscriptions** node, as shown:

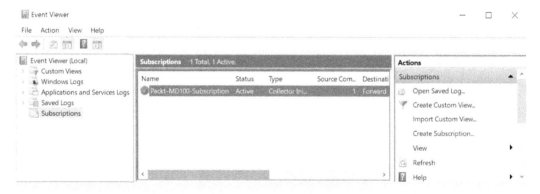

Figure 12.15 - The Subscriptions window that is created

In this section, you learned how to create an event subscription to gather remote logs for troubleshooting. In the next section, you will learn how to manage the performance of Windows 10 with different tools, such as **Resource Monitor** and **Performance Monitor**.

Managing performance

Within Windows 10, there are a variety of tools you can use to monitor and manage results. These programs give you a graphical layout of historical data. Other programs also provide a method for gathering and evaluating data on results over time.

To monitor the output in Windows 10, you can use the following tools:

- **Task Manager**
- **Resource Monitor**
- **Performance Monitor**
- **Reliability Monitor**

We will look at each of these tools in the following sections. Let's start with the Task Manager tool.

Monitoring performance with Task Manager

The Task Manager tool is one of the most frequently used software by end users and administrators to monitor system output and the use of resources on a computer. Task Manager is mainly a tool that is used to track performance, not to track reliability.

Task Manager can be managed in a variety of ways. The numerous ways of opening Task Manager are listed as follows:

- Right-click on the taskbar and select **Task Manager**.
- Press the *Ctrl+Alt+Del* keys, then select **Task Manager**.
- Use the *Ctrl+Shift+Esc* key combination.
- Type `taskmgr.exe` in Command Prompt to open **Task Manager**.
- Click **Start** icon, type in `taskmgr`, then press *Enter*.

The following screenshot shows you what the **Task Manager** app typically looks like:

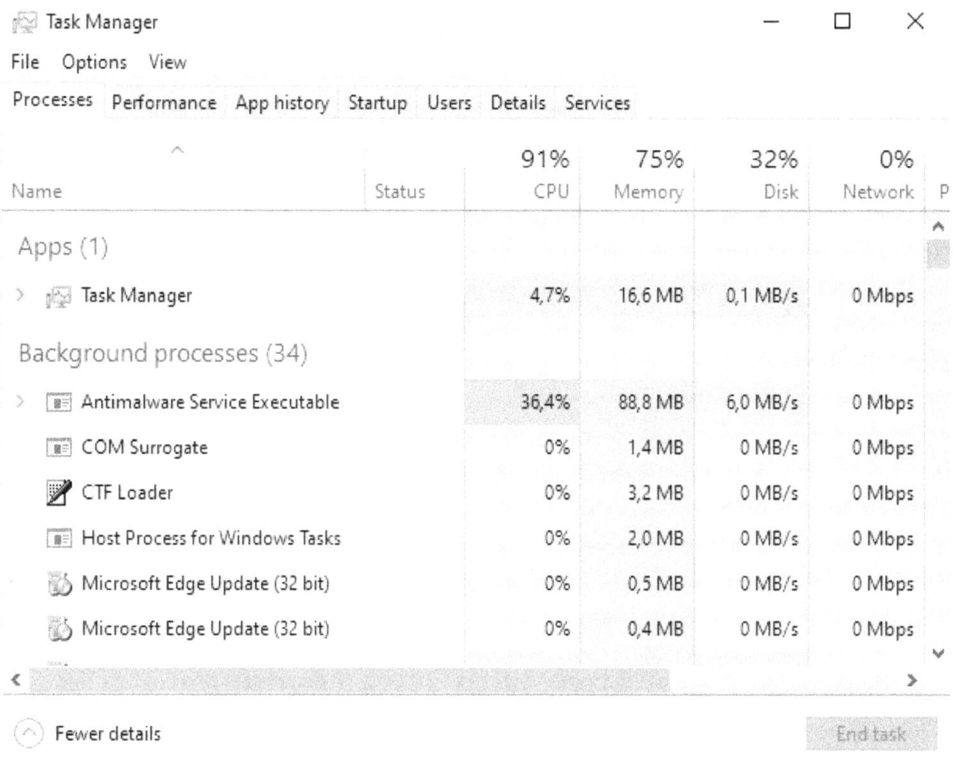

Figure 12.16 - The Task Manager app

From the previous screenshot, you can see that the Task Manager app that is built into Windows 10 shows you which processes (tasks) are running on your system and, most importantly, the use of performance-related system resources. If a particular task or process is not reacting or continues to run after an application has been terminated, you can use Task Manager to monitor this activity and force the unwanted task to stop.

When you first run Task Manager, it only displays the programs and processes that are running. If you click the **More details** button, the **Task Manager** window will expand and you will be able to view more information about the program's operation. The **Task Manager** window contains the following tabs:

- **Processes**: This tab shows a list of the running programs, subdivided into applications and Windows internal processes. This tab shows a description of the processor and memory use for each running operation.

- **Performance**: This tab shows a list of what the CPU, memory, and data on the network is using.

- **App history**: This tab shows the device statistics and resource usage. It is useful when trying to find a specific device that consumes additional resources.

- **Startup**: This tab shows applications that are running at startup time. You can disable any of these programs to stop them from starting up.

- **Users**: This tab shows per-user resource usage. You can also extend the user view to see more specific details about the particular processes that a user is running.

- **Details**: This tab lists all the processes operating on a server and offers information on the CPU, memory, and other resource usages. This tab can be used to control the running processes. For example, you can either stop a process, stop a process and all the related processes, or change a process's priority values. If you change a process's priority values, you decide the degree at which CPU resources can be used by the process. If the priority is increased, you allow the process to request more CPU resources.

- **Services**: This tab offers a list of relevant information on operating Windows services, including whether a service is operating and the running service's **Process Identifier** (**PID**) meaning. You can use the list in the **Services** tab to start and stop services.

When you first notice a problem with reliability, you can use Task Manager to see whether you can solve the problem. For example, you might review the start-up items to decide whether a specific program causes problems after it begins and search the processes for non-responsive applications.

Important Note

Task Manager displays the latest usage of the tools on the local computer. Task Manager cannot be used to track the activity on a remote device or to store operation and resource usage in a log file.

Now, you know what you can do with Task Manager. Let's take a look at what you can do with Resource Monitor.

Examining performance with Resource Monitor

Resource Monitor offers a device's output analysis with a description and four tabs with specific information for the main components of the device. These four tabs are as follows:

- **CPU** (processor)
- **Memory**
- **Disk**
- **Network**

When a Windows 10 device runs slowly, you can use Resource Monitor to monitor current activity in each of the four component areas and decide what has caused a bottleneck output. Resource Monitor, however, can only display resource use for the local machine, not remote or virtual computers.

The following screenshot shows the **Resource Monitor** app:

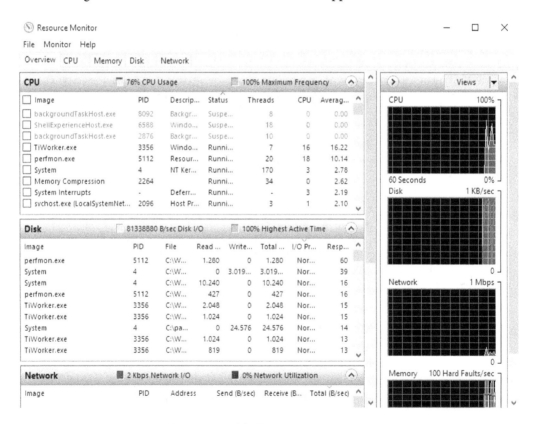

Figure 12.17 - The Resource Monitor app

Review each tab of the **Resource Monitor** app in the preceding screenshot. Each subcomponent offers additional components.

You can access **Resource Monitor** from **Task Manager**. You can also execute the following command on a Command Prompt window to access **Resource Monitor**:

```
perfmon /res
```

Compared to Task Manager, Resource Monitor's primary objective is to monitor system performance and the usage of the **CPU**, **Disk**, **Network**, and **Memory** resources. However, you can also use it to help recognize reliability issues, such as the inappropriate use of device resources or unresponsive applications.

So, you have now learned how to use Resource Monitor to troubleshoot problems in Windows 10. The next tool we will look at is Performance Monitor.

Monitoring performance with Performance Monitor

Performance Monitor is a snap-in of **Microsoft Management Console** (**MMC**) that you can use to see details about system results. You can use this tool to evaluate the performance impact of apps and services that you might have on your computer and to get an overview of the system performance or to collect comprehensive troubleshooting details. Performance Monitor has the following functionalities:

- **Monitoring Tools**: This section contains the performance monitor, which offers a visual view of integrated Windows output counters, either in real-time or as historical data.

- **Data Collector Sets**: A data collector set is a custom set of output counters, records of incidents, and data about system configuration. Once you create a combination of data collectors that explains valuable information about the system, you can then save it as a collection of data collectors, then run and display the results.

- **Reports**: You can use the **Reports** feature to view and generate reports from a selection of counters that you use to build data collector sets. Performance Monitor automatically generates a new report each time a collection of data collectors runs.

The following screenshot shows you a view of the **Performance Monitor** app:

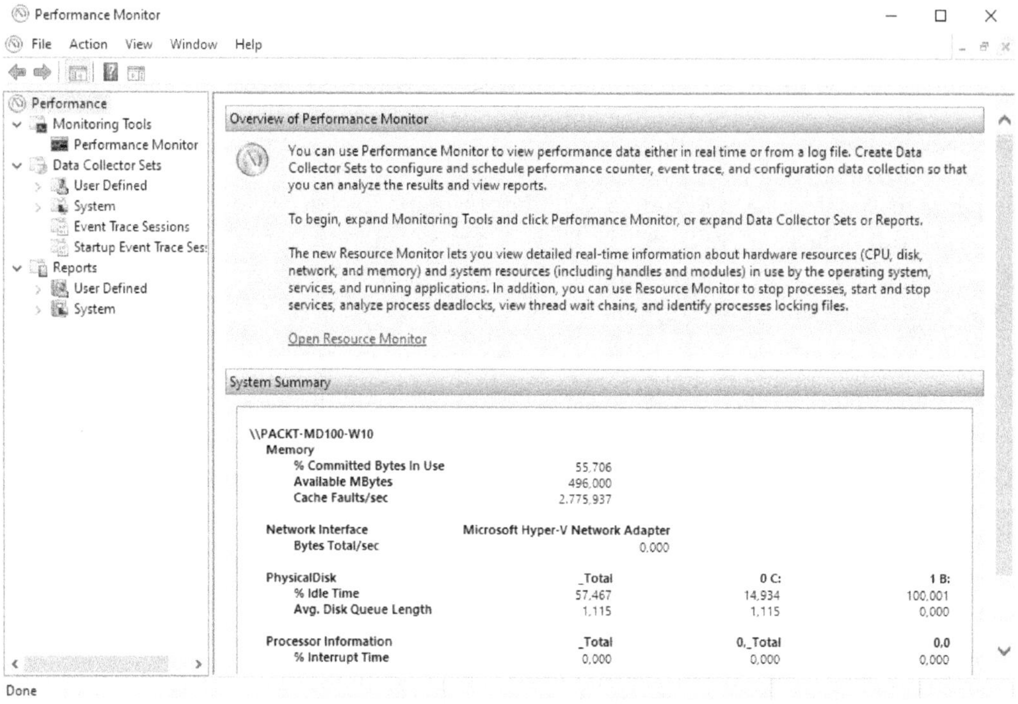

Figure 12.18 - The Performance Monitor app

Performance Monitor uses counters to calculate the state of operation of the device. The OS contains some performance counters, which can have additional performance counters for individual applications. Performance Monitor, by default, demands the current value of output counters every second at specified time intervals.

You can add Performance Monitor counters by dragging and dropping the counters or by building a collection of custom data collectors. Performance Monitor features several graph views that allow you to visually check the performance log data. In **Performance Monitor**, you can build Custom Views, which you can then export as data collector sets for use with performance and logging features.

A group of data collectors organizes multiple points of data collection into a single, portable portion. You can use your collection of data collectors, combine it with other sets of data collectors, and integrate it in to logs, or you can display it in Performance Monitor. You can configure a collection of data collectors to generate alerts when they exceed thresholds.

You can also configure a series of data collectors to operate at a specified time for a specific time or until a predefined size is reached. For example, to build a performance benchmark, you can run the data collector collection for 10 minutes every hour during work hours. If the collection exceeds a fixed limit, you can also fix the data collector to restart, so the output monitor generates a new file for each cycle. Regardless of whether Performance Monitor is initiated, scheduled data collection sets collect data.

You have now learned that you can use Performance Monitor to view performance data either in real-time or from a log file. You have also learned how to create custom collector sets to configure and schedule performance counters and event tracking so that you can analyze the results and view reports. Next, we will move on to Reliability Monitor.

Surveilling performance with Reliability Monitor

The Reliability Monitor app measures the functionality of a computer and its history of problems. It can be used to generate reports and charts in many forms that can help you determine the source of reliability issues.

You can open **Reliability Monitor** by following these steps:

1. Click on the **Start** icon.

2. Type in `reliability`.

3. Click on **View reliability history**. The following screenshot shows you what the app looks like:

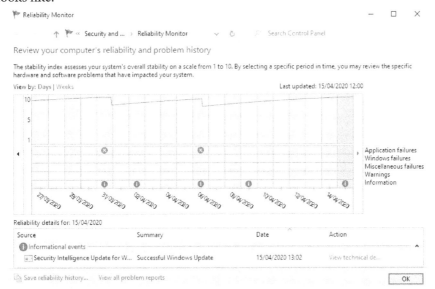

Figure 12.19 - The Reliability Monitor app

In the previous screenshot, you can see a timeline with historical data of when, for example, an update was installed. You can also see that two errors have occurred in a program.

In the following sections, you will learn and understand the techniques and tools that are used in Reliability Monitor—namely, a system stability chart, events in the timeline, and the Problem Reports and Solutions tool.

Understanding the system stability chart

The system stability chart in Reliability Monitor lists the annual performance of the system in regular increments. This chart shows some details, error messages, and alerts. Additionally, it simplifies the process of defining issues and states the date that they occurred on.

The system stability report includes details on each case in the chart, including software installations, software uninstallations, application failures, hardware failures, Windows failures, and other miscellaneous failures.

Recording key events in a timeline

Reliability Monitor monitors the main device configuration events, such as downloading new applications, OS updates, and drivers. It also helps you recognize the causes of reliability problems by monitoring events such as memory problems, hard disk problems, driver problems, application problems, and OS failures.

Reliability Monitor includes a timeline for device improvements and also reports on the reliability of a device. This timeline is used to determine whether a specific system shift is associated with the system instability initialization. The reliability database stores up to a year's history of these incidents.

Understanding the Problem Reports and Solutions tool

Reliability Monitor's **Problem Reports and Solutions** tool lets you monitor problem reports and any solution details that other resources have received. This tool is only used to help store knowledge. **Windows Error Reporting** handles all contact on the internet related to errors and solutions to those problems. The **Problem Reports and Solutions** tool lists the attempts made to fix issues with a computer.

To open the **Problem Reports and Solutions** tool, click on the **View all problem reports** option located at the bottom of the **Reliability Monitor** window. The following screenshot shows you the **Problem Reports** window:

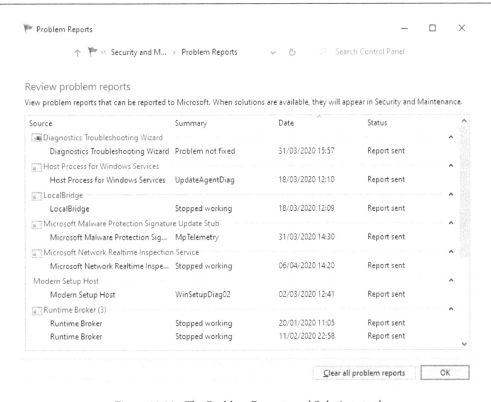

Figure 12.20 - The Problem Reports and Solutions tool

If an error occurs when an app is running, Windows Error Reporting prompts the user to choose whether they want to submit to Microsoft the error information over the internet. If there is information available that can help a user fix a problem, Windows will show a message to the user with a link to information about how to solve the problem.

The Problem Reports and Solutions tool can be used to monitor information about resolution information and to recheck and find new suggestions. You can start the Problem Reports and Solutions tool from the Reliability Monitor window. This tool includes options such as saving the reliability history, viewing all the problem reports, checking for solutions to all problems, and clearing the solutions and problem history.

So, you have now learned that you can review specific hardware and software problems with Reliability Monitor that have impacted your system with the help of different reports. This tool can advise you on how to solve a problem that has occurred.

The next section of this chapter will cover how you can manage a Windows 10 environment, including managing printers, configuring indexing, and managing services.

Managing Windows 10 environment

In your daily job, you may have to resolve problems with regard to the slow performance of Windows 10 as well as managing print servers. Many end-users complain that their Windows 10 is slow in performance and you will have to solve this. For this reason, in this section we will focus on how you manage printers, monitor and customize indexing, assess device reliability, and customize and manage services.

Monitoring and managing printers

Windows 10 provides you with some extra tools to handle your printing, as opposed to previous Windows versions. The new **Print Management** desktop app and the new **Printers & Scanners** option in the **Settings** app that have been introduced provide you with important print management options, such as adding, removing, and setting printers as default.

You can still access the previous printer tools in the **Control Panel**'s **Device and Printers** section or from the link in the **Settings** app at the bottom of the **Printers & Scanners** options. The **Devices and Printers** item in **Control Panel** has the same GUI as in the earlier **Windows 7** versions.

> **Important Note**
> This section focuses on the latest printing features in Windows 10, but you should also study the older printing tools for the exam.

You can manage printers with the **Print Management** console or with **PowerShell**. You will learn about how to do this in the following sections.

Managing printers with Print Management

Windows 10 can operate as a print server or you can connect and control printers remotely on Windows-based print servers via the **Print Management** console.

The **Print Management** console can be found in the **Administrative Tools** section of the **Control Panel**, so you can open it from there or type `printmanagement.msc` into the Start menu. The **Print Management** console will then open, as shown:

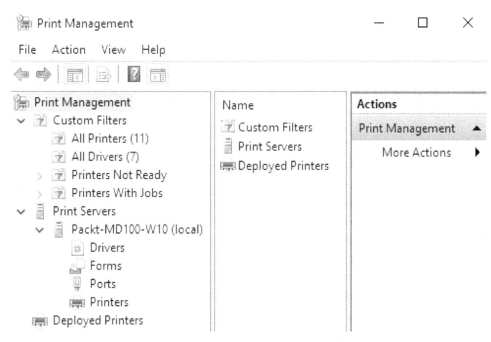

Figure 12.21 - Print Management console

The **Print Management** console offers a unified interface that helps you control several printers and print servers and perform several management tasks, which are as follows:

- Adding and removing print servers

- Adding and deleting printers

- Adding and managing drivers

- Managing print queues

- Viewing and modifying printers' statuses

- Creating a custom filter to view printers that match specific criteria

Let's look at these management tasks in more detail in the following sections.

Adding and removing print servers

When you first open the Print Management console, it is only linked to a local print server based on Windows 10. If you have sufficient permission and want to access other Windows-based print servers, you first need to add them to the Print Management console by right-clicking on the **Print Server** node and then selecting **Add / Remove Print Servers**.

Adding and deleting printers

On any print server that is connected to the Print Management console, you can connect or remove printers locally or remotely. You can connect printers using the **Network Printer Installation Wizard** page, which is similar to the **Add Printer Wizard** page in **Devices and Printers**. The **Network Printer Installation Wizard** page lets you perform the following tasks:

- Search the network for printers.

- Add a **Transmission Control Protocol/Internet protocol (TCP/IP)** or web service printer by IP address or hostname.

- Add a new printer by using an existing port.

- Create a new port and add a new printer.

Next, we will move on to adding to and managing the driver section.

Adding and managing drivers

Windows can also download a driver for the appropriate printing device while you are connecting a printer. For example, if you connect a **PostScript** printing device to Windows 10's 32-bit edition, a **PostScript 32-bit Windows 10** driver will be enabled. However, other users can also link to it while sharing the printer and are able to use the printer. You will also have drivers for the OS that they are using. For example, if someone is running a **64-bit Windows 7** version driver, you may want to add a 64-bit driver to your Windows 10 print server.

By running **Add Printer Driver Wizard**, the **Print Management** console lets you add printer drivers, as shown:

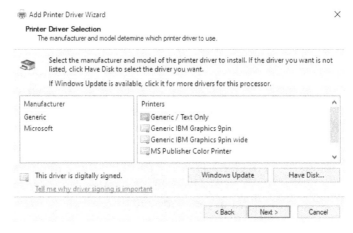

Figure 12.22 - The Add Printer Driver Wizard

You should be aware that users no longer need multiple drivers for various printers with **Type 4** printer drivers.

> **Important Note**
>
> A Type 4 driver is typically bundled with the OS or downloaded from Windows Update, while **Type 3** drivers are mostly downloaded from the website of the printer's manufacturer.

Printer drivers can't be downloaded from the print server, but instead, have to be downloaded from **Windows Update** or **Windows Update for Business**.

Let's move on to the next section on managing print queues.

Managing print queues

By clicking on the **Printers** node under the print server, you can view the printers that are installed on a specific print server. By selecting the **All Printers** node, you can also view all the installed printers on all the print servers that are connected to the Print Management console.

By right-clicking on the printer, you can view the printer queue. Then, select **Open Printer Queue**. The resultant window is shown in the following screenshot:

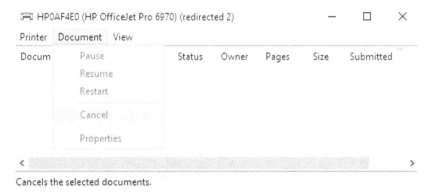

Figure 12.23 - Managing print jobs in the print queue

In the previous screenshot, you can see the **Pause**, **Restart**, **Resume**, and **Cancel options**, and you can reorder print jobs.

Let's move on to look at viewing and modifying printers' statuses in the next section.

Viewing and modifying printers' statuses

The **Printers** node shows information about each printer linked to any print server you attached to the **Print Management** console, as shown:

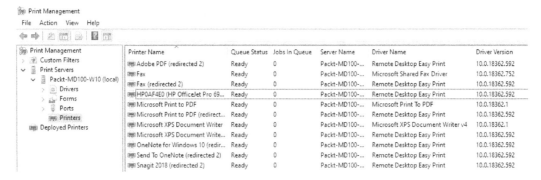

Figure 12.24 - All the listed printers under the Printers node

In the previous screenshot, you can see each printer's print queue status, the number of jobs in the queue, the driver name and version, and the type of driver.

Next, we will see how we can create a custom filter to view printers that match certain criteria.

Creating a custom filter to view printers that match specific criteria

By design, four custom filters are included in the **Print Management** console. They are as follows:

- **All Printers**
- **All Drivers**
- **Printers Not Ready**
- **Printers With Jobs**

You can add new custom printer or driver filters by specifying one or more conditions that a printer or driver needs to have when you are selecting a filter to appear on the screen. For example, you could build a custom filter to display printers at a specific location, irrespective of the print server they are linked to, or display printers in a print queue that have more than five print jobs.

> **Important Note**
>
> The **Devices and Printers** tool can only be used to handle printers on local Windows 10-based computers. In addition to printers that are connected to other Windows-based printer servers, you can control printers on local Windows 10-based computers by using the Print Management console.

In this section, you learned what you can do in the Print Management console. However, most of these actions can also be carried out with PowerShell.

Managing printers with PowerShell

Windows has more than 20 **PowerShell** cmdlets that can be used for printer management. The following are some of the most popular cmdlets:

- `Add-Printer`: Adds a printer
- `Add-PrinterDriver`: Installs a printer driver
- `Get-PrintConfiguration`: Used to get the printer configuration
- `Get-Printer`: Retrieves the installed printers
- `Get-PrinterDriver`: Retrieves the installed drivers
- `Get-PrinterProperty`: Retrieves the printer properties
- `Remove-Printer`: Removes a printer
- `Remove-PrintJob`: Removes a print job
- `Rename-Printer`: Renames a printer
- `Restart-PrintJob`: Restarts a print job
- `Resume-PrintJob`: Resumes a print job
- `Set-PrintConfiguration`: Sets the printer's configuration information
- `Set-Printer`: Updates the printer's configuration

To get a list of all the available cmdlets, type the following command into a PowerShell console:

```
Get-Command -Module PrintManagement
```

The output of the previous command is shown in the following screenshot:

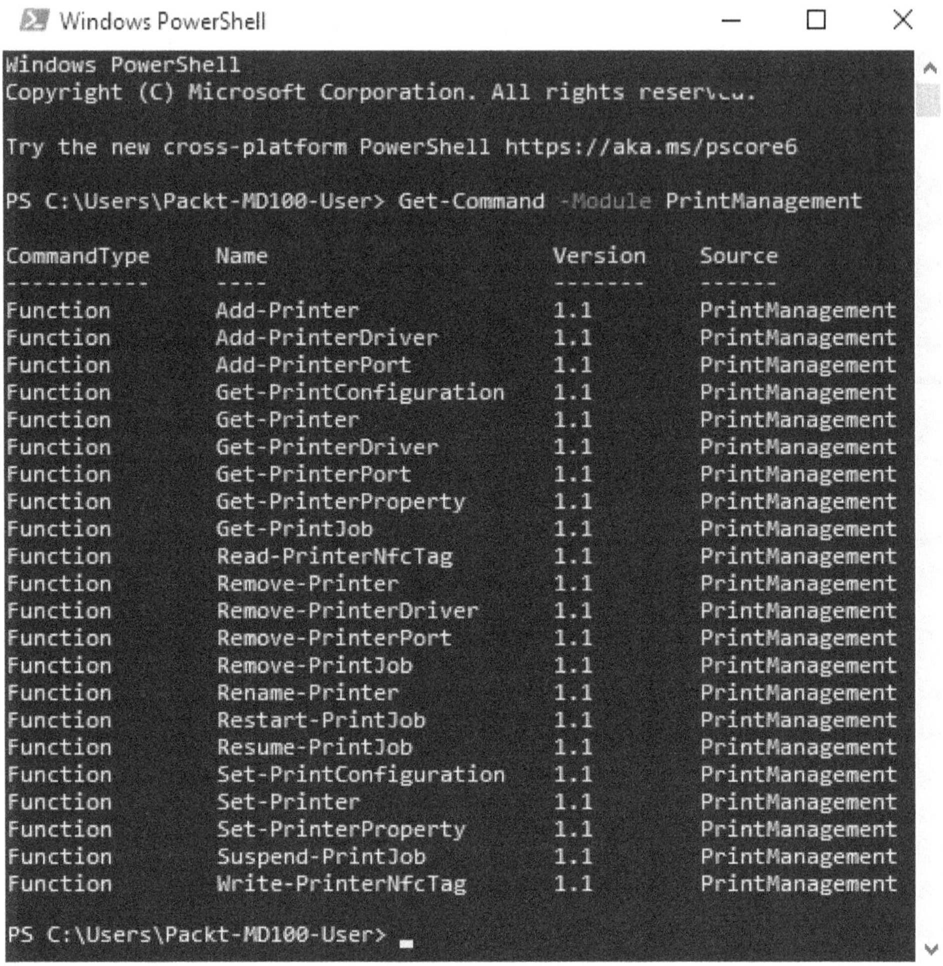

Figure 12.25 - The output of the PrintManagement PowerShell cmdlet

A few examples that will help you understand the previously listed cmdlets are as follows:

```
Add-PrinterDriver -Name "HP0AF4E0 (HP OfficeJet Pro 6970)"
```

The previous command installs the driver for the HP OfficeJet Pro 6970 printer. The next example is as follows:

```
Add-PrinterPort -Name "IP_10.168.14.29" -PrinterHostAddress
"10.168.14.29"
```

The previous command adds a local printer port with an IP address of `10.168.14.29`. We will see the next example:

```
Rename-Printer -Name "HP0AF4E0 (HP OfficeJet Pro 6970)"
-NewName "HPOJ6970_ITSupport"
```

The previous command renames the printer from `HP0AF4E0 (HP OfficeJet Pro 6970)` to `HPOJ6970_ITSupport`. We move on to the following example:

```
Get-Printer -Name "HP0AF4E0 (HP OfficeJet Pro 6970)"
```

The previous command gives the details of the `HP0AF4E0 (HP OfficeJet Pro 6970)` printer . Now, have a look at the next example:

```
Remove-Printer -Name "HP0AF4E0 (HP OfficeJet Pro 6970)"
```

The previous command removes the `HP0AF4E0 (HP OfficeJet Pro 6970)` printer . We will look at the last example:

```
Remove-PrinterDriver -Name "HP0AF4E0 (HP OfficeJet Pro 6970)"
```

The previous command removes the printer driver from the `HP0AF4E0 (HP OfficeJet Pro 6970)` printer.

In this section, you have learned how to manage a print server with PowerShell and Printer Management. The next section shows you how to configure the indexing options in Windows 10.

Configuring the indexing options

The system automatically indexes data to your computer in the background to improve the output of the Windows 10 search. This data includes the files, directories, and documents created by the user. Most users will never change the default indexing settings, but you can add new indexing areas and delete others. Popular areas include parts of your user profile and device data that you regularly access, such as the **Microsoft Office** apps.

When you store a lot of data in a storage space or removable drive, you can add this location to the Indexing Options to accelerate the output of potential searches to this location significantly.

To view your existing indexing locations, follow these steps:

1. Click on the **Start** icon.
2. Type in `indexing` and click on **Indexing Options**.

3.   Then, the **Indexing Options** dialog box will open up, as shown:

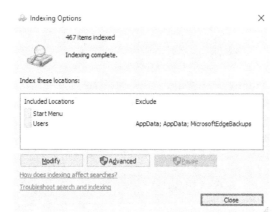

Figure 12.26 - Indexing Options dialog box

From the previous screenshot, you can see that you can add or delete locations using the **Modify** button. There is also an **Advanced** button.

When you click on the **Modify** button, you will see the localization overview in the **Indexed Locations** window. Clicking on the **Show all locations** button will reveal all the hidden locations in Windows 10, as shown:

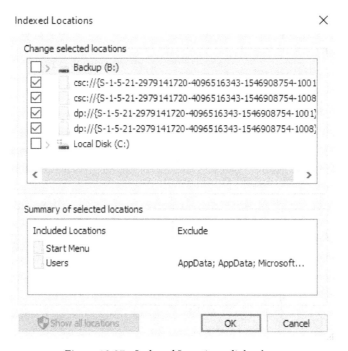

Figure 12.27 - Indexed Locations dialog box

The indexing process doesn't start directly after you make changes to indexing; rather, it acts as a background function while your system runs but is not being used. Although the indexing cycle is incomplete, the message in the dialog box shows that indexing is in progress, as shown:

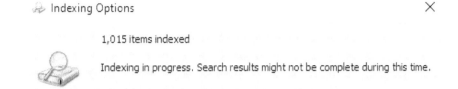

Figure 12.28 - Indexing is in progress

Now, the **Advanced** button in the **Indexing Options** dialog box allows you to customize **Index Settings** and indicate excluded file types. You can include or remove encrypted data, view similar words as different words, delete and re-create the index, and adjust the index location from the default `C:\ProgramData\Microsoft` location. In the following screenshot, you can see what the **Index Settings** tab looks like:

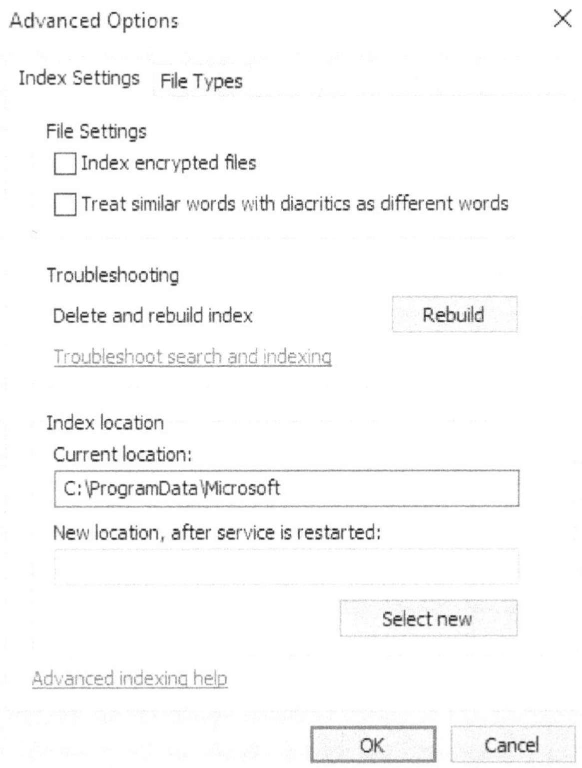

Advanced Options   ✕

Index Settings   File Types

File Settings
☐ Index encrypted files
☐ Treat similar words with diacritics as different words

Troubleshooting

Delete and rebuild index   Rebuild

Troubleshoot search and indexing

Index location
Current location:

C:\ProgramData\Microsoft

New location, after service is restarted:

Select new

Advanced indexing help

OK   Cancel

Figure 12.29 - Index Settings tab in the Advanced Options dialog box

You can remove file types from the index under the **File Types** tab and customize whether the index searches a file's contents or just the file properties. You can also manually add new types of files that are not automatically included in the index. In the following screenshot, you can see what the **File Types** tab looks like:

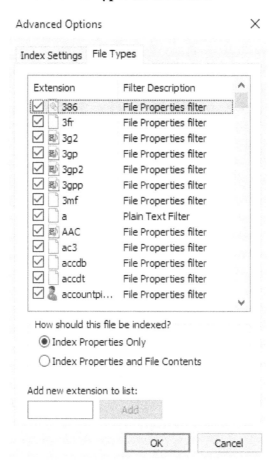

Figure 12.30 - File Types tab in the Advanced Options dialog box

In this section, you have learned how to configure **Indexing Options** to perform some speed enhancements in Windows 10. In the final section of this chapter, we will finetune Windows services.

Configuring and managing services

A service can best be defined as a component of the software that communicates with system drivers on one level and with app-level components on another. In a sense, services are located between apps and hardware devices and are considered a core part of the OS.

Windows 10 OS services have separate features that do not require user interaction. By using PowerShell and the management console, you can control resources in a variety of ways, including from the Command Prompt.

The best way to handle services is by using the **Services** management console snap-in, as in the following screenshot:

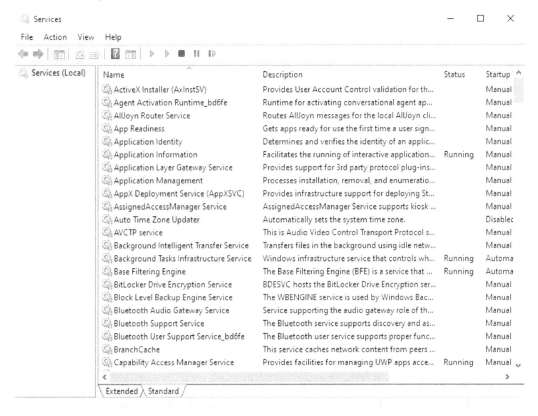

Figure 12.31 - Services management console snap-in

From the previous screenshot, you can see that you can use this console to view and manage services in the system. You can also manage the settings of a service by double-clicking on the desired service. In the **Properties** dialog box for the named service, you can then configure its properties, as shown:

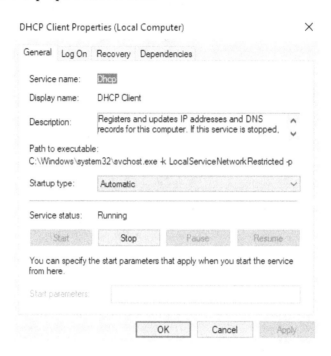

Figure 12.32 - The Properties dialog box of a service

Instead of using a **Graphical User Interface(GUI)** to configure services, you also can use the command-line tool to investigate and troubleshoot services. To use the commands, you have to open an elevated Command Prompt. The commands to do this are as follows:

- NET start: Used to start a service

- NET stop: Used to stop a service

- Sc query: Displays information for a service

- Sc stop: Stops a service

- Sc start: Starts a service

For example, if you want to stop the **Dynamic Host Configuration Protocol (DHCP)** service, as in the previous screenshot, the command will be as follows:

```
NET stop dhcp
```

Services can also be controlled with PowerShell. This is particularly useful because you can use PowerShell to control other computers and their services remotely. You can also script PowerShell cmdlets so that you can create administrative tasks for future use. To use the cmdlets, you must open an elevated **PowerShell** window.

In this section, you learned how to configure and manage services with the snap-in, PowerShell, and the Command Prompt.

Summary

In this last chapter, you learned how to understand event logs and their two different log types. You also familiarized yourself with working in the Event Viewer, how to read event logs, and how to use four different built-in apps to monitor the performance of Windows 10. You then familiarized yourself with how to track down potentially corrupted app installations or updates that could make a computer unstable, as well as how to manage and monitor printers. Finally, you learned how to carry out some speed enhancements in Windows as well as learning what a service is and how to configure it.

With the skills that you have learned in this chapter, you are able to configure and analyze event logs. You can now manage the performance of Windows 10 efficiently with configuring the indexing and the Windows services.

You are now ready to take the Microsoft MD-100 exam. Next, we will test the knowledge and lessons that you have learned from this book.

Questions

1. In **Event Viewer**, you will see a node called **Forwarded Events**. Is this node used to send logs to other computers?

2. To enable **Windows Event Collector**, can you use the `winrm quickconfig` command?

3. Can you use the `perfmon` command to open **Resource Monitor**?

4. Does **Reliability Monitor** measure the history of problems?

5. Can you use **Network Printer Installation Wizard** to install printers?

6. Are **Type 3** printer drivers downloaded from **Windows Update** during installation?

7. Can you change the index location of the indexing services?

Further reading

- **Windows Event Log**: https://searchwindowsserver.techtarget.com/definition/Windows-event-log

- **Windows Task Manager – The Complete Guide**: https://www.howtogeek.com/405806/windows-task-manager-the-complete-guide/

- **How to Get the Most out of Resource Monitor in Windows 10**: https://techtalk.gfi.com/how-to-get-the-most-out-of-resource-monitor-in-windows-10/

- **How to Use Performance Monitor on Windows 10**: https://www.windowscentral.com/how-use-performance-monitor-windows-10

- **Solving Problems Using Reliability Monitor in Windows 10**: https://www.petri.com/solving-problems-using-reliability-monitor-in-windows-10

- **Special Considerations with Windows Type 4 Print Drivers**: https://www.papercut.com/kb/Main/WindowsType4PrintDrivers

- **Starting or Stopping Windows Services from the Command Line (cmd)**: https://www.windows-commandline.com/start-stop-service-command-line/

- **Managing Services**: https://docs.microsoft.com/en-us/powershell/scripting/samples/managing-services?view=powershell-7

- **Managing Printers and Drivers with PowerShell in Windows 10 / Server 2016**: http://woshub.com/powershell-managing-printers-and-their-drivers-in-windows-8/

Mock Exam (A and B)

You must have learned about many new topics after reading through these chapters and gained insightful knowledge about Windows 10 and its components.

In this mock exam, we will be looking at questions regarding everything that you've learned by reading the chapters of this book. This will help you test your knowledge and will make you ready for the real **MD-100: Windows 10** exam. The mock exam has been divided into two sections: *Mock exam A* and *Mock exam B*.

The mock exam has a total of 40 questions. The answers to all the questions in this mock exam can be found in the *Assessment* section of the back matter of this book.

Let's start with exam A first, which provides test questions from *Chapter 1, Deploying Windows 10*, to *Chapter 7, Securing Data and Applications*.

Mock exam A

1. You are an IT support professional in a well-renowned organization and your company has upgraded 60,000 computers to **Windows 10 Enterprise** successfully. What amount of time, in months, will Microsoft offer support for?

    a. 12

    b. 18

    c. 24

    d. 30

2. Where can we find the settings/configuration for what happens when the **lid closes** on a Windows 10 device?

    a. Display options

    b. Power plans

    c. Ease of Access

    d. USB settings

3. Suppose you have a computer that runs on the Windows 10 **Operating System (OS)**. When you open the **Control Panel**, which items can you expect to see in the **Category** view? (select three answers)

    a. System and Security

    b. Appearance and Personalization

    c. Time & Language

    d. Ease of Access

    e. Network Security

4. If you want to remove the **Gaming** option from the **Windows Settings** app, which of the following options would help you accomplish this?

    a. Uninstalling Solitaire.

    b. Creating a group policy that hides the Gaming option.

    c. Right-clicking the Gaming option and selecting **Hide from view**.

    d. Removing the Gaming tile in the **Notification and actions** page.

    e. Logging in with a work or school account.

5. Suppose you are a support technician at a retail computer store. A customer has just requested that you upgrade their computer to **Windows 10 Home**. First, you need to verify whether the computer can be upgraded or not. Which Windows editions can be upgraded to Windows 10 Home? (select four answers)

    a. Windows 8/8.1

    b. Windows RT

    c. Windows 7 Ultimate

    d. Windows 7 Starter

    e. Windows 7 Home Basic

f. Windows 7 Education

g. Windows 7 Home Premium

6. If your organization has developed custom **Windows Store** apps, you will need to install them. What can you use to install them?

a. Windows Store

b. Windows Installer Package

c. Sideloading

d. Group Policy

7. Regarding the benefits of Windows 10, which of the following statements is not true?

a. Support for touch

b. Easier to use

c. Updates occur less frequently

d. Performance improvements

e. Consistent user interface and Universal Windows apps

8. Suppose the sales personnel in your organization use a variety of Windows 10 computers and devices. When using their desktop computers, which tile is not displayed in the **Action Center**?

a. Rotation lock

b. Tablet mode

c. Connect

d. VPN

e. Location

f. None of the above

9. You are a desktop support technician for your organization and you need to create a bootable version of Windows on a USB drive. Which Windows editions support the **Windows To Go Creator** feature? (select two answers)

    a. Windows 8 Pro

    b. Windows 8 Enterprise

    c. Windows 8.1 Pro

    d. Windows 8.1 Enterprise

    e. Windows 10 Pro

    f. Windows 10 Enterprise

10. Suppose you support 500 computers that run a mix of **Windows 8.1** and **Windows 10**. As an IT support professional, you are aware that device drivers are specific to the family of Windows operating systems. You need to view the list of installed device drivers on the Windows 10 computers. Which tool would you use to do this?

    a. `Driverlist.exe`

    b. `Driverquery.exe`

    c. `Drivers.exe`

    d. None of the above

11. Which of the following statements are true when referring to **New Technology File System (NTFS)** compression? (select three answers)

    a. Compression is an attribute of a file or folder.

    b. Volumes, folders, and files on an NTFS volume are either compressed or uncompressed.

    c. New files created in a compressed folder are not compressed by default.

    d. Compressed files or folders cannot be deleted until they are uncompressed.

    e. When you open a compressed file, the Windows OS automatically decompresses it for you.

    f. The compression state of a folder reflects the compression state of the files within that folder.

12. Suppose you are an IT support professional for the sales team in your organization. The sales team members need to easily project their **Personal Computers'** (**PC's**) screens to their customers' TVs and projectors. You plan to recommend **Miracast**. Which of the following is not an option when using Miracast?

   a. Mute screen

   b. Duplicate

   c. PC screen only

   d. Extend

   e. Disconnect

   f. Second screen only

13. You are configuring the storage for a Windows 10 computer. You format a 32 GB volume with **FAT32**. What is the maximum file size supported on this volume?

   a. 16 Exabytes

   b. 8 GB

   c. 4 GB

   d. 16 GB

   e. 2 GB

14. When signing into a web application, your users are asked if they want to store their password. You have identified that this password will be stored for future use in **Credential Manager** on their PCs. Which of the following statements is not true regarding Credential Manager?

   a. It saves the credentials entered by the users when accessing other computers and resources on local networks.

   b. Credential Manager is disabled by default on non-domain joined computers.

   c. It can be used to back up and restore credentials.

   d. It is built into Windows 10 Control Panel.

368 Mock Exam (A and B)

15. Suppose your organization has created several security groups. You need to assign permissions to one of the security groups that will allow the group members to see folder content, read files, and start programs. What are the minimum permissions that you must assign?

    a. Modify

    b. Read and execute

    c. Read

    d. Write

    e. Full Control

16. As an IT support professional, you need to create a network share that can be used by the executives. The folder that you are sharing is on a **Resilient File System (ReFS)** volume. Which of the following are features that you can take advantage of? (select two answers)

    a. Auditing

    b. Compression

    c. **Encrypting File System (EFS)** encryption

    d. Quota

    e. Security

    f. Volume shrinking

17. Suppose you need to set up an account that will be used to log on to a Windows 10 PC. This account needs to be able to synchronize files with **OneDrive**. What type of account do you need to create to do this?

    a. Domain account

    b. Local account

    c. Microsoft account

    d. None of the above

18. Suppose you are configuring a 64-bit Windows 10 Enterprise computer. Your organization discourages the use of weak passwords and storing passwords insecurely. Which of the following features can securely store OS secrets and prevent hackers from accessing them, even if the machine is already compromised?

    a. Windows Hello

    b. Credential Guard

    c. Encrypted File System

    d. None of the above

19. When troubleshooting hardware and drivers, which of the following registry hives is the one that you will likely edit the most?

    a. **HKEY_CLASSES_ROOT**

    b. **HKEY_CURRENT_USERS**

    c. **HKEY_LOCAL_MACHINE**

    d. **HKEY_USERS**

    e. **HKEY_CURRENT_CONFIG**

20. Suppose your organization is in the process of migrating users to **Office 365**. You have a mix of Windows 10 editions deployed. You are required to provide conditional access and **Single Sign-On** (**SSO**) from anywhere for the Office 365 users using **Domain Join** with **Azure Active Directory** (**Azure AD**). Which of the following Windows OS versions will support this?

    a. Windows 10 Pro

    b. Windows 10 Pro and Windows 10 Enterprise

    c. Windows 10 Enterprise

    d. None of the above

Now, let's move on to exam B, which contains questions from *Chapter 8, Configuring Various Networks*, to *Chapter 12, Managing Logfiles*.

Mock exam B

21. As an IT support professional, you have been assigned 25 Windows 10 computers in a workgroup. The computers receive a Microsoft Windows 10 update on **patch Tuesday**. One of the computers did not get the previous month's Windows update. What will happen when you try to apply the current month's update to that computer?

    a. The update will fail. You will have to install last month's update manually first.

    b. The update will complete, but the computer will be missing last month's updates.

    c. Last month's update will be downloaded and installed first, and then the current update will install automatically.

    d. The update will succeed because it is cumulative.

22. Suppose you need to approve and deploy updates after you've tested them, but not immediately after Microsoft has released them. Which tool allows you to do this from a centralized cloud-based service?

    a. System Center Configuration Manager

    b. Microsoft Intune

    c. Windows Updates

    d. Windows Server Update Server

    e. None of the above

23. You need to view both updates that have been applied and those that have failed to be applied. Where can you see the list of updates on a Windows 10 computer?

    a. Update log

    b. Check for updates

    c. Update history

    d. Task Manager

    e. Event Viewer

24. **Windows PowerShell** has several characteristics that make it ideal for local and remote management of one or more Windows 10 devices. As an IT support professional, you want to be familiar with this tool. Which one of the following options provides Windows PowerShell's main functionality?

    a. **Graphical User Interface (GUI)**

    b. Commands

    c. Processors

    d. Active Directory

25. Suppose users in the marketing department have specialized printers connected directly to their Windows 10 desktop computers. One of the marketing users' computer has several print jobs that have failed to print. Which tool can you use to manage printing on this user's computer? (select three answers)

    a. Device and Printers

    b. Print Management Console

    c. Print Server

    d. `PrintManagement` PowerShell cmdlets

    e. Windows Management Console

    f. Device Manager

26. Suppose you have a computer that runs on Windows 10 OS. You need to reset the computer. What can you do by using the **Reset this PC** feature? (select three answers)

    a. You can remove specific files.

    b. You can remove everything.

    c. You can restore from a backup.

    d. You can return/restore a device to its initial state.

    e. You can choose to keep your files.

27. Suppose the users that work from home for your organization need to be configured to defer Windows Updates. These computers have not joined to a domain. How can you manually configure these machines for the **Semi-Annual Channel**?

    a. Use a Group Policy

    b. Use the Settings app

    c. Use Windows Server Update Services

    d. Use Home Device Manager

28. Your organization recently upgraded to Windows 10 from Windows 8.1 and you want to use a familiar, wizard-driven tool to configure wired and wireless connections. Which tool should you use?

    a. Network & Internet

    b. Network and Sharing Center

    c. Network Setup Wizard

    d. Windows PowerShell

29. Suppose your organization has recently upgraded its wireless network access points. Wireless security is the main driver for the upgrade. Which of the following forms of wireless security should you avoid using when connecting your wireless devices?

    a. **Wi-Fi Protected Access 2 (WPA 2)**

    b. **Wired Equivalent Privacy (WEP)**

    c. **Wi-Fi Protected Access (WPA)**

    d. All three should be avoided

30. You are configuring a Windows 10 computer's firewall and you need to keep the computer from being visible to other computers. Which one of the following network location profiles should you select?

    a. Domain networks

    b. Private networks

    c. Guest or public networks

    d. None of the above

31. Suppose you are using the **New Connection Security Rule** wizard in **Windows Firewall**. Your organization requires the strongest level of authentication possible. However, you must not block connections if a remote computer fails to authenticate. Which one of the following options should you specify?

    a. Require authentication for an inbound and outbound connection

    b. Do not authenticate

    c. Require authentication for inbound connections and request authentication for outbound connections

    d. Request authentication for inbound and outbound connections

32. What criteria can you use to configure a firewall so that it blocks or allows traffic?

    a. Traffic source address

    b. Traffic source subnet

    c. Traffic source router

    d. Traffic source user

    e. All the above

33. You are preparing to troubleshoot a user's computer and you plan to gather information about the problem using the tools available on the computer. Which one of the following tools is not included in Windows 10?

    a. Reliability History

    b. Message Analyzer

    c. Event Viewer

    d. Task Manager

    e. All of the above are included

34. To protect your organization's data, you enabled System Restore points on your users' Windows 10 computers. System Restore points will be created automatically when which of the following actions occur? (select three answers)

    a. You install a new application or driver

    b. You change your password

    c. You remove programs

    d. You perform a backup

    e. You install updates

35. A user reports a problem regarding application failures and the user has indicated that this is not the first time they have experienced issues with this application. Which of the tools provided in Windows 10 can create a problem report that you can use to troubleshoot this application?

    a. Process Explorer

    b. Task Manager

    c. Event Viewer

    d. Message Analyzer

    e. Reliability History

    f. None of the above

36. Suppose users are reporting desktop app operation issues. You create a log and categorize these issues and you confirm that some users do not have access to a newly deployed application. Also, you suspect that file permissions might be insufficient. What is the most likely cause of this issue?

    a. Missing application features

    b. Poor performance

    c. Incorrect configuration

    d. Incorrect database connection settings

    e. None of the above

37. Suppose you are troubleshooting a Windows 10 computer and you need to stop a process and its dependencies. Then, you open **Task Manager**. Which feature in Task Manager will allow you to stop a process tree?

    a. Processes

    b. Details

    c. Performance

    d. Services

    e. None of the above

38. Suppose you are troubleshooting a Windows 10 computer and you open the **Event Viewer** to review each of the logs. Which of the following is not a type of event logged by Windows 10?

    a. Critical events

    b. Information events

    c. Warning events

    d. Error events

    e. System events

39. You need to launch the **Windows Recovery Environment**. Which of the following options are the methods that you can perform? (select three answers)

    a. Reboot and press the *F8* key before Windows starts to load.

    b. Boot using recovery media.

    c. From the login screen, click **Shutdown**, then hold down the *Shift* key while selecting **Restart**.

    d. In the Windows 10 Settings app, under **Update & Security**, select **Recovery | Restart now** under **Advanced Startup**.

40. Suppose you are troubleshooting a Windows 10 computer in which the Windows Store app cannot connect to the store. You have run the Apps troubleshooter but still experience the issue. What should you try next?

    a. Make sure your applications are up to date.

    b. Configure Windows Firewall rules so that the application functions properly.

    c. Clear the Windows Store cache.

    d. Synchronize application licenses.

That's all, guys! I wish you the best of luck for the exam. Good luck! If you have any questions, do not hesitate to contact me.

Assessments

Chapter 1 – Deploying Windows 10

Question 1

If you want to deploy **AppLocker** and **Windows Defender Credential Guard** on your school's network, can you install the **Windows 10 Education** version?

- Yes
- No

Answer

Yes. If you want to deploy AppLocker and Windows Defender Credential Guard on your school's network, then you can use the **Windows 10 Enterprise** or Windows 10 Education versions.

Question 2

Can you buy Windows 10 Enterprise from a computer store?

- Yes
- No

Answer

No. You cannot buy Windows 10 Enterprise from a computer store because this edition is only available for Volume Licensing—for example, for large companies or universities.

Question 3

If you have a 32-bit version of Windows 10, is it possible to install the **Hyper-V** feature?

- Yes
- No

Answer

No. You cannot install the Hyper-V feature on a 32-bit version of Windows 10. Hyper-V is only supported on 64-bit Windows 10 editions.

Question 4

Is it possible to boot and install Windows 10 from a DVD?

- Yes
- No

Answer

Yes. If you can find a computer with a DVD player on it or you can use an external DVD player, then it is possible to boot and install Windows 10 from a DVD. Another method is booting and installing from a USB.

Chapter 2 – Upgrading Windows 10

Question 1

Can you upgrade from **Windows 8 Pro** to **Windows 10 Pro** in just one step?

- Yes
- No

Answer

No. If you want to upgrade from Windows 8 to Windows 10, then you first have to install **KB2919355**. More information about this can be found at `https://support.microsoft.com/en-us/help/15356/windows-8-install-update-kb-2919355`.

Question 2

If you want to add text-to-speech and handwriting features to your Windows 10 device, can you install the language pack?

- Yes
- No

Answer

No. Text-to-speech and handwriting are **Features on Demand** features and cannot be installed by installing a language pack.

Question 3

Is it possible to upgrade from **Windows 8.1 Connected** edition to Windows 10 Education edition?

- Yes
- No

Answer

Yes. It is possible to upgrade from Windows 8.1 Connected to Windows 10 Education edition.

Chapter 3 – Customizing and Configuring Windows 10

Question 1

Can I open legacy web applications with Microsoft Edge?

- Yes
- No

Answer

Yes. You can open legacy web applications with Microsoft Edge by configuring the **Enterprise Mode** Site List via Group Policy or Microsoft Intune.

Question 2

To export the Start menu to a .xml file, is the following command correct:

```
Export-StartLayout -Path \\server\share\folder\StartMenuLayout.xml
```

- Yes
- No

Answer

Yes. That is the correct command to export a Start menu layout.

Question 3

Can you use Command Prompt commands in PowerShell?

- Yes
- No

Answer

Yes. You can use Command Prompt commands on Windows PowerShell. For example, you can run `ipconfig.exe` in PowerShell and it gives you the same result as if you had run it on Command Prompt.

Question 4

If you want help with a PowerShell command, is `Get-Help <PowerShell cmdlet>` the correct command to use?

- Yes
- No

Answer

Yes. This command gives you all the relevant syntaxes and parameters for a PowerShell cmdlet.

Chapter 4 – Managing Local Users, Groups, and Devices

Question 1

Can you fully manage a registered Windows 10 device in **Azure Active Directory** (**Azure AD**)?

- Yes
- No

Answer

No. If a Windows 10 device is registered on Azure AD, then you can only manage the corporate applications and data on that device. This means personal and corporate data are separated from each other.

Question 2

Is the local administrator account enabled by default?

- Yes
- No

Answer

No. The built-in local administrator account is disabled by default.

Question 3

Can you register a smartphone to Azure AD?

- Yes
- No

Answer

Yes. You can register a smartphone to Azure AD and it will be treated as a **Bring-Your-Own-Device (BYOD)** device. Corporate and personal data will be separated.

Question 4

What is the correct PowerShell cmdlet to use to create a new local group?

Answer

The correct PowerShell cmdlet to use to create a new local group is as follows:

```
New-LocalGroup -Name W10NewLocalGroup
```

Chapter 5 – Configuring Permissions and File Access

Question 1

Can the **FAT** file system support a partition size of 1 TB?

- Yes
- No

Answer

No. The FAT file system can only support a maximum partition size of 32 GB. **FAT32** can support up to 2 TB.

Question 2

Does the **Resilient File System** (**ReFS**) file system support the Quota feature?

- Yes
- No

Answer

No. The **ReFS** file system does not support the Quota feature.

Question 3

With the **Read & Execute** permissions, is it possible to start programs?

- Yes
- No

Answer

Yes. You can start programs with the Read & Execute permissions.

Question 4

When you copy a file within a single volume, will the copy of the file inherit the permissions of the destination folder?

- Yes
- No

Answer

Yes. The copy of the file will inherit the permissions of the destination folder.

Question 5

Is **File Explorer** also available on older versions of Windows?

- Yes
- No

Answer

Yes. On older versions of Windows, File Explorer is called **Windows Explorer**.

Question 6

If you remove all shared folders, will Windows 10 automatically delete the firewall rules?

- Yes
- No

Answer

No. After you removed all shared folders, the firewall rules will not be deleted.

Question 7

Can you use the `net use` command to set the shared folder properties?

- Yes
- No

Answer

No. You cannot use the `net use` command to modify or set the shared folder properties.

Chapter 6 – Configuring and Implementing Local Policies

Question 1

Is the `USERDIFF` binary file present by default on Windows 10?

- Yes
- No

Answer

No. The `USERDIFF` binary file is only used for Windows upgrades.

Question 2

Can you import or export registry keys?

- Yes
- No

Answer

Yes. You can import or export registry keys in Windows 10.

Question 3

Is **REG_DWORD_SZ** a valid value type?

- Yes
- No

Answer

No. **REG_DWORD_SZ** is not a valid value type.

Question 4

Can you set the maximum password age to 123 days?

- Yes
- No

Answer

Yes. The maximum password age can be set to any value between 1 and 999 days.

Question 5

Can you use the **RSoP** planning mode on a standalone Windows 10 device?

- Yes
- No

Answer

No. The RSoP planning mode is only available on Azure AD-joined devices.

Chapter 7 – Securing Data and Applications

Question 1

Can a standard user account reset the network adapter?

- Yes
- No

Answer

Yes. A standard user account can reset the network adapter without receiving a **User Account Control (UAC)** prompt.

Question 2

Are there four settings for UAC notifications?

- Yes
- No

Answer

Yes. The four settings are **Never notify me, Notify me only when apps try to make changes to my computer (do not dim my desktop)**, **Notify me only when apps try to make changes to my computer (default)**, and **Always notify me**.

Question 3

Can **WIP** automatically protect the content that is downloaded to a device?

- Yes
- No

Answer

Yes. WIP automatically protects the content that is downloaded to a device.

Question 4

Can **Encrypting File System** (**EFS**) encrypt an entire hard disk?

- Yes
- No

Answer

No. EFS will only encrypt single files or folders, not an entire hard disk or volume.

Question 5

Can **BitLocker** be used without a **TPM chip**?

- Yes
- No

Answer

Yes. BitLocker can be used without a TPM chip. However, a computer with a TPM chip can provide the additional security of pre-startup system integrity verification.

Question 6

Is AppLocker **Event ID 8023** a valid event ID?

- Yes
- No

Answer

No. AppLocker **Event ID 8023** is not a valid ID.

Chapter 8 – Configuring Various Networks

Question 1

Can you make use of a **Class E** network?

- Yes
- No

Answer

No. Class E networks are reserved for experimental use.

Question 2

How many hosts can you connect in a **Class B** network?

Answer

You can host up to 65,534 hosts in a Class B network.

Question 3

With which mechanism can you configure alternative IP settings?

Answer

You can use the **Alternative Configuration** tab in the **Properties** box from the network card to configure alternative IP settings.

Question 4

Can Microsoft provide you with a cellular plan?

- Yes
- No

Answer

No. Microsoft can't provide you with a cellular plan. However, Microsoft recommends different mobile operators in your region through the **Mobile Plans** app.

Question 5

Is **Internet Key Exchange (IKEv1)** a valid **VPN** protocol?

- Yes
- No

Answer

No. IKEv1 is not a valid VPN protocol, but **IKEv2** is a valid VPN protocol.

Question 6

Is **Wired Equivalent Privacy (WEP)** encryption the most secure Wi-Fi encryption that you can use?

- Yes
- No

Answer

No. **WEP** encryption is the weakest Wi-Fi encryption that you can use. Use **Wi-Fi Protected Access 2 (WPA2)** instead.

Chapter 9 – Configuring Remote Connectivity

Question 1

Is **Quick Assist** a remote management feature that you can turn on in the firewall?

- Yes
- No

Answer

No. Quick Assist uses the **TCP 443** protocol.

Question 2

Is the **Remote Desktop Protocol (RDP)** protocol used by **Microsoft Management Console (MMC)** to connect to remote hosts?

- Yes
- No

Answer

No. MMC does not use the RDP protocol to connect to remote hosts. You have to open the correct port in the firewall of the hosts to allow MMC.

Question 3

Can you start the **Remote Desktop Connection** app via the command line and specify specific connection properties?

- Yes
- No

Answer

Yes. You can start the Remote Desktop Connection app from the command line. You can also specify specific connection properties.

Chapter 10 – Understanding Troubleshooting and Recovery

Question 1

Is **Microsoft Azure Backup** a built-in tool on Windows 10?

- Yes
- No

Answer

No. Microsoft Azure Backup is not included on Windows 10. Instead, you have to download and install it on Windows 10.

Question 2

Does **File History**, by default, back up the Windows libraries?

- Yes
- No

Answer

Yes. File History saves files by default from the default Windows libraries.

Question 3

Can the recovery drive have a size of 4 GB?

- Yes
- No

Answer

No. The recovery drive should have a size of at least 8 GB to hold its contents.

Question 4

If you go back to a restore point that you created earlier, will your personal data be affected?

- Yes
- No

Answer

No. When you go back to an earlier-created restore point, only the system settings and system files are affected.

Question 5

Can you access **Windows Recovery Environment** (**WinRE**) with the *F8* key?

- Yes
- No

Answer

No. The *F8* option (or the *SHIFT+F8* option) does not work on Windows 10.

Question 6

Can you use the **Application Compatibility Toolkit** (**ACT**) tool to test your legacy software on Windows 10?

- Yes
- No

Answer

Yes. You can use ACT to test your software on Windows 10.

Question 7

Is the `IISReset.exe` command, the correct command to use to clear the **Windows Store** cache?

- Yes
- No

Answer

No. `IISReset.exe` is used to restart **Internet Information Services**. To clear the Windows Store cache, you need to run `WSReset.exe`.

Chapter 11 – Managing Updates

Question 1

Can anyone opt in to the **Windows Insider** program?

- Yes
- No

Answer

Yes. Anyone can join the Windows Insider program at any time.

Question 2

Is **Semi-Annual Channel (Targeted)** a valid servicing channel?

- Yes
- No

Answer

No. Semi-Annual Channel (Targeted) is not a valid servicing channel anymore. It was a servicing channel, but Microsoft removed it.

Question 3

If you manually check for updates, can you install them at a later time?

- Yes
- No

Answer

No. If you manually check for updates, then the updates are automatically downloaded and installed.

Question 4

Is it necessary to test and validate updates before you deploy them to the rest of your organization?

- Yes
- No

Answer

Yes. You need to test and validate updates before you release them to the rest of the company to make sure everything works on the hardware and the software.

Question 5

Are the **Background Tasks Infrastructure Service** and Windows Update services critical for Windows updates?

- Yes
- No

Answer

No. The **Background Intelligent Transfer Service (BITS)** and the Windows Update service are the critical services for Windows updates.

Chapter 12 – Managing Log Files

Question 1

In **Event Viewer**, you will find a node called **Forwarded Events**. Is this used to send logs to other computers?

- Yes
- No

Answer

No. This node is used for logs that are sent from remote computers.

Question 2

To enable **Windows Event Collector**, can you use the `winrm quickconfig` command?

- Yes
- No

Answer

Yes. To enable Windows Event Collector, you need to run the `winrm quickconfig` command.

Question 3

To open **Resource Monitor**, can you use the `perfmon` command?

- Yes
- No

Answer

No. You need to run the `perfmon /res` command to open the **Resource Monitor** from the command line.

Question 4

Does **Reliability Monitor** measure the history of problems?

- Yes
- No

Answer

Yes. Reliability Monitor measures the history of problems.

Question 5

Can you use **Network Printer Installation Wizard** to install printers?

- Yes
- No

Answer

Yes. You can use Network Printer Installation Wizard to install printers.

Question 6

Are **Type 3** printer drivers downloaded from Windows Update during installation?

- Yes
- No

Answer

No. A **Type 3** printer driver is usually downloaded from the printer manufacturer's website.

Question 7

Can you change the index location of the indexing services?

- Yes
- No

Answer

Yes. You can change the index location of the indexing services under the **Advanced Options** tab.

Mock Exam 1

Question 1

You are an IT support professional in a well-renowned organization and your company has successfully upgraded 60,000 computers to Windows 10 Enterprise. How long will Microsoft offer your company support for?

    a. 12 months

    b. 18 months

    c. 24 months

    d. 30 months

Answer

d – 30 months

Question 2

Where can you find the setting/configuration that decides what happens when the lid closes on a Windows 10 device?

    a. In the Display options

    b. In the Power Plan options

    c. In the Ease of Access options

    d. In the USB settings

Answer

b – In the Power Plan options

Question 3

Suppose you have a computer that runs on Windows 10 **Operating System** (**OS**). When you open the **Control Panel**, which items can you expect to see in the **Category** view? (Select the three correct answers:)

> a. **System and Security**
>
> b. **Appearance and Personalization**
>
> c. **Time & Language**
>
> d. **Ease of Access**
>
> e. **Network Security**

Answer

a – System and Security, b – Appearance and Personalization, and d – Ease of Access

Question 4

If you want to remove the **Gaming** option from the **Windows Settings** app, which of the following options would help you do this?

> a. Uninstall **Solitaire**.
>
> b. Create a group policy that hides the **Gaming** option.
>
> c. Right-click on the **Gaming** option and select **Hide from view**.
>
> d. Remove the **Gaming** tile in the **Notification and actions** page.
>
> e. Log in with a work or school account.

Answer

b – Create a group policy that hides the **Gaming** option.

Question 5

Suppose you are a support technician at a retail computer store. A customer has just requested that you upgrade their computer to **Windows 10 Home**. First, you need to verify whether the computer can be upgraded or not. Which Windows editions can be upgraded to Windows 10 Home? (Select the four correct answers:)

    a. Windows 8/8.1

    b. Windows RT

    c. Windows 7 Ultimate

    d. Windows 7 Starter

    e. Windows 7 Home Basic

    f. Windows 7 Education

    g. Windows 7 Home Premium

Answer

a – Windows 8/8.1, d – Windows 7 Starter, e – Windows 7 Home Basic, and g – Windows 7 Home Premium

Question 6

If your organization has developed custom **Windows Store** apps, you will need to install them. Which of the following methods can you use to install them?

    a. Windows Store

    b. Windows Installer package

    c. Sideloading

    d. Group Policy

Answer

c – Sideloading

Question 7

Which of the following statements about the benefits of Windows 10 is not true?

>   a. It supports touchscreen.

>   b. It is easy to use.

>   c. Updates occur less frequently.

>   d. It has performance improvements

>   e. It has a consistent user interface and universal Windows apps.

Answer

c – Updates occur less frequently.

Question 8

Suppose the sales personnel of your organization use a variety of Windows 10 computers and devices. When using their desktop computers, which tile will not display in **Action Center**?

>   a. Rotation lock

>   b. Tablet mode

>   c. Connect

>   d. VPN

>   e. Location

>   f. None of the previously mentioned options

Answer

a – Rotation lock

Question 9

If you are a desktop support technician for your organization and you need to create a bootable version of Windows on a USB drive, which Windows editions support the **Windows To Go** creator feature? (Select the two correct answers.)

a. Windows 8 Pro

b. Windows 8 Enterprise

c. Windows 8.1 Pro

d. Windows 8.1 Enterprise

e. Windows 10 Pro

f. Windows 10 Enterprise

Answer

d – Windows 8.1 Enterprise and f – Windows 10 Enterprise

Question 10

Suppose you support 500 computers that run a mix of Windows 8.1 and Windows 10. As an IT support professional, you are aware that device drivers are specific to the family of Windows operating systems and you need to view the list of installed device drivers on all of the Windows 10 computers. Which tool would you use to do this?

a. `Driverlist.exe`

b. `Driverquery.exe`

c. `Drivers.exe`

d. None of the previously mentioned options

Answer

c – `Driverquery.exe`

Question 11

Which of the following statements are true when referring to **New Technology File System** (**NTFS**) compression? (Select the three correct answers.)

a. Compression is an attribute of a file or folder.

b. Volumes, folders, and files on an NTFS volume are either compressed or decompressed.

c. New files created in a compressed folder are not compressed by default.

d. Compressed files or folders cannot be deleted until they are decompressed.

e. When you open a compressed file, the Windows OS automatically decompresses it for you.

f. The compression state of a folder reflects the compression state of the files within that folder.

Answer

a – Compression is an attribute of a file or folder, b – Volumes, folders, and files on an NTFS volume are either compressed or decompressed, and e – When you open a compressed file, the Windows OS automatically decompresses it for you.

Question 12

Suppose you are an IT support professional for the sales team in your organization. The sales team members need to easily project their **Personal Computer**s' (**PC**) screens to their customers' TVs and projectors. You recommend using **Miracast**. Which of the following is not an option that Miracast offers?

a. Mute the screen.

b. Duplicate the screen.

c. Show the PC screen only.

d. Extend the screen.

e. Disconnect the screen.

f. Show the second screen only.

Answer

a – Mute the screen

Question 13

You are configuring the storage on a Windows 10 computer. You format a 32 GB volume with **FAT32**. What is the maximum file size supported on this volume?

a. 16 Exabytes

b. 8 GB

c. 4 GB

d. 16 GB

e. 2 GB

Answer

c – 4 GB

Question 14

When signing in to a web application, your users are asked whether they want to store their password. You identify that their password will be stored for future use in **Credential Manager** on their PCs. Which of the following statements about Credential Manager is not true?

a. It saves the credentials entered by users when accessing other computers and resources on local networks.

b. Credential Manager is disabled by default on non-domain joined computers.

c. It can be used to back up and restore these credentials.

d. It is built into the Windows 10 Control Panel.

Answer

b – Credential Manager is disabled by default on non-domain joined computers.

Question 15

Suppose your organization has created several security groups. You need to assign permissions to one of the security groups that will allow the group members to see the folder's content, read files, and start programs. What are the minimum permissions that you must assign?

> a. **Modify**
>
> b. **Read & execute**
>
> c. **Read**
>
> d. **Write**
>
> e. **Full Control**

Answer

b – **Read & execute**

Question 16

As an IT support professional, you need to create a network share that can be used by the executives of your company. The folder that you are sharing is on a ReFS volume. Which of the following are features that you can take advantage of? (Select the two correct answers:)

> a. Auditing
>
> b. Compression
>
> c. EFS encryption
>
> d. Quota
>
> e. Security
>
> f. Volume shrinking

Answer

a – Auditing and e – Security

Question 17

Suppose you need to set up an account that you will use to log in to a Windows 10 PC. This account needs to be able to synchronize files with **OneDrive**. What type of account do you need to create to do this?

>   a. A domain account

>   b. A local account

>   c. A Microsoft account

>   d. None of the previously mentioned options

Answer

c – A Microsoft account

Question 18

Suppose you are configuring a 64-bit Windows 10 Enterprise computer. Your organization discourages the use of a weak password and storing passwords insecurely. Which of the following features can securely store OS secrets and prevent hackers from accessing them, even if the machine is already compromised?

>   a. Windows Hello

>   b. Credential Guard

>   c. **Encrypted File System (EFS)**

>   d. None of the previously mentioned options

Answer

b – Credential Guard

Question 19

When troubleshooting hardware and drivers, which of the following registry hives is the one that you will likely edit the most?

   a. **HKEY_CLASSES_ROOT**

   b. **HKEY_CURRENT_USERS**

   c. **HKEY_LOCAL_MACHINE**

   d. **HKEY_USERS**

   e. **HKEY_CURRENT_CONFIG**

Answer

c – **HKEY_LOCAL_MACHINE**

Question 20

Suppose your organization is in the process of migrating users to **Office 365**. You have a mix of Windows 10 editions deployed. You are required to provide conditional access and **Single Sign-On** (**SSO**) from anywhere for the Office 365 users using **Domain Join** with Azure AD. Which of the following Windows OS versions support this?

   a. Windows 10 Pro

   b. Windows 10 Pro and Windows 10 Enterprise

   c. Windows 10 Enterprise

   d. None of the previously mentioned options

Answer

b – Windows 10 Pro and Windows 10 Enterprise

Mock Exam 2

Question 1

Suppose as an IT support professional you are assigned 25 Windows 10 computers in a workgroup. The computers receive a Microsoft Windows 10 update on **Patch Tuesday**. One of the computers did not get the previous month's Windows update. What will happen when you try to apply the current month's update to that computer?

a. The update will fail. You will have to install last month's update manually first.

b. The update will complete, but last month's update will be missing on the computer.

c. Last month's update will download and install first, then the current update will install automatically.

d. The update will succeed because it is cumulative.

Answer

d – The update will succeed because it is cumulative.

Question 2

Suppose you need to approve and deploy updates after you test them, but not immediately after Microsoft releases them. Which tool allows you to do this from a centralized cloud-based service?

a. Microsoft System Center Configuration Manager

b. Microsoft Intune

c. Windows Update

d. Windows Server Update Services

e. None of the previously mentioned options

Answer

b – Microsoft Intune

Question 3

Where can you find a list of both the updates that are applied to a Windows 10 computer and those that have failed to apply?

    a. **Update log**

    b. **Check for updates**

    c. **Update history**

    d. **Task Manager**

    e. **Event Viewer**

Answer

c – **Update history**

Question 4

Windows PowerShell has several characteristics that make it ideal for the local and remote management of one or more Windows 10 devices. As an IT support professional, you need to be familiar with this tool. Which one of the following options provides Windows PowerShell's main functionality?

    a. The **Graphical User Interface (GUI)**

    b. The commands

    c. The processors

    d. Azure AD

Answer

b – The commands

Question 5

Suppose users in the marketing department have specialized printers that are directly connected to their Windows 10 desktop computers. One of the marketing user's computer has several print jobs that have failed to print. Which tools can you use to manage printing on this user's computer? (Select the three correct answers.)

    a. **Device and Printers**

    b. The print management console

    c. Print Server

    d. The `PrintManagement` PowerShell cmdlets

    e. MMC

    f. Device Manager

Answer

a – **Device and Printers**, b – The print management console, and d – The `PrintManagement` PowerShell cmdlets

Question 6

Suppose you have a computer that runs on the Windows 10 OS. You need to reset the computer. What does the **Reset this PC** feature do? (Select the three correct answers.)

    a. You can remove specific files.

    b. You can remove everything.

    c. You can restore your system from a backup.

    d. You can return/restore a device to its initial state.

    e. You can choose to keep your files.

Answer

b – You can remove everything, d – You can return/restore a device to its initial state, and e – You can choose to keep your files.

Question 7

Suppose the users in your organization that work from home need to configure their computers to defer Windows updates. These computers have not joined to a domain. How can you manually configure these machines for the Semi-Annual Channel?

    a. Use Group Policy.

    b. Use the Settings app.

    c. Use Windows Server Update Services.

    d. Use the home device manager.

Answer

b – Use the Settings app.

Question 8

If your organization recently upgraded to Windows 10 from Windows 8.1 and you want to use a familiar wizard-driven tool to configure wired and wireless connections, which tool should you use?

    a. Network & Internet

    b. Network and Sharing Center

    c. Network Setup Wizard

    d. Windows PowerShell

Answer

b – Network and Sharing Center

Question 9

Suppose your organization has recently upgraded its wireless network access points. Wireless security is the main driver for the upgrade. Which of the following forms of wireless security should you avoid using when connecting your wireless devices?

a. **Wi-Fi Protected Access 2 (WPA 2**

b. **Wired Equivalent Privacy (WEP)**

c. **Wi-Fi Protected Access (WPA)**

d. All three should be avoided

Answer

b – Wired Equivalent Privacy (WEP)

Question 10

If you are configuring a Windows 10 computer's firewall and you need to keep the computer from being visible to other computers, which of the following network location profiles should you select?

a. **Domain networks**

b. **Private networks**

c. **Guest or public networks**

d. None of the previously mentioned options

Answer

c – **Guest or public networks**

Question 11

Suppose you are using the **New Connection Security Rule** wizard in **Windows Firewall**. Your organization requires the strongest level of authentication possible. However, you must not block connections if a remote computer fails to authenticate. Which of the following options should you specify?

a. Require authentication for an inbound and outbound connection

b. Do not authenticate

c. Require authentication for inbound connections and request authentication for outbound connections

d. Request authentication for inbound and outbound connections

Answer

d – Request authentication for inbound and outbound connections

Question 12

What of the following criteria can you use to configure a firewall to block or allow traffic?

a. The traffic source address

b. The traffic source subnet

c. The traffic source router

d. The traffic source user

e. All of the previously mentioned options

Answer

a – The traffic source address

Question 13

If you are preparing to troubleshoot a user's computer and you plan to gather information about the problem using the tools available on the computer, which of the following tools is not included in Windows 10?

    a. Reliability History

    b. Message Analyzer

    c. Event Viewer

    d. Task Manager

    e. All of the previously mentioned options are included

Answer

b – Message Analyzer

Question 14

To protect your organization's data, you enabled system restore points on users' Windows 10 computers. System restore points are created automatically when which of the following actions occur? (Select the three correct answers.)

    a. You install a new application or driver.

    b. You change your password.

    c. You remove programs.

    d. You perform a backup.

    e. You install updates.

Answer

a – You install a new application or driver, c – Your remove programs, and e – You install updates.

Question 15

If a user reports a problem regarding application failure and they indicate that this is not the first time that they have experienced issues with this particular application, which of the tools provided in Windows 10 can create a problem report that you can use to troubleshoot this application?

    a. Process Explorer

    b. Task Manager

    c. Event Viewer

    d. Message Analyzer

    e. Reliability History

    f. None of the previously mentioned options

Answer

e – Reliability History

Question 16

Suppose several users report desktop app operation issues. You create a log and categorize these issues and confirm that some users do not have access to a newly deployed application. Also, you suspect that the file permissions might be insufficient. What is the most likely cause of this issue?

    a. Missing application features

    b. Poor performance

    c. Incorrect configuration

    d. Incorrect database connection settings

    e. None of the previously mentioned options

Answer

c – Incorrect configuration

Question 17

Suppose you are troubleshooting a Windows 10 computer and you need to stop a process and its dependencies. You open Task Manager. Which feature in Task Manager allows you to stop a process tree?

a. **Processes**

b. **Details**

c. **Performance**

d. **Services**

e. None of the previously mentioned options

Answer

b – **Details**

Question 18

Suppose you are troubleshooting a Windows 10 computer and you open Event Viewer to review each of the logs. Which of the following is not a type of event logged by Windows 10?

a. Critical events

b. Information events

c. Warning events

d. Error events

e. System events

Answer

e – System events

Question 19

If you need to launch **Windows Recovery Environment**, which of the following options can you perform to do so? (Select the three correct answers.)

   a. Reboot and press the *F8* key before Windows starts to load.

   b. Boot using recovery media.

   c. From the login screen, click **Shutdown**, then hold down the *Shift* key while selecting **Restart**.

   d. In the Windows 10 **Settings** app, under **Update & Security**, select **Recovery**, then click **Restart** under **Advanced Startup**.

Answer

b – Boot using recovery media, c – From the login screen, click **Shutdown**, then hold down the *Shift* key while selecting **Restart**, and d – In the Windows 10 **Settings** app, under **Update & Security**, select **Recovery**, then click **Restart** under **Advanced Startup**.

Question 20

Suppose you are troubleshooting a Windows 10 computer where the Windows Store app cannot connect to the store online. You have run the app's troubleshooter but it is still experiencing this issue. What should you try next?

   a. Make sure your applications are up to date.

   b. Configure the Windows Firewall rules for an application to function properly.

   c. Clear the Windows Store cache.

   d. Synchronize the application licenses.

Answer

c – Clear the Windows Store cache.

Other Books You May Enjoy

If you enjoyed this book, you may be interested in these other books by Packt:

Microsoft 365 Certified Fundamentals MS-900 Exam Guide

Aaron Guilmette

ISBN: 978-1-83898-217-1

- Gain insights into the exam objectives, test scenarios, and knowledge required before taking the MS-900 exam

- Understand the cloud services and SaaS models available in the Microsoft ecosystem

- Identify Windows deployment considerations using the Admin Center and User Portal experiences

- Implement enterprise mobility, device management, and application management within your organization

- Explore the reporting and analytics capabilities of Microsoft 365

- Discover various features of Azure Active Directory and other Microsoft 365 security tools

Microsoft 365 Mobility and Security – Exam Guide MS-101

Nate Chamberlain

ISBN: 978-1-83898-465-6

- Implement modern device services
- Discover tools for configuring audit logs and policies
- Plan, deploy, and manage Microsoft 365 services such as MDM and DLP
- Get up to speed with configuring eDiscovery settings and features to enhance your organization's ability to mitigate and respond to issues
- Implement Microsoft 365 security and threat management
- Explore best practices for effectively configuring settings

Leave a review - let other readers know what you think

Please share your thoughts on this book with others by leaving a review on the site that you bought it from. If you purchased the book from Amazon, please leave us an honest review on this book's Amazon page. This is vital so that other potential readers can see and use your unbiased opinion to make purchasing decisions, we can understand what our customers think about our products, and our authors can see your feedback on the title that they have worked with Packt to create. It will only take a few minutes of your time, but is valuable to other potential customers, our authors, and Packt. Thank you!

Index

www.ingramcontent.com/pod-product-compliance
Lightning Source LLC
LaVergne TN
LVHW081510050326
832903LV00025B/1437

9 781838 822187